BAIDARKA DIARIES

Voyages and Explorations:
British Columbia and
Alaska,
1992-2003

Réanne
Hemingway-Douglass

Published by Cave Art Press, Anacortes, WA 98221
An imprint of Douglass, Hemingway & Co., LLC
CaveArtPress.com

**Cave
Art
Press**

ISBN-13: 978-1934199-329

Editor and book designer: Arlene Cook
Maps by Lisa Wright
Additional editorial input: Lisa Wright, Kathleen Kaska
All photographs by Réanne Hemingway-Douglass and Don Douglass,
except where indicated.

To Don,

who has made life an exciting journey.

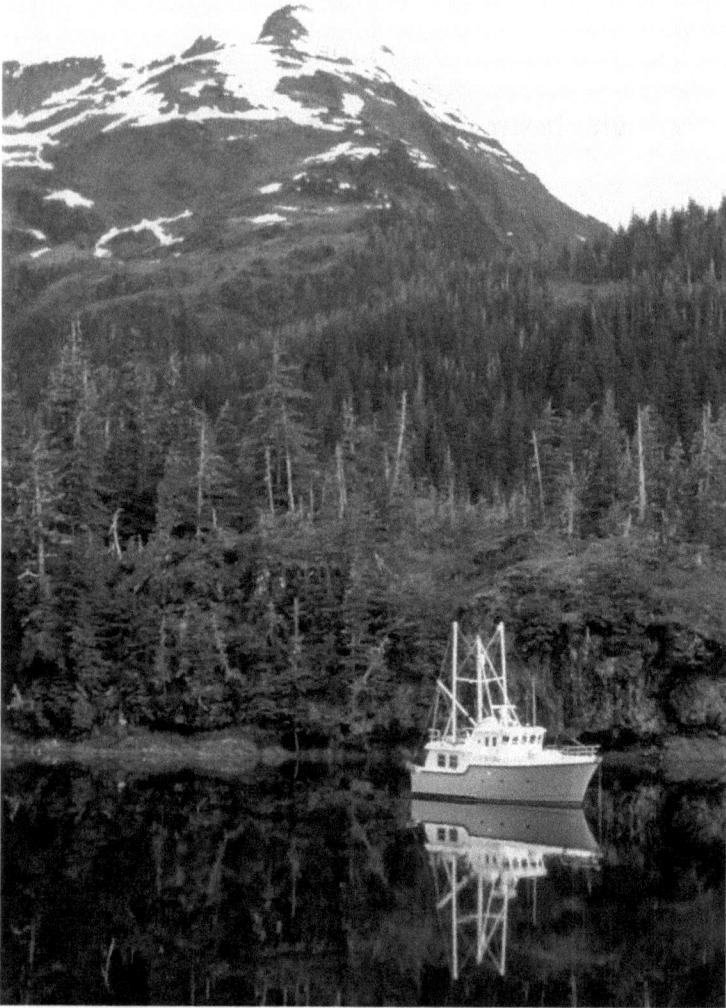

'Big' Baidarka *in Valdez Arm, Alaska, 2003*

CONTENTS

LIST OF MAPS

Note: The maps in this book have been included for geographical reference. They do not show all of the coves, inlets and other places mentioned. For more detailed maps consult *The Inside Passage Route Planning Maps* or the *Exploring* series of cruising guidebooks, by Don and Réanne Douglass (see Appendix, page 206).

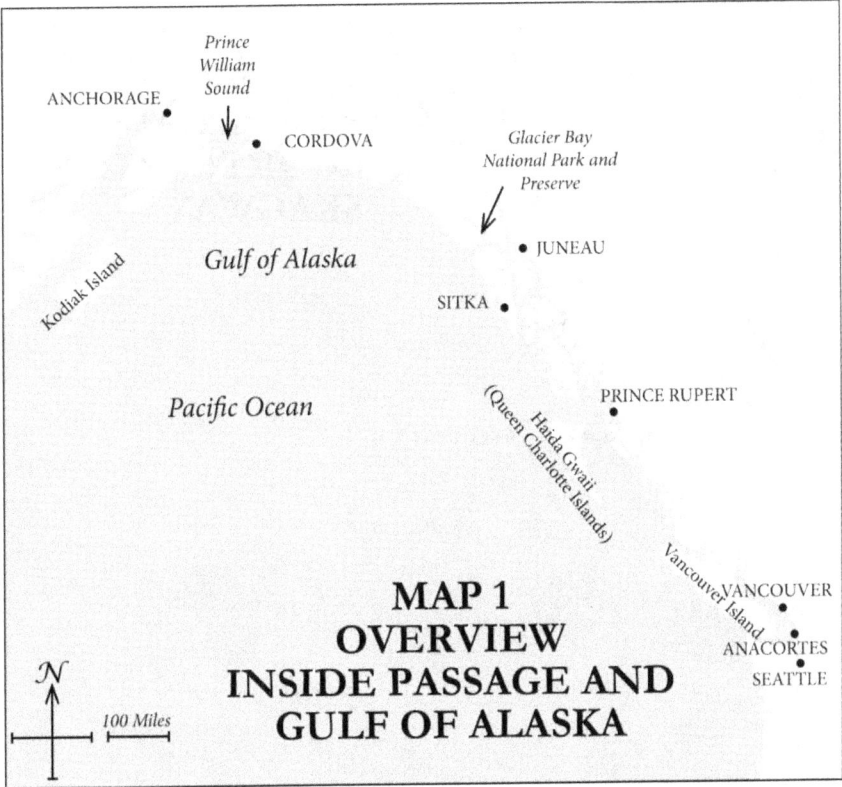

ANCHORAGE

Prince
William
Sound

CORDOVA

Glacier Bay
National Park and
Preserve

Gulf of Alaska

JUNEAU

Kodiak Island

SITKA

Pacific Ocean

Haida Gwaii
(Queen Charlotte Islands)

PRINCE RUPERT

Vancouver Island

VANCOUVER

ANACORTES

SEATTLE

MAP 1
OVERVIEW
INSIDE PASSAGE AND
GULF OF ALASKA

N

100 Miles

Auke Bay, Juneau

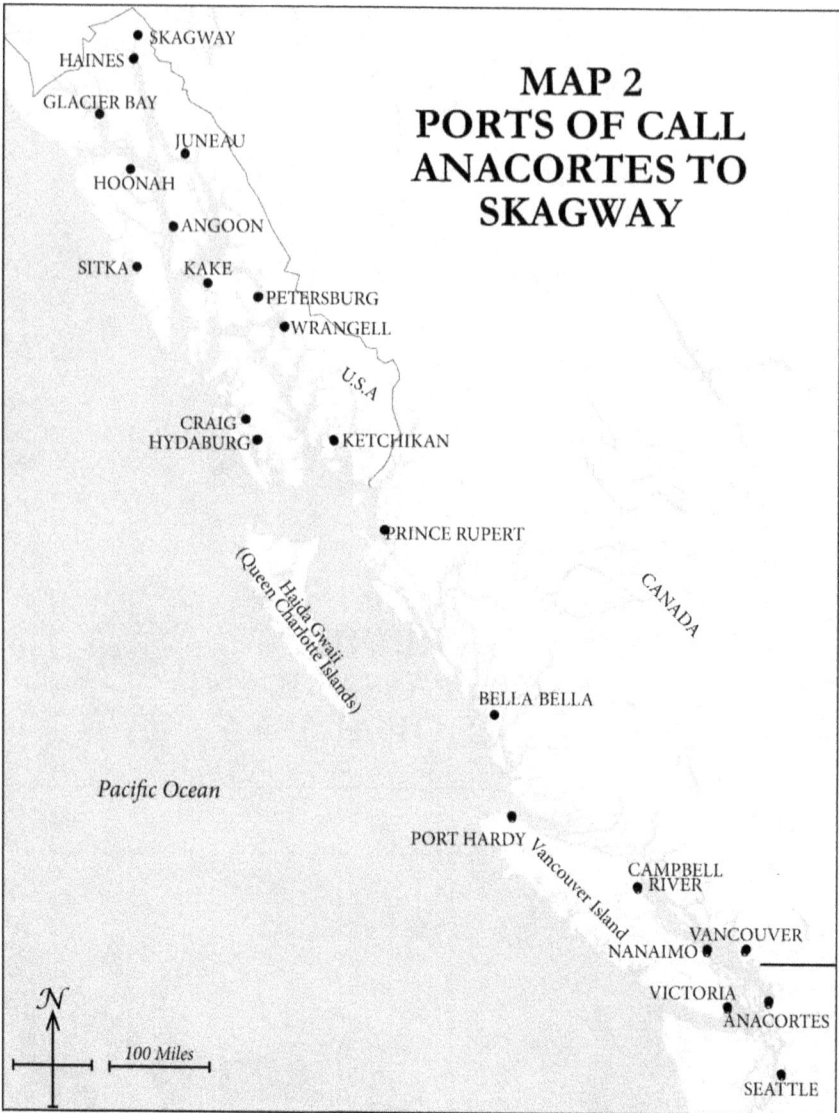

SKAGWAY
HAINES
GLACIER BAY
JUNEAU
HOONAH
ANGOON
SITKA   KAKE
          PETERSBURG
          WRANGELL
          U.S.A
CRAIG
HYDABURG   KETCHIKAN

PRINCE RUPERT

Haida Gwaii
(Queen Charlotte Islands)

CANADA

BELLA BELLA

Pacific Ocean

PORT HARDY   Vancouver Island

CAMPBELL
RIVER

VANCOUVER
NANAIMO

VICTORIA
ANACORTES

N

100 Miles

SEATTLE

**MAP 2
PORTS OF CALL
ANACORTES TO
SKAGWAY**

8

INTRODUCTION

The night I met Don Douglass, the man who would become my husband and to whom I am still married fifty-one years later, we asked one another what we considered to be the most important thing in life. "Love," I said. "Adventure," he said. It was Don's lifelong dream to sail around the world, via Cape Horn, and when I married him, I signed on "for whatever life would bring." However, since we had five kids between us and no money at that time, I was fairly confident that Don's dream would remain just that— a dream.

Eight years later, having built up a successful business, we set off from Los Angeles in our forty-two foot William Garden ketch, *Le Dauphin Amical*, on the greatest adventure of our lives. I kept a diary of that voyage, as I have done at various times throughout my life, and later used it as the basis for my 1994 memoir, *Cape Horn—One Man's Dream, One Woman's Nightmare*. I won't recount everything that is contained in that book, but at its heart is the night of February 26-27, 1975, when we were pitch-poled by "the ultimate wave," half way between Easter Island and Cape Horn. Don and I spent the next five weeks "rescuing ourselves," sailing under jury rig to the Chilean coast, then limping through the Patagonian channels—the South American equivalent of the North American Inside Passage—to eventual safety in Punta Arenas.

That was enough maritime adventure for me for a while! I returned to my teaching job, while Don picked up a new crew and continued sailing for the next year, crossing the Atlantic twice before returning home to Los Angeles. (This is documented in his book, *Beyond Cape Horn—The Atlantic Voyages of Le Dauphin Amical*.) We kept that boat for the next dozen years, sailing to the Channel Islands on weekends and on longer trips to Baja, until, in 1987, we decided to live full time in Bishop, California, in the Sierra Nevada. We moved on to new adventures, mountain bicycling, cross-country skiing, traveling in Europe and New Zealand, and writing and publishing guidebooks on outdoor activities under the imprint Fine Edge Productions (after Don's mantra of always living life at its limits).

Don and I both loved the Sierra, but we missed the water. In 1987, we chartered a sailboat with some friends and cruised from Comox, on Vancouver Island, to Desolation Sound and Princess Louisa Inlet, on the mainland British Columbia coast. This was our first foray into these waters, and we were entranced. It was like Patagonia, but without the drama.

9

After selling *Le Dauphin* in 1988, however, our only sea-going vessel for the next two years was a double sea kayak we named *Baidarka*—the Aleut word for kayak. We learned to paddle it in some of the lakes around Bishop, then took it on three separate trips—one to the beautiful Bowran Lakes Provincial Park, in central British Columbia, and two to the west coast of Vancouver Island, where we began doing research for a proposed kayaking guidebook.

On Vancouver Island, our first trip was a ten-day paddle around Barkley Sound, near Ucluelet, in 1988. The second trip, two years later, was a longer tour of the inlets around Clayoquot Sound, north of Tofino. The Pacific side of Vancouver Island is a beautiful but rugged place that gets a lot of weather, and in Clayoquot Sound we were subjected to both rain and gale force winds. But, in addition, we weren't paying much attention to the tides and one night we awoke to find the water lapping at the sides of the tent. We decided, after moving to higher, drier ground, that any further nautical research projects should be undertaken in a proper vessel. This idea was reinforced a day or two later when an extremely large marine animal surfaced in the water beside us. It was longer than our kayak, and although we found out later that it wouldn't have eaten us, Don and I were in full agreement: "We need a bigger boat!"

Don wanted a vessel that could take us to Glacier Bay in Alaska, since his daughter Dawn had given him a map of that area and he was keen to do some exploring. Dawn and her husband, Jeff Mach, were living in Juneau at that time, and Don suggested to them that we buy half-shares in a cruising boat. Don had recently traveled down the Inside Passage from Juneau in a twenty-six foot Nordic Tug, *Forevergreen*, with our friend Rod Nash, a professor from Colorado who kept his boat in Anacortes, Washington—a former mill town where Don had lived for several years as a high schooler.

Don liked the tug but thought a larger, thirty-two foot version would serve us better. Like Rod, we could keep the boat in Anacortes during the winter months and take it to Alaska in the summers, and Dawn and Jeff could use it up there, too.

We named the boat *Baidarka*, after our kayak, and throughout the 1990s we spent our summers exploring every nook and cranny of the Inside Passage, clocking up 5,000 engine hours and traveling over 35,000 miles. "What a life," you might think, but we worked from dawn to dusk every day, visiting small coves, collecting data on anchorage sites, and writing descriptions of every place we visited. Back home we'd do further research to fill in the details. The result was the series of cruising guidebooks that have become essential references for boaters who travel the Inside Passage.

The first of these books, *Exploring Vancouver Island's West Coast*, was published in 1995 and had its beginnings in our soggy kayaking trip of a few years before. But it came about seriously after we approached the Washington state-based nautical book wholesaler Robert Hale & Co. in 1994 about selling my *Cape Horn* book. Robert Hale was interested in *Cape Horn* but he said there was a definite market for a boater's guide to Vancouver Island if we could produce one. So we did, and the *Exploring* series of guidebooks grew from there. For over fifteen years we documented 5,000 places along the Pacific coasts of California, Oregon, Washington, British Columbia, and Alaska in six books of as many as 600 pages each, all published by Fine Edge. All of these books have been republished in updated editions. We also produced maps of the Pacific Coast for recreational boaters. Don and I were the principal authors of these publications, although a number of other people contributed to them also.

Our goal with the *Exploring* series was to help boaters explore and enjoy the waters of the West Coast by sharing our "local knowledge." Although the Inside Passage, in particular, comprises a relatively sheltered, boater-friendly environment, it is also a wilderness that requires constant and vigilant navigation. Boaters have to respect its wild and unpredictable nature and be prepared to handle whatever comes, in the knowledge that help may be a long time coming. Don and I did not intend our books to be used as navigational replacements for proper nautical charts, but we suggested numerous places for boaters to take shelter if they needed temporary anchorage sites in the event of fog, bad weather or unfavorable tides.

Each of the books included diagrams that reflected the particular routes and anchor sites we used. We would always enter small coves or anchorages at very slow speeds with me or someone else on the bow watching for submerged rocks or other hazards. We might not have observed all potential hazards, as we didn't always stay at a site for an entire tide cycle, but the information we presented was the best available, based on both our own observations and follow-up discussions with other boaters. We believed the books were of value because not all areas of the Inside Passage had been well charted at the time.

The cruising life met Don's need for adventure, and we found it to be highly social, also. Friends and family members joined us as crew for some segments of our trips, and we were always meeting people and making new friends. Most were fellow boaters, many of whom make cameo appearances in this book. Some of the people we met became enduring friends, including Warren and Laurie Miller, of Orcas Island, Washington, and Neil and Betty Carey, who lived in the Queen Charlotte Islands. Don was looking for someone with local knowledge on how to navigate Skidegate Channel, between Graham and Moresby Islands, the two main islands in the archipelago. Skidegate Channel is long and winding, with several shallow narrows and large differences in tide ranges between the east and west ends, which makes it extremely treacherous water for boaters. Someone told us Neil Carey was the man to talk to, and he was happy to share his expertise. "The safest way to do it," he told us, "is to find a vessel larger than yours, like a local fishing boat, and follow exactly behind them!"

Aboard *Baidarka*, as with *Le Dauphin Amical*, Don believed that preparedness was next to godliness. We might no longer be attempting to sail around Cape Horn, but plenty of things could still go wrong. His greatest fear, especially with our second, larger boat, was always that one of us would fall overboard with the other person not being aware of it. We could float a line behind the stern, but there would still be the problem of hauling oneself back on board singlehandedly. Don thought about this problem quite a lot and eventually came up with the idea of a sling device that would free up a person's hands for grappling. Of course, it would have to be tested, and I would have to be the guinea pig, as Don was stronger and could pull me aboard if I couldn't do it myself.

We were anchored in Squirrel Cove, at the entrance to Desolation Sound, when Don decided we should try out his sling. There were a lot of other boats there too, many of them bigger and more luxurious than ours, but we were moored to one side of the cove and no one had any reason to pay any attention to us. While Don fooled around with the sling, I put on my swimsuit and went for an extended swim. When I returned to the boat Don told me to try and use the sling to get aboard. He thought he had a workable design, but my feet kept slipping under the boat and I was unable to get a grip. Don got madder and madder, thinking the problem was with me rather than the sling. "Keep your feet straight and behind you, goddammit," he yelled, but this didn't do much good as I was becoming exhausted and cold.

Eventually a guy from another boat came over. "I'll save you!" he shouted. Clearly he thought Don was trying to murder me! We explained the situation to him, but he wasn't convinced. Later, after Don pulled me out of the water, he sent me over to the guy with a free copy of one of our *Exploring* books, but he refused to take it.

Don thought some more about the sling in the meantime, and changed the design, and we tried it the next day, with me on the far side of the boat where no one could see me. This time the sling worked, but in all our years of boating after that we were fortunate we never had to use the thing for real. Nor did Don ever seriously try to murder me, and I never murdered him—though there were certainly times over the years when I thought about it!

For whatever reason, the sling episode does not appear in my diaries. Though I tried to keep a daily personal record of each of our *Baidarka* voyages, I did not always succeed. Some diaries started or stopped mid-voyage. Some have gaps because we "parked" the boat in Juneau or Sitka and flew home for a few weeks to tend to business. On other voyages, I kept no personal diary at all. But on many voyages I did, and when I revisited them this past year they brought back countless memories of good times—and some not so good—with Don and various friends, family members and fellow boaters in a truly spectacular and special part of the world, where I feel blessed to have spent so much time.

As presented here in edited form, the *Baidarka Diaries* offer a behind-the-scenes version of the work and experiences that went into our *Exploring* books. There are the expected entries on boat handling, sea and weather conditions, and the suitability or otherwise of various waterways for passage and anchoring. But the diaries also contain observations of nature, conversations with Don, encounters with fellow boaters and shore inhabitants, recurring battles with seasickness, occasional misadventures, bouts of frustration and tedium, shopping for provisions in various places—even onboard recipes!

Whether or not you are familiar with our *Exploring* books—and even if you're not a boater—I hope you find the *Baidarka Diaries* interesting and enjoyable. Please bear in mind that because they are indeed diaries, they are snapshots in time, written "in the moment." Some of the places mentioned remain timeless, others will doubtless have changed over the years since we last visited them, as they changed from year to year even when we were regularly cruising. The same applies to the people we encountered along the way, and perhaps to their boats. Though Don and I keep in touch with many of them to this day, I have made no effort in this book to provide follow-up information as to where they are now. I apologize for any misspellings of names—people or boats—and for any other inaccuracies.

- RHD, Anacortes, 2018

'LITTLE'
BAIDARKA

MAP 3
ANACORTES AND
SAN JUAN ISLANDS

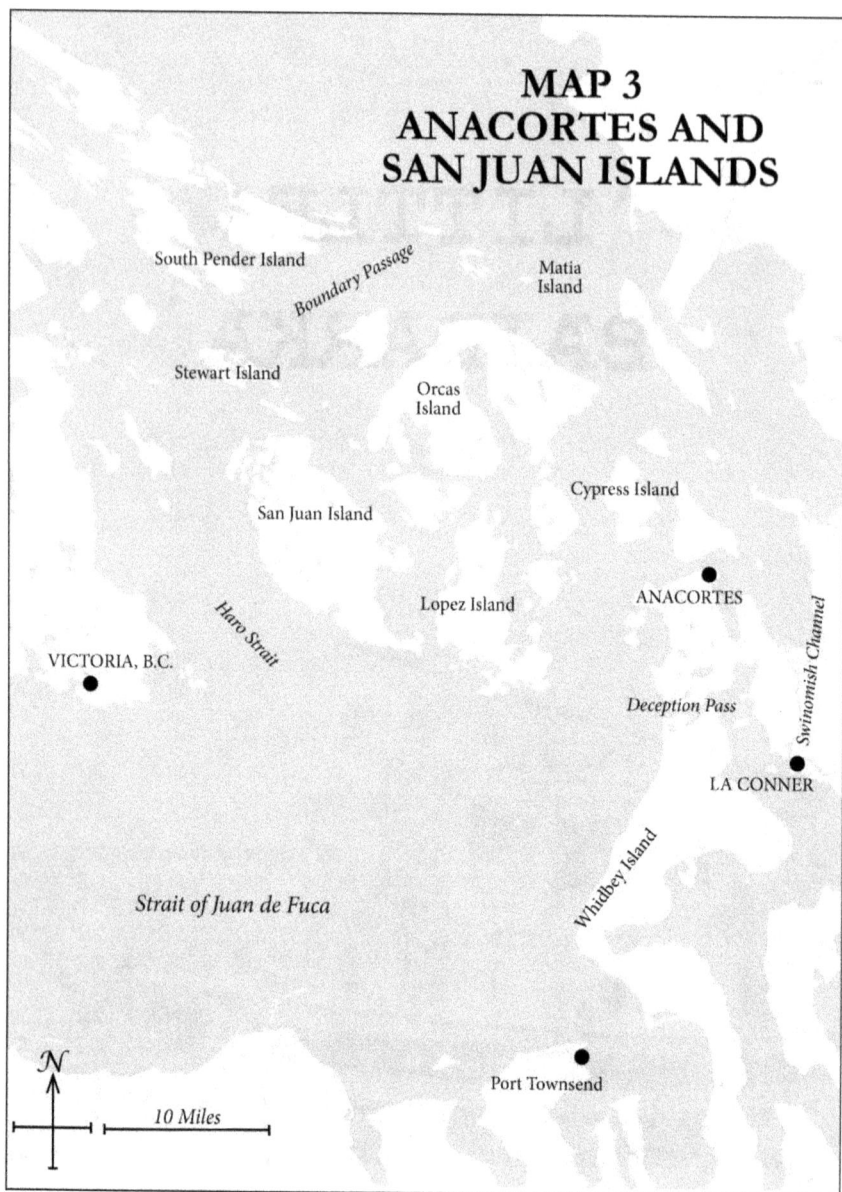

South Pender Island

Boundary Passage

Matia
Island

Stewart Island

Orcas
Island

Cypress Island

San Juan Island

Haro Strait

Lopez Island

ANACORTES

Swinomish Channel

VICTORIA, B.C.

Deception Pass

LA CONNER

Strait of Juan de Fuca

Whidbey Island

𝒩

10 Miles

Port Townsend

ANACORTES AND VICINITY, 1992

January 1, 1992: Crossing Boundary Passage between Pender and Stuart Islands. Gale force winds. Don whoops and hollers.

"You always sing when the weather's the worst," I say.

"Could be I'm whistling my way through the graveyard," he replies.

The boat leaped and rocked and fell into six-foot holes. The galley table flew across the salon and landed against the starboard bulkhead; everything not nailed down flew. I was sure the microwave would go next, so I flattened my front against it and wrapped my left arm around it and stood for an hour fixing my gaze on the horizon, taking deep breaths and periodic sips of water, in hopes that I'd prevent seasickness. Luckily we hit slightly calmer waters at the critical point for my stomach and I was able to let go and lie down!

We were both surprised at how well the boat took the rough seas. That's not something I'd like to do for a whole day or more, however.

February 15: The boat will have to go back to the manufacturers for massive electronic repairs. The new battery which was installed at the end of December has shorted out, as well as all equipment which depends on that battery: the tape recorder, the electronic starter for the stove, the heater, the water heater, the bilge pump. Good hull, lousy wiring. The employee who wired the boat was fired midway through the project. However, instead of sending him out the door immediately, the president (an ex-PE teacher who has NO business experience) told him to finish the wiring on our boat. We figure he purposely sabotaged the job.

If we can get the correct repairs done, we'll return to Victoria.

March 1: Yesterday we did nearly seventy miles, as we did the day before. Today was a nice slow-paced day. We started at 0730 hours in heavy fog with our radar going full blast. The fog lifted several hours later and we had wonderful filtered sun for three hours as we pulled into La Conner, a lovely little tourist town on the Swinomish Channel, dredged to create access to Anacortes without having to use the "infamous" Deception Pass. La Conner has a marvelous bakery, the Calico Cupboard, that serves breakfast and lunch seven days a week. We've stopped to buy pastries several times but had never eaten there. The dine-in food was as good as the baked goods. We had salmon benedict served on a croissant. Salmon is caught and smoked by the Swinomish Indian Tribe, which owns part of the land at La Conner.

Because the Channel is so narrow, the tide runs through it at quite a clip and to tie up at the dock is a mental and physical feat. This morning as we paddled in toward the dock, I grabbed the bow line and poised to spring onto the dock. I thought I heard Don yell "jump" when we were about three feet from the dock. It seemed a bit far but I jumped anyway. It was too far! And as I jumped my feet hit the dock and slid right off. I landed feet-first—in the water—bending my upper torso at a ninety-degree angle splat against the dock. It nearly knocked the wind out of me, but not enough to prevent a three-second exit from the water. So rapid that I was sure I hadn't even soaked my shoes and pants. Wrong! Fortunately the current was so strong running against the bow that it kept the boat off the dock and prevented my being crushed. The whole scene was video material. One of those "learning experiences" we hope not to repeat. I'm black and blue and very sore, but in good shape otherwise.

La Conner is an historic town. Don remembers it from the 1940s when his family lived in Anacortes, and in those days "you did not go to La Conner!" All the 1930s buildings have been beautifully restored and each one sells lovely handcrafted or imported products for the pretty people who drive up from Seattle to browse, eat and watch the boats go through the Channel.

We anchored at 1430 this afternoon after having motored through Deception Pass at slack tide. Shortly afterwards a gentle rain started and we are sitting here comfortably rolling and listening to the rain on the deck.

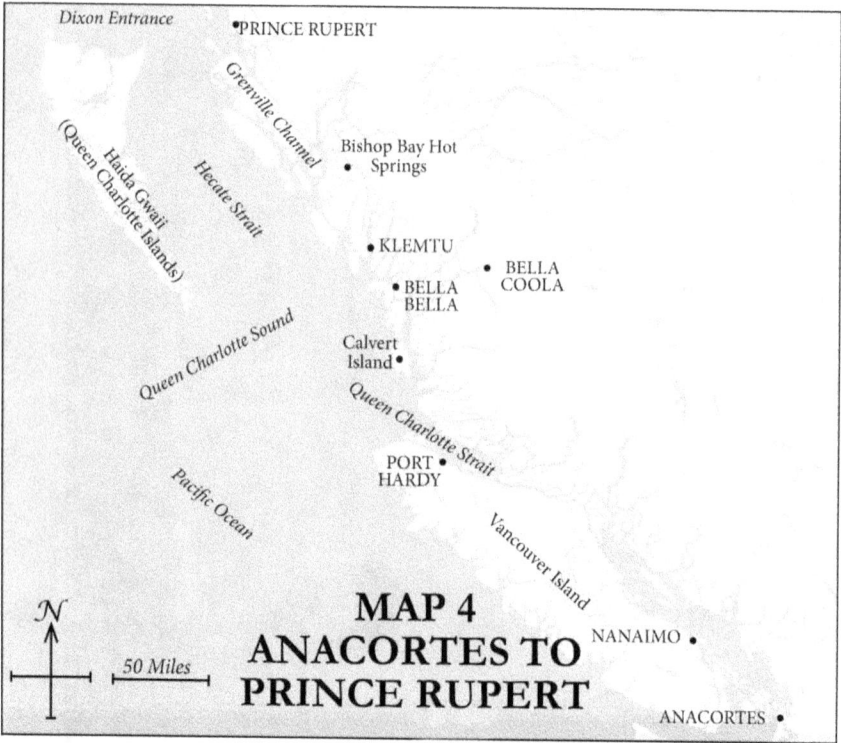

Dixon Entrance

•PRINCE RUPERT

Grenville Channel

Haida Gwaii
(Queen Charlotte Islands)

Hecate Strait

Bishop Bay Hot
• Springs

• KLEMTU

• BELLA
COOLA

• BELLA
BELLA

Calvert
Island •

Queen Charlotte Sound

Queen Charlotte Strait

Pacific Ocean

PORT •
HARDY

Vancouver Island

N

50 Miles

**MAP 4
ANACORTES TO
PRINCE RUPERT**

NANAIMO •

ANACORTES •

ANACORTES TO GLACIER BAY, 1992

May 1, 1992: Left Anacortes at 1800 hours and anchored off Pelican Beach, Cypress Island, for the night. In March, we had the whole place to ourselves. Now the boats and kayaks have come out of the garages and slips for the season. The beach was covered with tents of kayakers and two other boats were anchored offshore.

May 3: Nanaimo. Anchored off Newcastle Island. Gently rocking from the swells of the last ferry boat of the evening leaving Nanaimo, half a mile away. Tomorrow, we pick up Geza and Rusty[1] at Nanaimo.

The heater works like a dream and we now seem to have enough battery power for all our equipment. We run the refrigerator all the time, have lights and water pump on much of the time, and so far no problem at all with low voltage.

At noon we anchored for three hours at Princess Bay, on Wallace Island. Sat on the fan tail and had our lunch (Greek salad) in the sun, watching the clams shoot water five to eight feet high. Ravens landed among the tidal rocks, picking up seaweed and depositing it to the side to look for mussels and clams. Don says the clams were ejaculating.

Yesterday we saw dolphins. Today, we spotted seals, with smooth and silky silvery coats.

Saw tube worms this morning at Conover Cove, Wallace Island. Deep red "feathers" recoiled into the tube when I touched them.

Tonight we spent three hours sorting out the charts, $600 worth, "cataloguing" and rolling them. Stowed away all the provisions and stuff we'd brought for us so Geza and Rusty would have some room. I installed hooks in most of the lockers so we can hang hats, gloves, etc., as well as a hammock for our extra clothing.

Had two visitors tonight from the *Sea Crews*, of Anchorage, AK, which is headed north with five Icelanders. The captain is married to an Icelandic woman, lived in Iceland for eleven years building an air base. The man who came aboard with him works for Icelandic Air as maintenance crew. He said all aboard the *Sea Crews* do the same.

---

[1] Our longtime friend Geza Dienes and his then-girlfriend Rusty, whom he subsequently married.

We anchored at Princess Bay as the tide was going out—witnessed by lessening of water along shore, though the surface water was still coming in. Don says it must have been a function of cold versus "hot" water.

May 6, Wednesday: Squirrel Cove to Cameleon Harbour, Sonora Island. On Monday, after picking up Geza and Rusty in Nanaimo, doing laundry, going shopping, filling up the water, and going to the port office, we took off for Lasqueti Island. Tuesday, we continued on to Squirrel Cove, with stops to check out the fish plant (closed) at Lund; Savary Island; lunch at Copeland Islands; and the store at Squirrel Cove, where we looked for cheesecake for Don's birthday before entering Squirrel Cove and anchoring off the creek.

Off North Rendezvous Island, we saw six American widgeon—black and white heads with a rust breast.

1400 hours. Yuculta and Dent Narrows. Saw five eagles circling. A ring around sun with the outer ring a rainbow. A tug pulling logs, with another tug at the end of the jam pushing to maneuver through the rapids. A fishing village with a dozen houses. Area is full of fishing lodges. It looks like Patagonia, with high wooded hills; many are clear cut.

Through Dent Rapids we follow a fishing boat, fifty feet behind in his wake. He almost broaches; we pass. These are the heaviest rapids we've ever been in—full of whirlpools. Before we entered, Rusty said "Hey look though the binoculars at that foot of water across the channel."

Washed hair—three pints of water to lather and rinse.

Divona Sea is anchored in Squirrel Cove also, a fifty-three foot power vessel . Owners have a grocery store in Sechelt.

May 7: Today we pass Chatham Point, "the last 'civilized' point where the men are separate from the boys," Don says.

Blind Channel—Greene Point Rapids. Edgar and Annemarie Richter have the marina and restaurant. Restaurant is open from June to September (Labor Day). Annemarie and her husband look to be in their late sixties. They have lived there for twenty-two years. Their older son was twenty-one, the youngest ten when they moved there. What they bought was a shack. They built everything else. Edgar designed all the buildings. The end wall of the store is curved, made of cement and glass bowls with openings that point outward. There are collages of stuff Annemarie has picked up all over the beach. Each finger of the dock has a collage, as well as the end of the dock which has a big one. Wall hangings in the restaurant are crocheted hangings. Daughter-in-law makes bread, tends garden. They sell lettuce in summer. We bought some bread—yummy. Wished for more.

Greene Point Rapids was the worst, most exciting yet. We went through against the current. Some of the whirlpools were four feet deep. We watched a fishing boat and followed it to avoid rocks. After we had gone through the worst we decided to pull over to the north shore and anchor for a few hours and wait for the current to reverse. Cordero Channel flood runs east; the ebb runs west. After dinner (lentil soup with potatoes, onions, carrots, garlic, ginger, basil), we went on through Whirlpool Rapids in Wellbore Channel, which is wider and not as treacherous as Green Point.

May 8: Left Douglas Bay (our overnight anchorage) at 1046 hours and bucked four-foot chop in Sunderland Channel for three hours, then came into Port Neville, where the first store north of Vancouver was built to serve farming families, and then loggers. The sawmill was destroyed by fire in 1925, when ten families were farming near the head of the inlet.

Lorna Chesluk is a descendent of the original Hansen family, of Port Neville. Her grandfather came to Canada in 1891. Her father, Ole Hansen, was born in 1909, came to live in Port Neville in 1916. The store opened in 1924 and was run by Ole's sister until 1960. Ole and Lily have four children, of whom Lorna is the youngest. She has lived on the island since she was born. Her daughter, Erica, is about to start primary school by correspondence. The school headquarters are at Comox; a teacher will fly out periodically to check students' progress. Lorna also did her schooling through correspondence.

Of kayakers, the Hansens say: "Damn environmentalists."

May 9, Saturday: Don was in his element during the morning as we worked our way through Broken Islands, Chatham Channel, then, after stop for breakfast at Minstrel Island marina, through the Blow Hole, a narrow, short passage leading to Lagoon Cove, then to Beware Passage. Names like Caution Cove, Dead Point, Care Rock, Beware Rock… Using the echo sounder, radio, chart and extreme caution we worked our way through very slowly, with Don and Geza discussing "that's this islet; no, that's this point, it just looks like an island", etc., etc.

People at the Minstrel Island marina were friendly and cordial. "No menu… I have pancake mix, sausage and eggs, toast…" said the waitress. The guys ordered the sausage and eggs; Rusty and I had apple pancakes.

On display in the restaurant: Northwest Art by Sam Johnson, who lives on Gilford Island just north of Minstrel Cove. We saw two masks and a large "sea otter" with sea urchin on its back. The asking price for the sea otter was $2000 Canadian.

We passed an abandoned Indian village, Mamalilaculla, on Village Island, where there were beautiful weathered cedar houses. We laughed when we saw "yacht club" on the chart, but were amazed when we passed it—a beautiful two-story building with a dock, and three boats in the harbor. Farewell Harbor Yacht Club has a lodge, presumably for rich fishermen who fly in from Vancouver, Seattle, Portland, etc.

We had planned to anchor at Goat Island, but with a change in weather forecast we anchored for only two hours, then pulled up anchor to make more northwesterly progress toward Port Hardy and avoid having such a long day on Sunday.

At 1400 hours Don had asked, "would you be mad if we went on?"

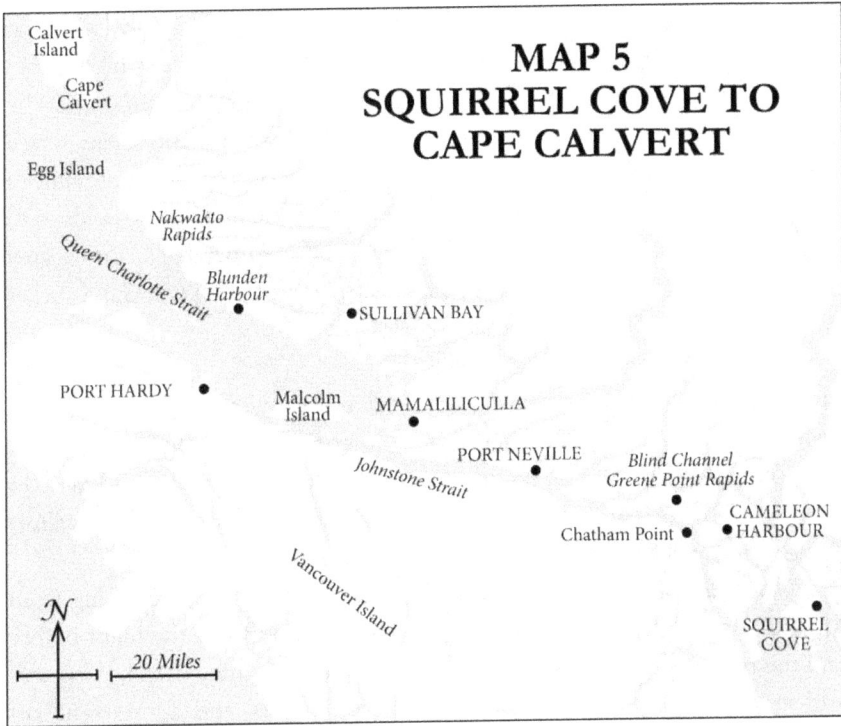

MAP 5
SQUIRREL COVE TO
CAPE CALVERT

Calvert Island
Cape Calvert
Egg Island
Queen Charlotte Strait
Nakwakto Rapids
Blunden Harbour
• SULLIVAN BAY
PORT HARDY •
Malcolm Island
MAMALILICULLA
•
PORT NEVILLE
•
Blind Channel
Greene Point Rapids
•
Johnstone Strait
CAMELEON
• HARBOUR
Chatham Point •
Vancouver Island
•
SQUIRREL COVE
N
20 Miles

"How many hours?"

"About two."

"Okay."

Rusty and I were planning a birthday party for Don and trying to get little things done, like cut-outs of "60" and decorating a crown for Don, and I was planning a good meal—pork roast marinated in ginger, garlic, orange juice, Worcestershire sauce, soy sauce, etc., roasted onions and potatoes, plus a dessert of hazelnut chocolate cake, which Rusty and I cut in the shape of a tug, laced with brandy and fake whipped cream. Don may have suspected something but he didn't let on. We taped the foil "60s" Rusty had cut out onto the windows and pillows, and Don was truly touched when he saw. "I'm going to take a shower to celebrate this," he said. He came up smelling like an aftershave lotion factory. We had tied up at the government float in Mitchell Bay, on Malcolm Island, by this time. Took a walk through rainforest after dinner; the guys checked out all the abandoned machinery—three boats with propellers intact, for which they devised a "plan" to steal them.

25

There's a beautiful new grey Victorian style two-story house located at the end of the government wharf. Rusty could see in the dining room where they have handmade cabinets of a wood she thought might be cherry. The lawn around the house was nicely mowed, and there was a truck and a car. Several other houses are nearby, nicely kept up but without the luxurious look of the first. We speculated that the grey house belongs to the owner of the logging outfit. A young girl hopped bareback onto a grey horse tethered in the yard and rode him in the pouring rain without a slicker to another house down the way.

May 10: At midnight the wind had veered and we were slamming into the dock so badly that we got up and moved to anchor off the head of the bay. We bobbed and rocked all night. Don didn't sleep after 0330, and at 0515 he weighed anchor and we left. Now, at 1030 hours, we're anchored calmly and securely, an hour from Port Hardy.

We pulled in at 0907 hours after a three and a half hour crossing from Mitchell Bay. No one was hungry after the rich food from the night before and the poor night's sleep. We dozed most of the morning, had hot brown-and-serve bread, then got the kayak down. Geza and Don went off paddling for an hour, then Don and I. We followed the shore west for several small bays, landed on one point where we saw an unfinished log cabin. We climbed up the hill to examine it. Only about a meter high, it was overgrown with arbutus, ferns and small evergreens. Below it were two pools of muskeg water which could have been bathing pools. A path, newly clipped, ran along the edge of the cliff and from the log cabin a crude ladder about fifteen feet high had been attached to the cliff to allow you to climb up. We followed the path for an eighth of a mile and speculated that it might have been an Indian path.

The shellfish and sea life are abundant: Starfish of purple, vermillion, pink; crabs; lined chiton, hairy chiton, whelks, urchins, sea squirts that look like tired penises, anemones. The sea-life here is more abundant than in the tropics, but less colorful in variety.

Geza and Rusty go ashore tomorrow to catch 8:45 a.m. bus to Nanaimo. I will miss them. They've been *great* boat companions. Geza and Don laugh like kids together—they're on the same wavelength—and Rusty is bright, down to earth, practical and so observant.

May 11: Up at 0530 hours. Weighed anchor at 0610 and headed around to Port Hardy, where we discovered that nothing opens before 0800. (We arrived at 0725.) The marina didn't even open until 0900.

Beautiful day—sunny, with gusty winds, scattered clouds. After accompanying Geza and Rusty to the bus station, we took on fuel, water and propane, and bought groceries. Spent $130 at the supermarket on cookies, bread, vegetables, and fruit.

1850 hours. Anchored in God's Pocket, I count twenty-three bald eagles, some of which are young ones. The female has a light brown head with tan spotted breast. God's Pocket is a small cove just off Scarlett Point, the take off point for crossing Queen Charlotte Strait. You can look out into the Channel and see the white caps flowing past, watch the eagles ride the thermals, and sit here tranquilly, gently rolling at the mooring buoy. To bed now, for tomorrow will be a long day—up early and sixty-plus miles to go.

May 12, Tuesday: Anchored at 1438 hours in Pruth Bay, after leaving God's Pocket at 0440. The first part of crossing Queen Charlotte Strait was the worst, but this lasted no more than four hours. I was queasy by 0600 so lay down on the settee for two hours. As we passed Egg Island, we heard a radio conversation with a woman "manning" the light station there. They welcome visitors in good weather, but not many people stop. They grow vegetables for their own use; this year has been mild but with lots of rain, so the bugs are horrible after a lack of frost in winter to kill them off.

When we hit Cape Calvert, on the southern end of Calvert Island, rollers from the open sea were no longer a problem and we had a slight dry east wind, so that passage which is normally choppy in north-westerlies was almost glassy. We were on our way to check out a small possible anchorage between Sweeper and Blair Islands when Don spotted two kayakers. We headed toward them and invited them to come on board. A young couple from Kitimat, B.C., they started a six month trip last October from Kitimat, kayaked till December, then took off again this spring. They will kayak till July, go home for ten days, then go on again. They have two Tofino kayaks—one a double which he is paddling, carrying all his camera equipment; she is paddling a single. They had come out of Pruth Bay, crossed Fitzhugh Sound and were heading down the mainland. She has a fantastic attitude about all the hardships, looks at it as an adventure and privilege to be able to see all the beauty and wildlife.

After checking out a spot near Sweeper Island, we decided it was not good enough for anchoring and crossed to Pruth Bay—a five-mile longer entry due east-west with a three-fingered anchorage, the best being off the west finger. (There is also good anchorage in the first cove east of Keith.) We dropped anchor and flopped, sleeping for two hours. Then we went to shore in the kayak and crossed through the forest on the well-worn path to the beach on the western shore. Caretakers of the Hakai Fish Company have a house at the end of Pruth Bay and keep up the path, which goes through muskeg a lot of the way. We spent over two hours on the beach, which is a beautiful crescent shape with dunes along the northern side and stone bluffs along the south side. The beach has singing sands like Saugatuck[2]. The water was so green and clear you could see light through the breakers, unlike at the beaches in southern California. Miniscule fish played in the inch of water that washed up on the sand. There were hermit crabs of every size, two millimeters to two inches, pink and green sea anemones; sea urchins; whelks, limpets, scallops. Sweet pea, wild strawberry, huckleberries, arbutus, sedge grass, grew along the sand dunes, and in the forest, arbutus, ground dogwood, ferns, mosses among the cedar and hemlock. The forest had been practically destroyed by logging in the early 1980s and the growth is only six feet high in many places. It's as if, once the trees are gone, there isn't room for any more big ones to grow. Huge trees were sacrificed. Sad, sad.

Hecate Island, the north end of Calvert Island, and the large island north of Calvert (Hunter) have been designated as a B.C. park, comprising over 100,000 hectares.

May 13, Wednesday: On our way to Fitz Hugh Crossing we checked out Goldstream Harbour, at the north-east end of Calvert Island. It was a great place to anchor and just south of lighthouse, so it would be good in foul weather because it's located so near the light.

The wind kicked up into a nice stiff breeze and as we anchored in Koeye Cove the white caps on Fitz Hugh looked as if the wind had increased to twenty-five knots. After a nap we kayaked one and a half miles up Koeye River, past an old lime camp—three abandoned cabins, piles for

---

[2] Michigan, where I spent summers as a child.

tie up, etc. We saw dozens of Canada geese, common goldeneye, and a snow goose or swan with a green tag around its neck—a solitary bird, without a mate. We paddled to convergence of two rivers then decided should get back to boat as wind was kicking up. It was spooky, it was so wild.

Don remarked on how white the sun was as it set because of lack of air pollution.

We spend so much time just "surviving" on the boat we don't have a lot of "disposable" time for the computer and portable piano. Tonight was the first time we took the piano out of its case. I'm wondering if it was worth the expense.

May 14, Thursday: Up anchor at 0455 hours. Leave Koeye Cove. Depth sounder set for six feet kept going off.

Observation: Logs at edge of horizon appear much larger than they actually are. A log that appears like a basking whale from one and a half miles off is no larger than ten feet long with a root two feet high. What looks like a boat coming over the horizon turns out to be a log.

1440 hours. Anchored in Boat Inlet of Cecilia Island, east of Milbank Sound. A long passage of fifty-two nautical miles today. Visited Codville Lagoon, recommended by people on *Julie Ann*, from Anacortes. It is a landlocked lagoon, an isosceles triangle with an island in middle. Sagar Lake is only a quarter mile walk from the east end of lagoon and offers good swimming with warm water, so we were told. Instead of following the regular route, Don took Gunboat Passage which connects Fisher Channel with Seaforth Channel, east of Bella Bella.

Coming down Reid Passage to Boat Inlet was another interesting problem of avoiding rocks and shallow parts. The good old echo sounder with its line picture of the bottom is big help. Again, we are alone.

After supper, a one hour paddle in the kayak out to the channel and around Boat Inlet. We saw millions of miniscule fish (one to two centimeters) in schools making ripples. Others two to four centimeters long swam near the surface making "wakes" like boats. We saw a Penpoint Gunnel—a fish which resembles an eel. This one was bluish grey with "feathers" along its spine. Usually green, they can be brown, red, or yellow. Commonly they are the shade of eel grass, with lines running down the sides. We first spotted one as we kayaked near shore, then another swam by the boat several times. There's no one else in this inlet. We saw one small pleasure boat pass through the channel as we kayaked. The evening is flat calm. The only indication that we're a boat is the turning on the anchor and the slight flap of the kayak against the starboard beam.

May 17, Sunday: 2155 hours, Bishops Bay. Pulled in last night at 2000 hours after a long day of eighty miles. Picked up one of the two mooring buoys off the hot springs float, where some locals were having a party.

We slept till 0900 hours, safely tied up and gently rocking. This morning we read, cleaned and put away tools, and did chores. When we moored last night I started to do dishes and found no pressure. Don opened the engine compartment and found it full of water. A connector from the hot water feeder tubing had loosened, so we lost all water from main tanks. The forward tank wouldn't feed into the other tanks because they're vented and have only air in them. The pump sucks in air instead of pulling in the water from the other tank. At least, we think that's the problem. We will go into Prince Rupert on Tuesday and fill up on water to see if that does the trick. If not, it's the water pump.

The hot springs here are clean, hot and perfectly clear. The Kitimat Yacht Club and other private groups have built a house out of cement block on three sides. The fourth side is the natural rock against the cliff where the water comes on. The bottom has been cemented in, a few large rocks have been set in the bottom to sit on, and three ropes are suspended from the rafters beneath the tin roof so kids can swing from them. The depth of the water is about three feet. An outer tub, through which the "house" water empties, can be plugged so you can soap up and not spoil the larger "room." Crews of pleasure vessels have painted their names all over the rafters.

A path from the house leads uphill to a covered camping area with outside picnic table, stacked wood and metal fire grate, and from there up a path to an outhouse (which needs emptying!).

At the south-east side of the end of the bay a beautiful waterfall tumbles down a granite face. Birch and alders line the route of the falls.

The M/V *Julie Ann* from Anacortes, which we saw in Pruth Bay, came in this morning and we spent several hours tonight talking on their boat. Margie and Frank Fletcher. Both are seventy-three years old. He was a radio operator for Pan Am during WWII in Alaska, near the Yukon River, for one and a half years. He first went to Alaska at age fifteen, in 1933. She went with him in the '40s. He and Don, who spent his later teenage years in Ketchikan, found a lot to talk about, reminiscing about Ellis Airlines (now Alaska Airlines), Juneau, and Ketchikan. She was a nurse. They have four grown children, one son in Albuquerque who is a biologist for the Forest Service.

Klemtu has wonderful water, according to Margie, and the tribe encourages visitors. The store there is good if the steamer has just made a delivery; otherwise it has an okay supply of dry and canned goods. The café is good, too.

Coming off the Fletchers' boat, we prepared to kayak back to *Baidarka*. "We want to see how you do this," they said.

"We'll give you a good laugh," Don said. And we did. Don usually gets in the kayak first to stabilize it. Instead, I stepped in first and Don didn't even have the stern line in hand although he'd unhooked the bowline. I hadn't sat down yet and lunged for the dock as the kayak swung out. Into the drink. Frank, Margie, Don and another Canadian man ran to pull me out, soaking wet. This nullified all the wonderful soaking I'd done in the hot springs.

"Damn, now I've had a fresh water bath and a saltwater bath," I said.

They suggested I go have another bath but since my clothes were so wet I didn't want to, and we paddled back to the boat.

May 18, Monday: Off moorage at 0630 hours and up Ursala Channel, around Gribbell Island, and down Verney Passage, where the tides meet and separate at all but high water. We're now in the "true north", Don says. High, snow-covered mountains, black granite cirques, sheer-walled domes. Verney Passage is very reminiscent of Chile's Patagonian channels. However, here the winds seem to be lesser than those in *Magallenes*. There were gale warnings, winds thirty-five to forty knots outside, for today so we may get some heavier weather later, but so far it's fairly calm and another beautiful sunny day. To date we've had only two days of rain.

We've been reading the Introduction to Vancouver's journals (283-plus pages!). Most of the names of the inlets, sounds, major coves and bays are from Vancouver's "complement" or benefactors of his voyage. Johnstone (of Johnstone Strait) was his sailing master.

May 19, Tuesday: Anchored during the day in Lowe Inlet, off a waterfall. It's like Yosemite. *Julie Ann* was also there, and Bob Sampson, a solo kayaker from Gig Harbor, Washington. Last year Bob went from Seattle to Chatham Point. This year, Chatham to Ketchikan. He said the most difficult part of trip is "the camping." The paddling isn't even so bad compared to the camping. At home, his wife kayaks with him in a double. Bob had dinner aboard *Julie Ann* last night, then spent the night ashore.

A hike to the falls and a lake started as a hike through a forest, where big black bear were probably were hiding.

Spent the night in Prince Rupert Yacht Club. We had a wonderful shower, did laundry, grocery shopping and had dinner with Margie and Frank at Smiles, a seafood cafe.

Weather was kicking up before we got into the yacht club. Don turned into the wrong finger and it then took twenty minutes to turn around because of wind. A few worried faces. Don kept his cool throughout. I was proud.

May 21, Thursday: Behind Gilanta Rocks, a cove with an off-white sand beach. Don thinks his Uncle Phil Fallis stayed here in 1936, when he paddled with three Sea Scout buddies in two canoes from Seattle to Skagway during the Great Depression. We looked for the totems Phil mentioned but could find none. They were probably hauled away years ago by researchers or government officials.

Don is a real explorer. He senses, observes, studies and comes to the correct solutions. What a pity he wasn't born two centuries ago. He might have been a Captain Cook or Vancouver.

The sounds of the mussels on drying rocks is like rain on pavement.

In Foggy Bay, we find Margie and Frank again in *Julie Ann*, also Tom and Trudie King, aboard *Kings Ransom*, a 42-foot Westsail. They're live-aboards who have cruised four times to Alaska. They spent four years in the South Seas, including New Zealand and Australia. When they got to Brisbane they shipped their boat back to US ($25,000). Like me, they like visiting the places, not the passages to get to them.

Saw a bear and her cub on shore. Also two martens as we were paddling close to shore in the kayak. They're curious little animals who peek out, lift themselves up on their front legs, and stare and sniff.

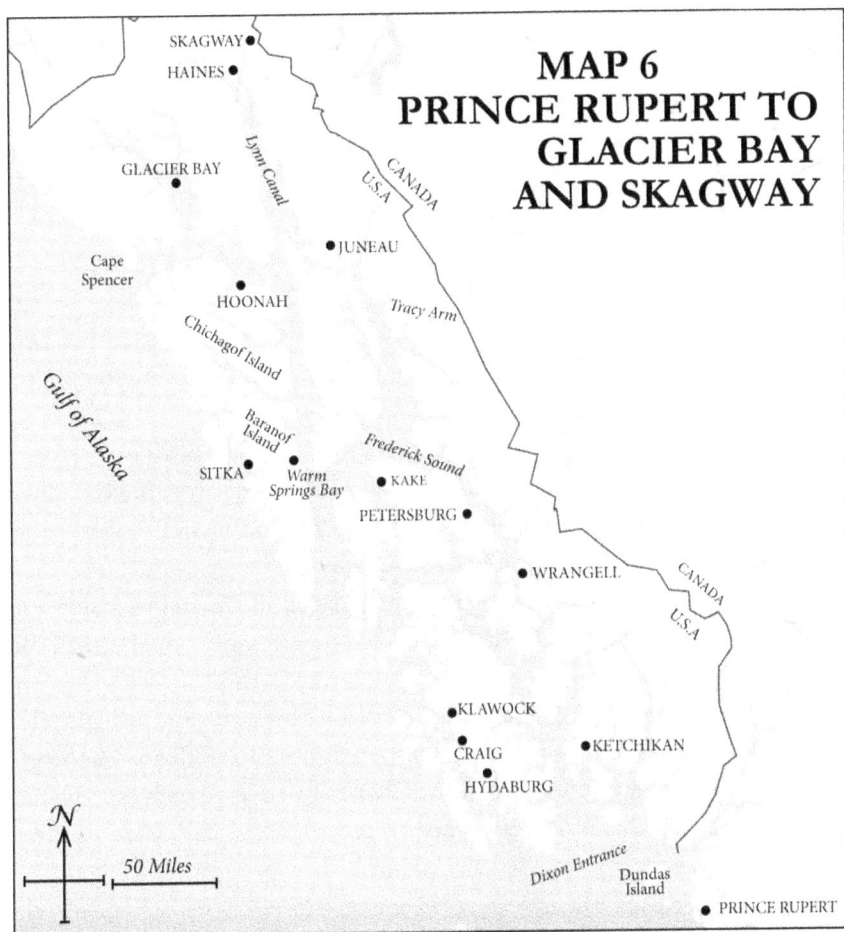

MAP 6
PRINCE RUPERT TO
GLACIER BAY
AND SKAGWAY

May 23: Ketchikan. We're back in redneck country, though the main part of town caters to tourists. The market sells things in big quantities.

Picked up Sally Ridley at the airport, after tying up at a float a hundred yards from the terminal.

May 24, Sunday: Misty Fiords. Overhanging gardens, granite domes, waterfalls, hanging valleys, vertical faces. "From snowfield to seaweed," Don says.

May 25: Moored in Walker Cove. A twenty-foot wide cascade is choked with snow. Chickamin River is full of glacier melt which flows green into the main channel. It looked almost menacing—cold, frightening. The scenery is so overpowering at times I feel uncomfortable, and the constant mist, rain and clouds just add to this feeling.

May 26: Spent the night in Yes Bay, in a calm, serene anchorage south-east of a lodge. Earlier we anchored in Anan Bay, where the US Forest Service maintains a bear observatory. There's a cabin on shore which fishermen can rent (and was being rented). We kayaked around the inner lagoon up to some rapids. Flat calm.

Anchored south of Green Point, Wrangell. Fishing boats—*Icy Queen, Spicy Lady, Siren, Odin, Dream Maiden*—pass us going north to unload their catch. "You can tell what's on their minds by the names," Don says. "They're no wimps. We're back where men are men."

All these fishing boats are going to port laden down and we can't buy a piece of fish for ourselves—it all goes to the canneries to be frozen or canned.

We pass houses along the shore, accessible by boat only at high tide. They have neat metal roofs with junky yards—motors, floats, gas cans, fishing nets, lines, kids' toy cars—casually, messily, covered with blue plastic tarps that are half blown off. "I suppose our yard would look like this if we lived here," I say.

May 27: Visited Wrangell for four hours. It's a cute small town which is still unsophisticated and less geared to tourism than Ketchikan. The harbormaster is a young man of about thirty who sold us huge prawns, four pounds for $20. Fees for tying up at the dock: free first night, $3.20 a night after that, with a discount for ten days or more. Little boys were fishing at the dock—one had "bagged" a Dolly Varden trout at least fourteen inches long. A beautiful rainbow to the north of Wrangell as we left.

We're anchored off the south-west end of Wrangell Narrows for the night.

May 28: Through the Narrows, which has over sixty-six navigation markers. At night because of its flashing red and green lights it's called "Christmas Tree Lane." The Alaska ferries use the Narrows also. We had

Wrangell.

fun navigating the channel. Visibility was at least ten miles, so we had no problems.

The sun came out in spots as we cruised in to Petersburg and could see the upper topography surrounding it. Petersburg is a cute, clean, well-manicured town, with houses painted cream and blue or pink and white. The market had beautiful produce, all the dry goods we needed, and a section of Norwegian imported goods.

Crossed Frederick Sound to anchor in Thomas Bay, where tomorrow we'll visit Baird Glacier. Rain held off as we crossed and the mountain peaks (Cosmos Mountain) to the east were all visible. We also could see a huge glacier to the south-east. It had two levels and we wondered whether it could be Le Conte.

Now we're anchored behind Ruth Island listening to the rain pour down.

May 29, Friday: Up early and off for a kayak ride to Delta Creek. We tied the kayak and walked through the overgrown road shown on the chart. The creek crossing used to have a bridge over it but this has been washed out. There were logs across it and as we watched the creek a little marten came running across the log, got two-thirds of the way across, stopped upon seeing us, then ran back. She repeated the two-thirds crossing three more times, each time getting a little closer. On the fifth try she looked straight at Don, kept coming on the log, then right by him and jumped down right beside him, scampering away. At the south point of the land we saw two blue herons with the brown coats. We tried to go up the Patterson Glacier terminal river, but the current coming down was too strong so we couldn't get a view of the glacier. The water was sandy brown with silt near the outlet. Canada geese are migrating north now. Lupine growing along the shore where it gets sun were two feet high, like they are in a good moist year in the Sierra.

While we kayaked for two hours the weather was beautiful. Huge clouds that resembled thunderheads piled up to the south—fleecy grey and white clouds, with holes of blue sky peeking through and then bright sun that fries you. Within fifteen minutes of getting the kayak back on *Baidarka* it was raining.

Baird Glacier: we go in to three fathoms to have a look. The sky was clouded in so the blue ice doesn't stand out as it does when under sun.

May 30: Tracy Arm of Holkham Bay. North and South Sawyer Glacier are at the head of bay. We encounter "bergy" bits before the entrance to Tracy Arm. They come in all sizes, ranging from one-foot-high cream puffs to forty-foot goliaths. U-shaped valleys at the back have sharp peaks—snow-covered, vertical granite faces with glacial markings.

Two miles from the head of the arm we started to encounter pack ice. We lay ahull for an hour; saw the tour boat *Glacier Spirit* go through, then heard him on the radio, so now we are trying to work our way through also.

I say, "We'll have glacial striations on the hull."

Don says, "I don't know if I have the courage to go through these things," as the chunks hit the hull.

The bergs: some are filled with holes and look like lava or moon rocks or Swiss cheese; some have sun cups; cuts are vertical, horizontal; cornices; some have shapes—polar bear, camel, swans, a duck.

Water in this channel is a most beautiful aquamarine. There are vertical faces where every crevice is filled with plants, bushes, shrubs.

We work our way through the pack ice till we have a view of just the tongue of North Sawyer Glacier, then we can't go any further and we turn around.

We go to bed at 2130 hours with two bergs headed our way. We get up several times during the night to check. At 2300 the bergs were a hundred yards off our port bow, but they headed toward shore. Don had put out the fenders in case of an iceberg attack.

May 31, Sunday: Weather: a small craft advisory of up to twenty-five knots with six-foot seas just off the corner of Stephens Strait (the Five Finger Lighthouse), so we stay put all day, reading, talking and eating. Breakfast: potatoes, onions and ham, basted eggs. For dinner we cook the rest of the prawns and make a big shrimp salad.

At 1800 hours we get the southeast storm that's been predicted all day. Don lets out 200 feet of anchor line and we think about Puerto Hombre, north of Punta Arenas, where we had to ride out two days of storms. It has intermittently poured rain—last night and today—the most we've seen yet.

Two other boats are in here—the *Frontier Queen* (here last night, then off this morning), and *Rainbow*, from Portland, OR.

A twenty-foot high berg sits at the entry to the little cove here. It's nearly 2100 hours, and we hit the sack after having made three (Don) plus two (me) trips out to the bow to secure the capstan, let out more line, and secure the kayak bow line. *Nasty* weather, but exhilarating.

There were hundreds of surf scoters earlier, when it was calm. They took off from the point by the creek. Their wings make a singing sound as they fly.

June 1: Leave Northwest Cove, Tracy Arm, through icebergs. About a quarter mile inside the entrance there's a turbulent tide rip, with leaping, heaping chop. We line up ranges on Harbor Island, then turn west when we are past the shoals off the two points.

Bergs appear in the shapes of swans, dinosaurs, crystal chandeliers, punch bowls.

A fog bank lies east-west across Stephens Passage. One very light hole shines where the sun shows through the bank. Today everything is blue, purple, white, pink: the clear outline of the mountains against the sky, snowfields, glaciers. Whales spout and breach, dive so their dorsal fin shows vertical along the horizon. Sometimes one does a continuous breach, six to ten times. The sun against his back glistens like sun on wet polished lava.

Arrive at Taku Harbor and tie up at the float dock. The "walk way" along the upper tide line is a series of recently placed planks and an old boardwalk. There are bog-orchids, marsh marigolds, shooting stars, forget-me-nots, and skunk cabbage not yet in bloom. An old cannery pier is reduced to ruins, the pilings still standing by the dozens, with small gardens growing on their summits. An engine, long-since abandoned and overgrown, sprouts a lone shooting star.

2015 hours. Sally spots river otters on the dock—we count seven of them. One swims back and we notice its chirping sound.

This is the first afternoon I've had a bad attitude toward Don. Perhaps he's had enough of having two women aboard. He has his rules, and his misplaced anger. He's angry with *me* because "my" friend is incompetent as crew.

June 2: Into Taku Inlet up to sixteen fathoms, where we can see the glacier curving around from Hole in the Wall. Why should we call it Yosemite-like? Why is Yosemite not Alaska-like?

Tracy Arm.

June 3: Juneau. Native dances. Old couples hold hands. There are at least 300 of them in the hall. The majority are Native American or mixed Tlingit or Haida. There's a diversity of "costumes." The women are beautiful.

June 7, Sunday: Anchored in a bay north of Hoonah. Hoonah is a native village with two grocery stores, several bars, one liquor store, one marine store, a large town harbor across a small island from government float. Men and couples were preparing for opening day of halibut season Monday spending hours, if not entire days cutting up bait and skewering the pieces onto hooks. Lines were coiled into tin pails and washtubs.

June 8, Monday: Arrived in Glacier Bay and signed in at the Visitors Center in Bartlett Cove. Don and I took the one-mile Forest Trail loop through spruce and hemlock forest, passing muskeg where the water lilies have yellow blossoms. Sphagnum moss and strewn lichen. Plants that grow in bogs share features with xeromorphs—plants adapted to dry conditions. Along the walkway from Park Headquarters to the lodge we saw five types of berry bushes: wild strawberries, currants, salmonberries, nagoon berries, and blueberries. Nagoon berries grow singly on a single leaf close to the ground. The air was perfumed by the odor of narcissus—it can't be that, but whatever it was, it was wonderful.

Today we saw our first coyote on shore, off Park Headquarters.

Anchored at 1630 hours in the South Bight of North Arm, Fingers Bay. The sun has come out and our two Alaskans (daughter Dawn and son-in-law Jeff Mach, picked up in Juneau) are "sunbathing." I'm sitting on the stern of the boat facing a valley where I hear a cascade and see snowcapped granite "hills."

June 9, Tuesday: Reid Inlet. We took the kayak to go look at the glacier. Don said, "It's like being back in the Pleistocene era." An under-glacier river coursed out. Streams ran everywhere carrying down silt and rocks— the beginning of the Pacific waters. The soil is so new that only small, thin willow shoots and shrubs grew along the streams. You couldn't even call them shrubs, they were so scrawny. New, raw land.

We kayaked in Johns Hopkins Inlet, also, under Lamplugh Glacier, with the uncomfortable feeling that at any time it could fall over on us. Glacier polish can be seen on Jaw Point, off Johns Hopkins Inlet, near the Lamplugh Glacier.

A mother harbor seal raised herself eighteen inches out of the water to look around. Then we understood why. We heard a baby seal crying as it swam from berg to berg. It tried to climb up on one berg and couldn't, whining and crying. Still, part of the training for the young.

Most of the inlets we've been to thus far were blocked by glaciers a hundred years ago. In fact, half of Glacier Bay was blocked before 1860.

We wouldn't have gotten more northerly than Geike Inlet today if it were 1860. In 1750, the entire bay was blocked by glaciers.

The sun shone all day. No clouds, even at 2040 hours, as I write.

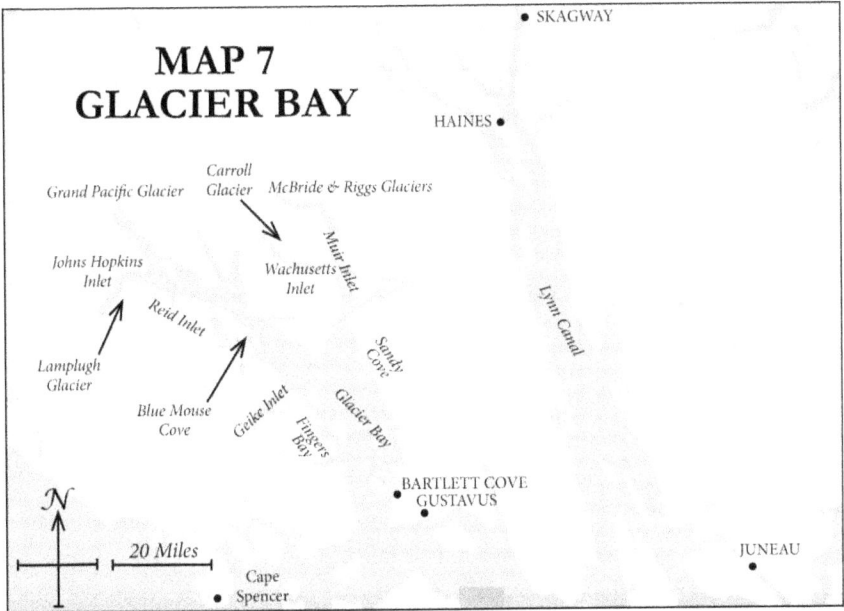

MAP 7
GLACIER BAY

SKAGWAY

HAINES

Carroll
Grand Pacific Glacier   Glacier   McBride & Riggs Glaciers

Muir Inlet

Johns Hopkins
Inlet   Wachusetts
Inlet

Lynn Canal

Reid Inlet

Sandy
Cove

Lamplugh
Glacier   Geike Inlet   Glacier Bay

Blue Mouse
Cove   Fingers
Bay

BARTLETT COVE
GUSTAVUS

N

20 Miles   Cape
Spencer   JUNEAU

June 10: Great Pacific Glacier, on another day of beautiful clear weather. *Reggae Princess* and *Westerdam* came into the head of the bay; then *Highlander* with its helicopter (*Highland Fling*)–Malcolm Forbes' "capitalist tool"—on the aft deck.

Jeff says the ice melting sounds like Rice Krispies in a bowl. The glacier to the left (west) of Pacific is quite active, doing the most calving we've seen to date.

Blue Mouse Cove overnight, next to a National Park Service floating cabin.

June 11: Muir Inlet. McBride and Riggs Glaciers are at the north end. Riggs is now a tidewater glacier at high tide only. McBride has receded. The entire north end of the inlet was filled with glaciers until 1929. The barren land is raw, prehistoric–looking. Nothing grows on it. Waterfalls of brown water race down the sides of the slopes. The land looks like the most barren of mined hills in Nevada—brown with streaks of burnt orange; fine like coal. In dinghy and kayak, we all went to Riggs to take photos, then landed on the beach below McBride, where six or seven creeks ran into the inlet. The glaciers calved making horrendous claps on the water and setting up three-foot waves. "Do you want to go into the cave?" Don asked, meaning a cave at the foot of the Riggs overhang. "No way," I replied.

June 12: Friday. Anchored at the south side of Wachusett Inlet, just inside Muir Inlet. In the morning, we motored toward the head of the inlet to Carroll Glacier, whose snout is far from the water. We couldn't get near because of silt and shoaling. Dawn and I took the kayak and followed the south shore. The entire inlet is raw land—waterfalls everywhere; no trees. A few willows and alders are taking hold; fireweed, yellow flowers and white ones which we couldn't identify from fifteen feet offshore.

June 13: Anchored in South Sandy Cove at night, then weighed anchor for Bartlett Cove where we had lunch at the lodge. Goodbye to Glacier Bay. I loved it!

Glacier Bay

KETCHIKAN TO ANACORTES, 1992

September 21, 1992: Weather: pouring rain in the morning and all last night while we were at the dock in Ketchikan. We went for gas and water before dropping Bob and Anna Mae Botley at the airport. Bob and Anna Mae had been with us since September 11. Great crew; they had good attitudes and Bob with his calmness and thoughtfulness was a particularly good complement to Don. Bob has many more facets than we knew—entrepreneurial, philosophical—and he and Don had some good conversations. Bob is also a good navigator and helmsman. We came fifteen nautical miles from airport and anchored at north end of Cascade Inlet, which we'd reconnoitered on our way north.

Highlights of trip with Bob and Anna Mae: Tracy and Endicott Arms with an overnight in Ford's Terror—along with a floatplane flight over the Sawyer glaciers. The weather that day was spectacular. I was overwhelmed—awed—by the experience, so that I could hardly speak as we overflew all the canyons and waterfalls we'd seen from below as well as the lakes we'd guessed were higher up. We saw mountain goats on the peaks. Bob and I stayed aboard while Don and Anna Mae took their flight first. Then I maneuvered the boat through iceberg "bits" to the mouth of North Sawyer Arm. This was good practice for me because I caught on to bringing the stern around in reverse.

1830 hours. Don sees calm water outside in Revillagigedo Channel; wants to head on down tonight. I'm too tired. No sleep last night and high adrenaline this morning.

September 22, Tuesday: Anchored in Cascade Inlet, inside Ham Island—a narrow opening we'd explored on ourway north in May. Left in heavy fog which cleared for thirty minutes, then socked in "properly" to fifty yards of visibility. Made it to Foggy Bay under radar, echo sounder, and chart following the compass. Hairy!!

It's rained all day, *heavily* since 1500 hours. All this rain. Can't it be "canned" and sent south?

Troubles with electricals: engine would start only on "both" batteries yesterday and today. Negative terminal on forward, small battery was loose.

We see bright lights crossing the opening to Foggy Bay—a fishing boat, probably. At home, no one goes out in this weather. Here, what can

Tracy Arm from the air.

they do? It's their livelihood and pouring rain, fog, etc. can't stop them if they want to make a few bucks.

September 23, Wednesday: Decided to weigh anchor in Foggy Bay since the weather was supposed to change—the wind shifting from south-east to south-west. We left in fog, rain and chop with the barometer descending. As we approached middle of Dixon Entrance, the wind did indeed bear to the south-west. Tonight it's supposed to bear north, as gale winds. We checked out Brundige Inlet, on the north end of Dundas Island, then decided to continue to Prince Rupert. As we neared the north-east point, however, we remembered we go back to Pacific Daylight Time in Canadian waters, so the Customs office would be closed before we arrived and we'd have to remain on the boat. So we came back to the head of Brundige Inlet. I'm exhausted today. The combined mental skills needed to navigate in fog and the rolling and pitching are almost more tiring than a heavy day of hiking.

September 24-25: Brundige Inlet to Prince Rupert. Tied up at Prince Rupert Yacht Club before noon, cleared Customs by 1300 hours. A hot shower with high pressure water. To Eddie's to buy magazines, Safeway to stock up on groceries—the first of three trips—and to the liquor store.

Donna at PRYC does washing for $6 Canadian, so we took her our duffel-full. Ate at Smiles Cafe, where we met a French couple, Genevieve and Jean-Louis Doudeau, who are traveling in B.C. by rental car. They drove to Banff, Jasper etc., then up through Quesnel and Prince George to Prince Rupert. From here they are taking the ferry to Port Hardy. We found many interests in common. He is a pilot, flies Airbuses. They travel a lot and, like us, prefer to make their own itinerary to untraveled places. They have five grandchildren and want to bring them next summer to Utah and Great Basin. We invited them down to the boat afterwards for a short visit.

Visited the Northern British Columbia Museum, which has a great collection of baskets, utensils, masks, "clothing," etc.; also an impression of a life-size petroglyph located off Robinson Island, outside Prince Rupert. It's called "the man who fell from the sky."

September 26: Crossed Chatham Strait and into Grenville Channel, which seems like a river compared to the "open" water. Pouring rain all last night and intermittent rain today, plus fog until Lowe Inlet, where the weather began to clear. Blue sky by suppertime. Now we're anchored off Verney Falls in four to five fathoms with the current running at an amazing two knots against us. The water rushes past the stern as if we're at full r.p.m. We're both exhausted. I forget how much energy it takes to survive each day on a boat.

Saw a great blue heron and three red-headed mergansers (two females, one male) at the outlet of a creek just along outer edge of shore, diving continuously for shellfish. The male seemed to protect the females' territory from the gulls who were "working" the same area. Merganser: russet head, long yellow bill, sandy streaked feathers, white breast.

Union Pass: a fifty-foot entrance into a huge bay, then many smaller bays off the main passage. Saw a black bear and her two cubs—the only bear we've seen on this trip.

September 28: Second day in Bishop Bay. Arrived yesterday with a falling barometer and gale warnings. Tied up at the dock, which has been damaged, as if someone neglected to clear their bowline and pulled the first dock off the logs. A B.C. Fisheries boat and another fishing boat tried to push the logs under the dock—they worked for about forty-five minutes but gave up. We tied up to the square dock, which is chained to the bottom.

Verney Falls at high tide.

Don was worried that with all the boats tied up—two rafted to the B.C. Fisheries vessel, plus two fishing boats behind us on the "loose" dock—we might be crushed in the middle of night. There's never a let up. Rain has poured all day with some weakening but mostly torrential. Both buckets on stern overflowed. We have no way to capture the water, unfortunately.

Tom Frazer, captain of the *Coast Ranger*, the B.C. Fisheries boat, and his friend, Barry, came on board for a glass of port after dinner last night. Tom has worked the B.C. coast for fifty years, since age fourteen. He knows all the inlets, including those in the Queen Charlottes. Barry was a tree-feller until four years ago when he suffered an accident—head injury, with broken neck and back in two places. He loved his work, could fell a tree every ninety minutes.

Tom and Barry saw a four-point buck swimming off the entrance to Bishop Bay.

1450 hours. The top plank of the walkway is three inches under water. The hot springs house has water up to the entry way and into the tub. Don thinks the "high tide surplus" is due to rain. Prince Rupert gets twenty-three to twenty-four feet a year, Bella Bella nineteen feet or more. A fishing boat came in twenty minutes ago; we told them about the dock and they're now trying to pull it to shore.

More rain here in twenty-four hours than I've seen in ten years in Bishop. What a shame we can't capture it.

1530 hours. Don says, "This is the longest continuous rain I've ever seen in my life." My sentiments too, but to hear it coming from him surprises me.

1545 hours. If I thought it was pouring thirty minutes ago, what do you call what it's doing now?

We sight two sea (or river) otters, four western grebe, and a surfbird on the dock or perhaps it's a plover.

2000 hours. The swell from outside was quite pronounced for a while. Still we rock.

September 29: Leave Bishop Bay at 0740 hours in heavy but not torrential rain, amidst gale warnings. Choppy on Frazer Reach. The cascades along the mountainsides have gone wild—waterslides, whitewater. Our buckets are full again.

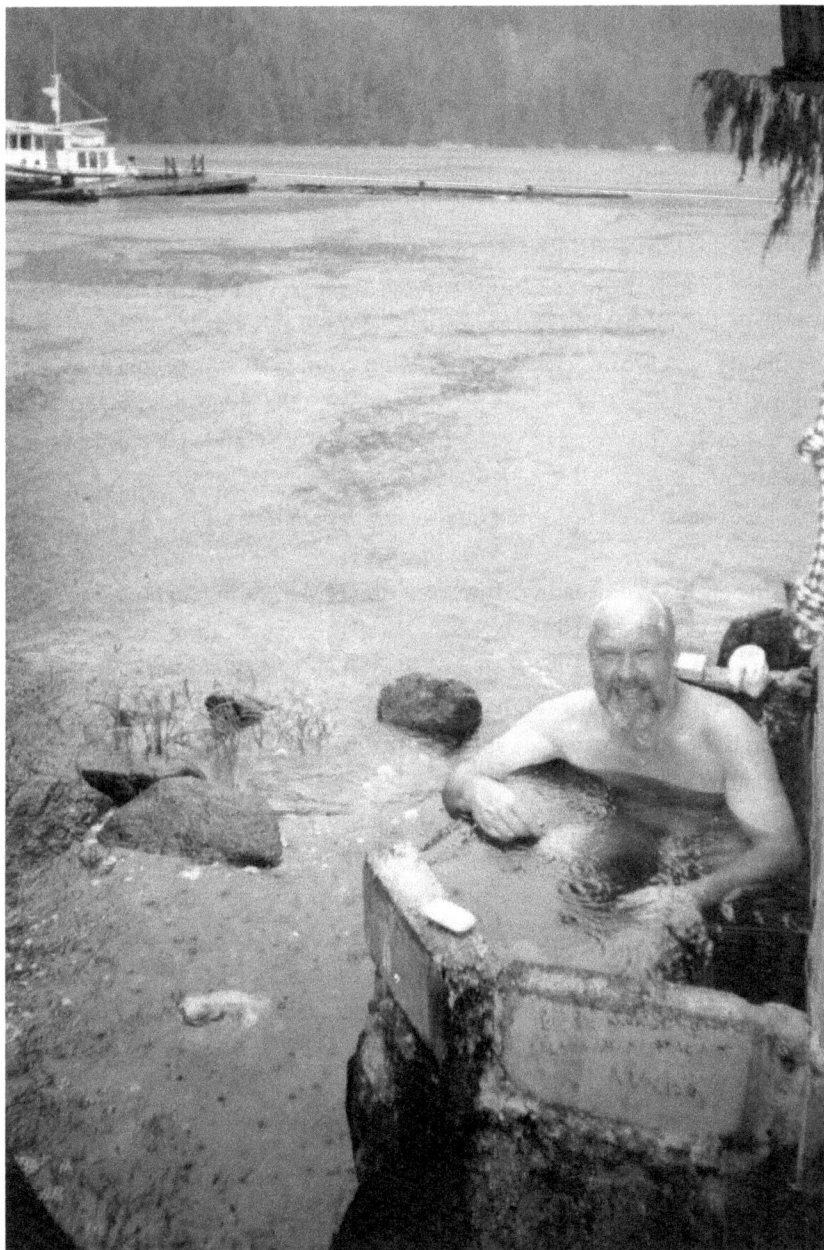

Bishop Bay in the rain.

I lay awake a long time last night creating stories about what could happen if the swell got too heavy in Bishop Cove. I also wondered how to categorize the force of the rain: heavy torrential, medium torrential, light torrential; heavy, medium-heavy, light-heavy; medium; light mist.

One of the fishermen in Bishop Cove last night had a young girlfriend or wife with him. We've seen a number of boats with just the skipper plus wife or girlfriend, and so many of the women look extremely young. Don says, "It's a sign of the economic times." Boats can't afford two paid crew, so the skipper takes his wife or girlfriend along.

Every crack and crevice has water coming down, occurring every hundred feet or less. We've seen two fantastic falls along the Frazer Reach west "shore." The first fall was so picturesque it would draw tourists if it were inland.

Trees have been uprooted due to supersaturation and gale force winds.

September 30, Wednesday: En route down Matheson Channel. Long day yesterday—eleven hours to Jackson Pass, then anchoring in Rescue Bay without charts. The rain decreased to light, then ceased at night. No rain fell at all during the night for the first time in a week.

High clouds today—all shades of grey, grey-blue, silver grey, smoke grey, mauve, violet.

October 1, Thursday: Anchored last night inside Fury Island, on the east side of Fitzhugh Sound, in Schooner Retreat. We entered at about 1800 hours under rain and chop, with waves breaking over all the reefs and islets. *Brigadoon* (which came in to Prince Rupert while we were there) followed us in, as arranged, since they didn't have the detailed chart. I was amazed they had the faith to follow Don, although Don kept giving them LOPS as we passed key islands, etc. They have GPS but no radar. Inside we found a small cove with a sandy beach to the west on the north-east side of Fury, almost completely protected on all sides.

Brigadoon is a thirty-seven foot cutter, owned by Kathy and Bill. They rafted alongside for about two hours so we could visit. They're on their way round the world. She is a psychologist who was in private practice. He was a manager of a woodworking manufacturing company. They sold everything, much as we did, to finance this trip. She said the hardest part was cutting the "personal" cord, not leaving the material things behind.

They sailed from North Carolina through the Panama Canal to Hawaii, then to Alaska and down the Inside Passage.

"Why Alaska?" I asked.

"I was born in Fairbanks and wanted to see Southeast," Kathy said.

Bill lived much of his life in California. Our visit was too brief to get all the details we wanted, but we hope to see them again. Don thinks they're "parking" the boat for the winter, then continuing.

Last night was our first night of zero rain, and was followed by a beautiful sunrise. Today we made good time down Queen Charlotte Strait in gentle seas, but hit fog just south of Egg Island. We were headed directly into the sun, which created blinding fog so we navigated by compass and radar. I'd been at the helm all morning and at 1300 hours Don told me to take a break. Visibility had increased by then to about a quarter of a mile. I lay down, fell fast asleep for an hour, woke up to zero visibility and Don blowing the horn. I took the helm so he could watch the radar, since he'd noticed a large boat or barge on the screen. Don blew the horn again since the boat was going to mow us down. Immediately after Don blew the horn, the other boat blew theirs and it was the sound of a big one. Don got on Channel 16 to call him. Another boat said, "I think he's on 71."

Don went to Channel 71 and asked if the skipper saw us on radar. He radioed back, "This is the *Columbia*. Yes, we see you."

Don recognized the name as that of the Alaska ferry. In fact, he recognized the sound of its horn. "It would have been nice if you'd given us a call on 16," he said.

"If you're gonna be in the traffic lanes you'd better monitor 16," the skipper said.

Don was pissed. "Damned Americans. The Canadians aren't like that."

We came into Blunden Harbor by radar. Another maze of rocks, islets and islands. When we got inside the fog began to burn off and by the time we anchored the sun was shining and it was beautiful all the rest of the afternoon. We were too exhausted, though, to go kayaking or do anything except rest and snooze again.

The quarter moon is now hanging lazily over the western horizon. It's quiet and still, not a ripple. I almost miss the sound of the rain. We heard on the local radio station that upper BC has extensive damage due to "torrential rains." So—the rains weren't just ordinary.

October 2, Friday: Blunden Harbor. I found four blue Indian trade beads on shore. Don found an abalone shell "bead." We visited "Grave Island." Don found the graves, with skulls and a few leg bones, etc.

October 3, Saturday: Layover at Blunden till noon. A kayak trip in the morning to Deer Cove, then tidal falls to Bradley Lagoon, then back to the beach where we found five more beads. I found another small abalone button in the water. Birds: puffin, grebe, great blue heron, oystercatcher, loon, scoters.

Hauled up the CQR anchor and "steamed" to Mamalilaculla, where we anchored just north of the old government pier. This is the village we passed with Rusty and Geza in May, but we did not go ashore then. It has beautiful old houses—circa 1930—but now abandoned and in ruin. The villagers had their own generator plant and water system. The village was built on top of *twelve feet of middens*. There are four totems—three right in the village and one near the creek-end of the village, just above the beach. Several of the totems were in salvageable shape. The one near the creek had what appeared to be a wolf's head at top; another that was fairly well preserved appeared to be a bear sitting on the head of a raven or eagle. We saw fresh bear scat, and on the island across from the village we saw bear prints going through the clay and into the water, which indicated bear swam across this morning. Two islets off the village had burial grounds—Don examined them and found skulls. Three islands have block house crypts without markers. It's sad to see the ruins of what was obviously a lovely village—fruit trees, berry bushes, mint.

The beach has been picked over and obviously has had more visitors going ashore than at Blunden Harbor. The beads we found probably date to early nineteenth century—not the eighteenth century—and in some cases are extremely valuable according to a book Don has been reading about the Tlingits.

October 4, 1992. Minstrel Island for lunch and water fill-up. The sea otter potlatch box was still for sale. Don made an offer and we bought it. Did washing while we had lunch and visited with Sylvia and Grant Douglas, owners of the resort since 1989. She is very bright and interested in politics. They've both done a beautiful job of renovating the place and adding activities etc. Financial conservatives, like us, they dislike government restrictions and unhelpful attitudes toward small businesses. They say everything's worse here in Canada than in the US.

Continued on to Port Neville, where there are over fifty boats anchored or rafted to the dock, etc. Gillnetting and seining season starts tomorrow at 7 a.m. We were fortunate to get a space at the dock just as a boat pulled out. A fishing boat that came in afterwards rafted against us—a lone fisherman, young and courteous.

October 5, 1992: Port Neville. A visit with Lorna Hansen Chesluk. She says:

- Petroglyphs are located at Robbers Knob in Port Neville.

- The deer here are "wild" but so tame you can almost feed them from your hand. Right now they're nervous, Lorna thinks because there are cougar or wolves about.

- The house at the north-west entrance was built by a group who are building a fishing camp at Robbers Point.

- The seiners have just one day (today) to fish. Gill netters have four days, through Thursday.

The barometer today is a full inch above where it was in the storm on September 26: then it was 996 millibars, now it's 1027.

From Port Neville, we made good time through all the rapids today:

1) Whirlpool on Wellbore Channel

2) Greene Point Rapids (where we saw the biggest whirlpools yet on our way north – Chancellor Channel and Mayne Passage)

3) Dent Rapids

4) Yuculta

We anchored in Squirrel Cove but made such good time we kept pushing on. Now we're almost sorry. We're back in real civilization in Desolation Sound and feel like the horse heading for the barn. I love the wilderness motoring and anchoring, even though we have some uncomfortable moments from time to time. Now we're back in the banana belt. My jeans were too hot and I'm now in a short-sleeved shirt for the first time. Don is in shorts and bare feet.

"Where are we headed for tomorrow?"

"Lasqueti Island."

"I don't remember where Lasqueti is."

"South of Texada. Don't you remember that's where we saw the Chinese junk, that beautiful boat. It's the island with the beautiful houses on it."

"Every island down here has beautiful houses... You remember the important details about all the islands and coves. I remember people's names and how to get around cities. But I do remember most of the places we visited up in Alaska and upper B.C."

October 6: Squitty Bay on Lasqueti Island. Have to cross the entrance, which has six-foot depths with a width of fairway of about forty feet. We started in with Rusty and Geza in May, but lost courage when we saw how shallow it was. Once in, Don had barely enough room to turn around to face out. The island is non-commercialized and the residents we talked to were very wary, cautious about talking about their property. We met Rena, an East German woman who escaped from that country in 1962; three others were shot during the escape attempt. She married a Dutchman. He was drowned off Lasqueti after four years of living there. She raised their daughter and son on the island. She seems to be a wonderful, spontaneous and very independent woman. Her car battery was dead so she had to go back around Point Young to her house by outboard.

October 7: Nanaimo for four hours to buy charts and books. Lunch at Scotch Bakery on Bastion Street. We also buy Okanagon port, groceries, and make phone calls. Tie up at the float in Pirates Cove, De Courcey Island.

October 9, Friday: Headed back across Boundary Pass. The sky is overcast with a waffled pattern that gives real depth to the view. A shaft of light, as if from a searchlight or beacon, leads us to the south-east end of Johns Island. The islands look brown and dry. We've had five minutes of rain in the last three days.

At 1500 hours we picked up a buoy on east side of Cypress Head Marine Park. By 1700 we were surrounded by four other power boats. I feel as if we're in a fish bowl now. Don's concerned that we'll have "buoy watch" in the middle of the night. What a disappointing last night. It might have been quieter in Anacortes.

October 10: 1200 hours Tie up N dock #66, Cap Sante Boat Haven marina, Anacortes.

ANACORTES TO SITKA 1994

April 22, 1994. Leave Anacortes at 1715 hours with Peter and Anita McMullen aboard. Anchor at Turn Island overnight, then head to Friday Harbor for breakfast. Nita and Peter take the ferry home from there. Don and I head for Victoria, arrive at the Customs dock at 1504 hours. They tell Don we're the first boat of the day to have phoned prepared with ship's documentation. I provision at Williams. There's a jazz festival going on with musicians, etc. along the quay.

April 28: Between Ripple Shoal and Helmcken Island we hit 14.7 knots across the ground, in smooth water over the shoal.

Port Neville by 1351 hours. A trip in Ole Hansen's boat to Robber's Knob to see the petroglyphs. Two fellows were clearing land there. Lorna Chesluk asked if their property was for sale. "It's on the market" one guy said, "But we're gonna spend the summer clearing." The area burned in 1925 when the mill burned down. The north shore is covered with alder that sprang up after the fire. But in nearly seventy-five years of regrowth, the firs and cedars have not come back. The alders choke out the evergreens.

Piles along dock at Port Neville are covered with white feathery plumrose anemones.

Birds sighted today: golden eagle, bufflehead, puffins. Yesterday and the day before: harlequin, Bonaparte gulls, goldeneye, scoters.

April 29: Matilpi. Plants ashore: *huge* maples and cedars, alder, gooseberry, red elderberry, salmonberries, snowberry, wild rose.

May 4, Wednesday: Egg Island light station. Light-keepers Stan and Judy Westhaver have been here for seventeen years. Before that they were at Estevan Point for two years, and before that Langara Island, Bonilla Island, Cape Scott and Victoria.

Egg Island is actually two islands connected by a bridge. The small island holds the helipad and houses the light station. Between the two islands the tide runs at high tide and the ravine is choked with huge logs, some of which have been here since before Stan and Judy came.

Judy told the story of one light-keeper who lived on Egg Island with his woman friend before she and Stan took over. He was paranoid that she might go back to her husband. One time she went to town; the weather worsened and she radioed to him she "wouldn't return the next day, she'd return the day after." The radio transmission was so bad he got only the first part of the message and was so distraught he committed suicide. He's buried on the island; a cross marks his grave.

Judy gets off the island two or three times a year. They have one son who was eight when they came to Egg. The most difficult aspect of Judy's life is not being able to see her family.

May 5: Thursday. Smith Sound. Landed at Open Bight in the morning. Beautiful sandy beach.

At Big Spring, there's a huge renovated ferry boat with a trailer-like top that provides accommodation for forty-eight guests. It has a swimming pool, garden deck. Caters mostly to Germans. Minimum cost of stay $4500.

Went as far as Dawson's Landing. Rusty and I got all excited, made our grocery list—potatoes, onions, pudding, fresh milk, mayonnaise, etc. When we got to the store, we found it to be fantastically outfitted, with groceries and boat equipment, clothing, household goods, etc., but so expensive we decided to buy only onions and a two-liter jar of bread-and-butter pickles ($10). Onions were 80 cents a pound. Geza bought a liter of Cinzano (Italian aperitif) for $10.95; the government regulates alcohol prices.

Anchored in Fifer Bay, off Blair Island.

May 6: Joe's Bay. Anchored with CQR to be secure while all four of us went up The Rapids in the dinghy. High tide was supposed to be 1120 hours at Bella Bella; we started up at 0930 when the water was still running out. After four tries within an hour we finally made it through. We had to cut the motor, and Rusty and I paddled through the shallowest, rockiest portion. Behind the tidal rapids was a huge lagoon with miles of shoreline. We headed in for two to three miles, until Don said, "We'd better go back or it's two hours till our next chance." We were too late. So, without food or emergency gear, we headed up to Elizabeth Lagoon, found a muddy beach, tied the dinghy and tramped through the brush. The ground was so spongy we sank down six inches, then the ground sprang back like a trampoline. We saw wild azalea, bunchberry, salal, cedar, hemlock, pine, skunk cabbage in bloom.

As we headed back the wind had kicked up and we took spray over the bow. The clouds had gathered over and it got a bit chilly.

A pair of canvasbacks at the Rapids flew back and forth perhaps to guard a nest on the little island at the entrance.

Anchored at Addenbrook Island. Don and Geza went ashore to visit Mike and Dawn Kovacs, who are the assistant light-keepers for Egg Island. The head light-keeper, Sam, said that during the 1984 hurricane spray came fifteen feet over the house on shore. Two guys on a twenty-six foot sailboat perished in spite of wearing dry suits. The theory is they died because there was so much spray and water in the air they couldn't breathe.

May 10: In Mathieson Channel we saw hundreds of horned puffins. They took off as we approached, kicking up white froth in the channel and creating a great whooshing-whirring sound as they took flight.

Mathieson Channel has dozens of beautiful waterfalls. The area above Kynoch Inlet to Mussel Inlet and up Sheep Passage is included in the 93,000-hectare Fiordland Recreation Area, part of the B.C. parks system.

Yesterday, as we headed west in Milbank Sound, then made a turn north into the rock-infested passage east of Ivory Island (Perrin Anchorage), seas were fifteen feet high and breaking off the rocks to the east of the passage—a beautiful but frightening display. Don, as usual, was excited, whooping and hollering, "Look, look! Did you see that, did you see that?" while the rest of us looked nervously at the echo sounder.

The head of Mussel Inlet shoals just ten feet from the shore. We were able to pull the boat in very close—the depth below the bow was about three feet; the depth at the stern was over thirty feet. The falls just south of the head of Mussel Inlet are the widest we've seen (300 feet) and look like a series of stairs.

We saw only one other boat after we came north in Mathieson Channel, drifting by the waterfall. In the middle of Mathieson we saw the Nordic tug *Sidekick*. At the south-east end there were whale-watching tour boats, also a small rusty tug carting away four or five huge logs that had been cut on shore.

In Griffith Passage: recent clear-cuts on the east shore, south of older clear-cuts. Looking south, we can also see clear-cuts. When we pull into the cove south of Lime Point (which is too deep too close to anchor) we hear the hum of chainsaws.

Rain most of the day, varying from mist to gentle rain.

Butedale: There seems to be a lesser volume of water in the falls. The black rock shows much more than we've seen in previous visits. The buildings are in a more pitiful state each time we return, also.

Fraser Reach, 1516 hours: A following wind. Small white caps are beginning to build. I'm alone at the helm. Don and Rusty are sleeping; Geza is reading.

Bishop Bay Hot Springs: Five boats at the float. A new float was installed just last month and it already has spray-painted "graffiti" on it. According to a Canadian couple from Prince George, fishing vessels are ruining the place. "It's advertised now… Every boat that's heading to Alaska stops here."

There's a new sign—a disclaimer—in the bathhouse and already people have spray-painted their names all over it. The gangway is a brand new aluminum structure. The Canadian couple we talked to said that when they were here in mid-April a fishing vessel pulled in. The five guys aboard got absolutely plastered and vomited all over the bathhouse. This couple feels very sad about what's happening because they and all the other Kitimat, Prince George and Prince Rupert residents try to keep the area nice. "What can you do?" the wife said.

Rusty and Geza just came back from the bathhouse and said there were four drunken guys throwing beer cans out the window.

Don is undecided about whether or not to mention the Bishop Bay hot springs in our *Exploring the North Coast of British Columbia* book.

May 11, Thursday: 1120 hours. Chugging up Ursula Channel to Verney Passage on the way to Weewanie Hot Springs. Vancouver and company knew about the hot springs in Goat Harbour, which are at least six feet below the high tide line.

May 12: Last night we tied to a mooring buoy in Coghlan Anchorage. Supper: spaghetti, made by Rusty. Terrific. Rain during the night, hard at times. I woke in the middle of the night with a splitting headache, then nausea this morning. I slept for an hour before noon. Sinuses acting up? Weather? Now we're anchored off west side of Lewis Island, north of Kelp Passage. No one else is here. Rusty and I put up a birthday sign for Don over the pilot berth so he'll see it in the morning.

May 13, Saturday: Between 2400 and 0300 hours the wind blew like hell—forty-plus knots. Don and Geza were up and down. Waves slapped very noisily all night long and there were heavy squalls at times. *Time Thief* at Kumealon Island had a more comfortable time with only twenty-five-plus knots—fifteen knots less than what we had.

Prince Rupert. Don went off to find the "Man who Fell from the Sky" petroglyph off Robinson Point, which he feels sure is a woman. He sold two books to Sea Sport marina, another two to the Star of the West bookstore, then filled up on water and diesel. I provisioned at Safeway, $235 Canadian.

Geza took us to dinner at the Crest Hotel. Hors d'oeuvre: seafood platter and fried zucchini.

May 14, Sunday: Left Prince Rupert at 0515 hours. *Time Thief* followed us out of the Venn Passage short cut. Anchored in Port Tongass and slept almost all day, wiped out after very little sleep Saturday night.

At 2030 hours we were about to turn in again when we heard a voice—two runabouts—one towing another asking if we had any gasoline. The guy being towed let the stern of his boat bump into our bow. They kept asking where they were. Don asked if they had a radio to call for help. They did. They said they knew there was a resort "around the corner." We couldn't figure out what they were doing out at that time of night. Foolish, foolish! The towing boat "captain" wore a dry suit. A girlfriend with him didn't have one. They had Canadian accents, but the second boat had Alaska registration.

May 16, Monday: 1130 hours. Today on shore we walked around to the west side of Tongass Island to look for evidence of the Indian village that was once there. We went across through the forest at the south end, ankle-deep in wild lily of the valley. The forest is alders, thin spruce and hemlock. The west side shows evidence of where the village might have been—a hundred yards into forest there are no large trees, just berry bushes springing up from the soft spongy undergrowth. Don thinks he might have found a plank or half logs standing about ten feet high, evidence of something man-made.

Spent two and a half hours ashore at low tide. Startled a tree-full of eagles, which were probably feeding on a seal we found dead on shore.

61

May 17: Ketchikan. *Sumdum.* Geoff Simmonds and Marzette Ellis, who is the granddaughter of Bob Ellis, of Ellis Airlines. (When he was eighteen, Don worked for Ellis Airlines in Ketchikan as a radio operator. He still tells stories about it.)

May 19: Docked at Point Baker, on the far side of Port Protection, after our longest day yet—over seventy miles. Sumner Strait, two years ago, with Bob and Anna Mae Botley, was wild. Today it was quite benign, so much so that I was able to work on the computer as we went.

This is a picturesque little settlement. The post office has mail pick-up almost every day. Water is available but it has to be boiled for ten minutes. The store has limited hours and supplies. There's a coin-operated laundromat, also a telephone (which doesn't work). There's a floating dock but you may not be able to tie up for lack of room, so you may have to raft or be prepared to anchor in the bay, which is well protected from all winds.

Seven otters go from one float to another.

Joe Sebastian, a fisherman who lives here, told a story about living in Bishops Bay. The RCMP stopped at the hot springs and wanted to know if he had checked into Canada. He was stark "necked" and didn't know whether to get dressed or not as he talked to them.

"You don't have clearance?"

"No, I'm just on my way home…"

They kept questioning him. Finally he asked, "Shall I put on my pants or not?"

May 20: Through Rocky Passage at high tide. It seems much different from last time, and more difficult to go through than two years ago with the Botleys. We could see no more than about four feet down into the water. Dawn and I were on the bow the entire time but we could see very little, other than kelp, which came in twenty- to thirty-foot-long streamers. The day was overcast, with good visibility but no sun.

A little marten swam from shore toward the boat, curious. Don started talking to him, and he turned around at once and started swimming back to shore as fast as he could. He climbed up on the rocks, shook himself, then watched as we moved away down the pass.

Lots of seals, eagles, crows and song birds, Canada geese. Jeff and I sighted two whales in Keku Straits. Birds sighted in Keku Strait north end: loons, surf scoters, grebe, pigeon guillemot, sandpipers.

In Chapin Bay, we sighted a "black" bear—actually golden brown with a yellow nose—along shore. He poked around as we watched, then stood on his hind legs to try to pick up a scent. Don scared him by shouting "Bravo!" and he ran into the brush.

May 21: Warm Springs Bay, Baranof Island. We tie up at the public dock along with *Matatua*, from Sydney, Australia. They're a family of four—husband, wife, and two daughters, one nineteen years old, the other twelve. They came across the Pacific—Solomon Islands, Cook Islands, etc. This is their first touch in the U.S., after checking in at Sitka. They plan to visit friends in Nanaimo.

We also meet Eméric Fissett, a French adventurer and author, thirty-two years old. He plans to kayak across the Gulf of Alaska to Anchorage, take dog sleds to the west, then to Siberia where he'll use reindeer, camels, etc. to get to Moscow. We wonder how much of all this he'll really do.

Anchored after fourteen miles in Ell Cove and had nice evening, with a huge Greek salad for supper. Ell Cove is small and L-shaped. The inner basin looks landlocked with sides fairly steep-to.

Don mucked up the Powerbook by inserting the diskette upside down. Fortunately we have only two more days to go on this trip.

Entrance to Rocky Pass

"OUTSIDE PASSAGE"
HAINES TO ANACORTES, 1994

August 13, 1994. 7:30 a.m. flight from Seattle to Juneau. A one-hour wait, then a thirty-five minute flight in a five-passenger plane to Haines. Our Seattle check-through luggage arrived on same flight; our brief cases, which we had to check in Juneau, did not, creating real anxiety until they were located and sent up on the afternoon flight. All our manuscripts, diskettes etc. were in Don's briefcase.

We unloaded, fueled and headed to Haines market; they delivered our groceries to dock. We took off by 1600 hours for Skagway and were tied up by 1800. Skagway is quiet compared to Haines, which was in the midst of its fair.

Lynn Canal was named by Vancouver for his birthplace (King's Lynn) in Norfolk, England.

August 15: Chichagof Island. The west coast is beautiful. High peaks with sharp summits covered with forests. Fog shrouded peaks give it a South Seas aspect, or else a Japanese or New Zealand flavor.

August 17: West coast of Chichagof Island, headed down Salisbury Sound into Peril Strait with the sun shining. The difference between the coastal mountains and those of the interior is apparent. Inland, the mountain tops appear to have been eroded smooth. Their tops are rounded and worn. Along the west coast, many of the peaks are cone-shaped and sharply vertical. A lot of the shore is rosy granite. In some cases the sides of the mountains are so steep that avalanche paths, or perhaps ancient glacier paths, have worn the sides smooth so they have the appearance of green velvet. These places are more pristine than the inner waters, which have been logged.

Spotted a family of at least ten sea otters off Kruzof Island, at head of Salisbury Sound.

1950 hours. Heading down Hoonah Sound with the sun at our backs and an almost full moon to the east. We're back in the Alaska of immensity—wide channels, massive rounded mountains with bands of clear-cuts obvious. I liked the west coast of Chichagof—the solitude, the striking but lonely beauty. Not the awesome, overpowering aspect of the Alaska Inside Passage. I liked the intimacy, the clean air and the greenness.

August 20: Hole in the Wall, Prince of Wales Island. Aquamarine water at the entrance. We enter with just a few feet below the keel. Inside, the sides are vertical with a convoluted base of holes and caves. Trees hang on the vertical cliffs. To the east, the basin opens up at the base of a grey rounded granite summit.

Old growth forest: spruce, hemlock, cedar; devil's claw; purple flowers along the overhead cracks. Threads of moss and lichen; black and green.

Inner Shakan Cove opens up into a Yosemite Valley with huge granite domes to the north. The air smells of evergreens. The north-east side is clear-cut.

In Sarheen Cove, a Clark's nutcracker flies from treetop to treetop warning the other birds. Soon a chorus of nutcrackers is clicking through the trees. Salmon cruise off the stream at the north-east end, jumping— their silver bodies gleaming and curved, waiting, waiting for the rains to flood the creeks so they can head back to their natal ground.

Prince of Wales is the largest island in Southeast Alaska, measuring 135 miles long by 45 miles wide. It has 990 miles of coast, and 1,000 miles of roads due to extensive logging. There's a ferry service to Hollis, forty-five miles west of Ketchikan.

August 21, Sunday: Yahku Cove, Tuxekan Island. This is not recommended by *Coast Pilot*, but it is north-facing and almost entirely landlocked. A reef across the entrance protects from any fetch and completes the protection. A "Douglass find!" Old growth lines the shores—spruce, cedar, hemlock, alder. A substantial creek (dry today) flows in at the north end.

Klawock. There are totems here, brought from farther north on Prince of Wales Island, twenty-one in total. My favorite has a twelve-foot Killer Whale mounted atop the figure of a Brown Bear. Another has a Raven atop a pole with a giant clam halfway down.

Craig. A full service town , population around 1700. Thompson House Market is neat, clean and nicely stocked, with a liquor store next door. It's one of the more reasonably priced grocery stores we've come upon, and they will deliver. Groceries come across the island from Hollis. You can also buy film and kitchen supplies. The Market and liquor store are open seven days a week; most stores are closed on Sundays. The payphones are busy on Sunday!

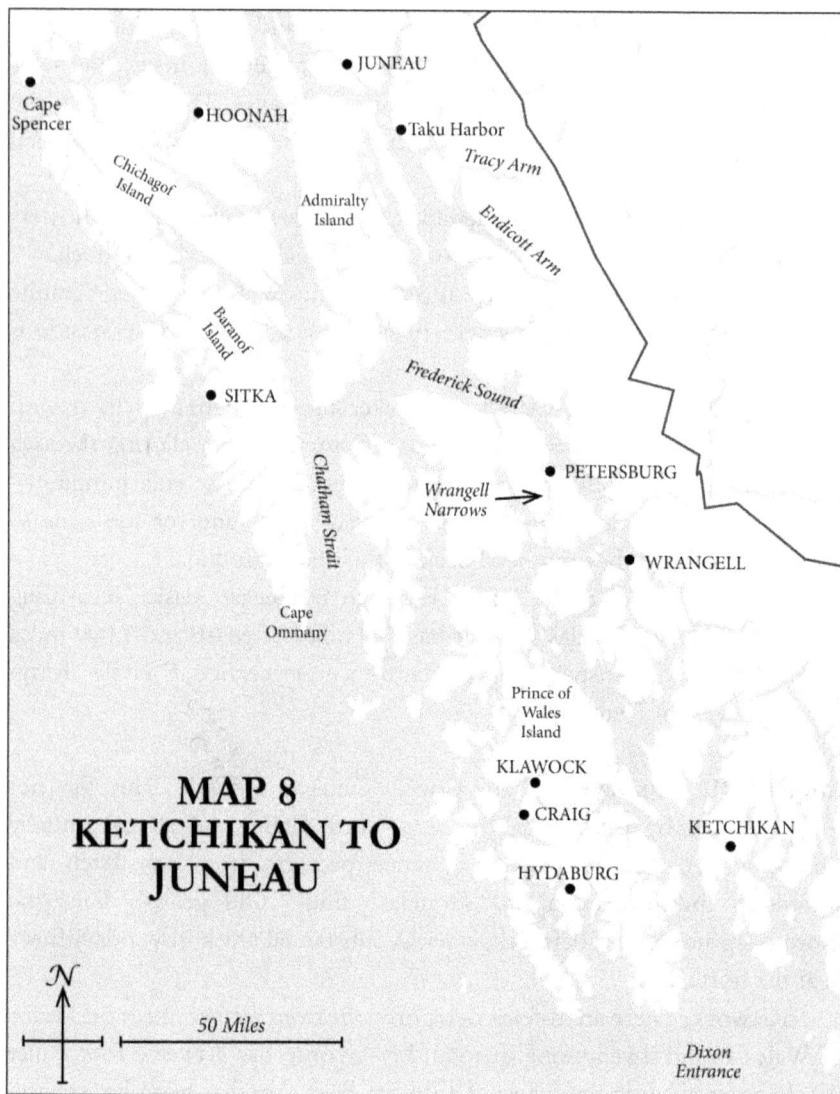

MAP 8
KETCHIKAN TO
JUNEAU

August 22: Hydaburg. Noon. We dock and plan to go "uptown," but on the way up the dock we encounter two women cleaning fish—Coho salmon. Don asks if we can buy one. "No... but if you fillet your own you can have one," says Judy, of TJ's Café. So Don, who's never filleted a salmon before, pulls one out of a six-foot cubic container and sets to work. The other woman's jaw drops. "You waste a whole lot... Oh, well, you learn by experience."

Judy says it takes ten days to smoke-dry the fish. Then they have to be frozen, because they're so fat they spoil otherwise. These Coho are lean because they've already started their run, so they make for better drying.

We visit the Hydaburg totems, then walk down to TJ's—a small purple and pink building. TJ is short for Totally Judy's. I asked Judy at the dock if her café was open. "No," she said, "here's the cook."

"When is it open?"

"When the cook doesn't have to come down here and work."

The kids congregate at Hydaburg River. They throw three-pronged hooks on line over the bridge. Some kids along the rocks of the bank net the fish. One little boy of about eight reels in his line with each throw, a salmon at the end. He knocks the fish senseless, then throws it back in. All the kids appear to be catching just for sport.

At the head of old main pier there's a post office and the Do Drop In, which is open seven days a week and sells groceries. People here are fairly friendly.

There's a telephone at the south side of the bridge, another at the foot of the microwave antenna above the Do Drop In. I called Aunt Lois. "Are you in Hydaburg?" she asked. I love it. She's always so interested in what we do, where we are.

August 23: Nichols Bay, Burt Millar Cut-Off. The *Coast Pilot* says there's a channel, thirty yards long, ten yards wide. We see a "channel" of bull kelp between two rocky ledges, and enter it with the tide against us. I go to the bow, Herb (Nickles) runs with the boat hook from starboard to port beam, sets the big fenders out on either side. I calculate the channel is more like twenty feet wide from side to side, with a maximum of eight feet under us. Don drops all his writing, just remains at the helm with the starboard door open. One misstep and we're on the rocks.

Heading back towards the opening of Nichols Bay, we see a skiff heading out through Burt Millar. Then we see a great blue heron standing on the kelp through which we struggled.

Anchored for the night in the first anchorage after spending the afternoon in the second. The crew nixed anchoring behind the reef at the entrance if the captain wanted barbecued salmon for dinner.

August 24: Prince Rupert. The *John Brix*, an ocean-going tug, long and green, is tied up at the fuel dock. It makes a ten-day round trip from Prince Rupert to the Whittier terminus of the Alaska Railroad, carrying 110 railroad cars. It takes almost a day at the Chevron dock to refuel. In 1993, they had an oil spill in the harbor.

The tramway to the top of the hill no longer runs to the top of Mt. Hayes. Rupert gets two weeks of snow, maximum. On a clear day you're supposed to be able to see the Queen Charlottes peeking over the horizon from the top of Mt. Hayes.

August 25: Left Prince Rupert Yacht Club at 0945 hours for Lawson Harbor, anchored by 0100 hours. Made radar and GPS approach. A fishing boat with its anchor light on made the approach easier. It was anchored at the very spot Don had programmed as the waypoint for anchoring.

August 26: Up and underway about 0730. Down Ogden Channel, then Petrel Channel. Don and I were at odds about what needed to be done for the *North Coast of British Columbia* book. "Write about the here and now," he said and went on ad infinitum in his lecture mode. We've seen some pretty spots today—"Squall Cove," Hodgson Cove, Moolock Cove, which was "infested" with huge jellyfish. The water was dotted, spotted white with the creatures, which we thought at first were rocks, they were so large.

I feel an emptiness today. Is it because of our dispute this morning? Is the lack of serene beauty and grandiose scenery? Is it the fact that one must start early for good work? I don't know. But I'm not happy. Today was a downer, as they say. Also, we've seen hardly any wildlife. A few dolphins, lots of gulls, a family of grebes.

Spent the night in Monckton, inner inlet. We bought four pounds of frozen shrimp (a mistake!) in Rupert, and an eight pound ling cod. We barbecued both tonight and had to throw away the shrimp—too mushy—but the cod was great and we had enough for a gourmet fish salad, using the last of the Hydaburg salmon.

August 27: Mel Bacon, of Mel's Mobile Marine Service, Sidney, B.C. We met him in the north end of Higgins Passage. His boat: S/V *Nawitka*, steel, forty feet. His dog: Stormy. Mel single-handed to Queen Charlotte. On the way back he got into northwest winds and seas and his motor mounts broke. His engine slipped six inches. He had to cut wooden blocks and shims out of beer cans.

Don asks, "Are you single-handling?"

"Yes!"

"Great!"

"No, it's the shits. I'm gonna advertise for a woman and tell her to send a picture of her boat."

He had a girlfriend who went with him on two or three weekend trips. Then she was on the boat for four days. When they got to Queen Charlotte Strait, she hated it. It was either her or the boat, she said. So, she left.

Nawitka is not pretty but it's a good cruising boat. Mel has weather clothes, an auto pilot, extra gear to repair. He trained his dog, a Sheltie, to pee on the starboard side of the boat by peeing himself on some net, then training the dog to pee on the net on the starboard side, then he got rid of the net when the dog was trained.

When we saw him he was towing an inflatable dinghy, as well as an eighteen foot sailboat, which he towed across Queen Charlotte Strait.

"Would you do it again?" I asked.

"No. It was foolish." The sailboat filled with water when the seas picked up to ten feet and Mel was sure he'd lose it. But because its bow was riding high, it never filled more than three-quarters full. He didn't expect to see it in the morning.

August 28: Kynumpt Harbour. Scott Davis, of Nordland, WA. His vessel: *Chrystal Vision*, a twenty-five foot wooden rowing skiff. He has been rowing for six months, plans to return to Port Townsend by October, has rowed 2000 miles to date. He rowed to Glacier Bay, then outside Chichagof, Lisianksi Strait and outside Prince of Wales. Did Dry Pass and Burt Millar Cut-Off, Higgins, Rocky Pass. Went up the Stikine, Skeena through Telegraph; Anger Island; Campania Island. He carries no GPS, only charts, but has LORAN and a handheld radio. He stresses that it's important not to skimp on gear—his raingear is Patagonia.

2120 hours. Anchored off Fury Island. Came in under radar, GPS and depth sounder. Good day today. Quite calm seas through Fitz Hugh.

At Bella Bella we met two kayakers—Alex Frid and Gail Rothenberg, from Haines Junction, YT. She is an environmental historian, he is a photojournalist.

The liquor store in Bella Bella is closed on Sunday. A sign at the Market says it's closed Sunday too, but it was open, perhaps because there were so many fishermen. Boats were coming in with their seasonal subsistence catches of Coho and Sockeye. Don took pictures of one of the guys across from us on fuel dock. (It took almost forty-five minutes to wait in line for fuel.) Just before we left—as I was walking back to the dock after making phone calls—I saw Don carry a salmon to the boat. I thought, "Oh no, I'm going to have to clean it." But he did the gutting and cleaning, then Al (Ryan) filleted it. I baked it in the oven with sesame, ginger dressing and lemon as sauce. We had salmon sashimi beforehand dressed with soy sauce.

The salmon had roe, which the Haida said to bake in the oven. I had the roe sitting on a piece of foil and later when Al was ready to prepare it, I couldn't find it. I must have inadvertently thrown it in with the rest of the garbage. Or maybe Don did.

Scott Davis saw sandhill cranes in Higgins. So did Alex Frid and Gail Rothenberg.

August 29: 0900 hours. Anchored in north bight (nine fathoms) off Egg Island. Seas are like a pond; never have we seen it so calm. Al and Don went ashore since Don didn't go last time (May) when Rusty, Geza and I went.

MAREP (Marine Information Reporting) from Cape Scott came on Channel 69 asking for weather reports from vessels in the area. I called and talked to Cheryl, gave her a report, and told her we'd be passing in a day or so and would like to visit the lighthouse. She said we should anchor in Experiment Bight, row ashore, and walk one mile to the lighthouse. The anchorage is usually okay, she says. She and another woman, Sheila, man the station year round.

I have been having bouts of feeling sorry for myself, thinking the kids don't care. They do, I know, but they're so wrapped up in their sixty-hour work weeks and their own families to be able to care. Aunt Lois is the only one who asks pertinent questions about the trip, who studies our itinerary and follows it. "She's the only one who has time," Don says. But she and Uncle Bob have always taken time to learn about us, even when they were both still working. A sign of our times, all this. It's perhaps when we realize our own mortality that we begin to appreciate our parents. I think back on the things I would have liked to have photographed—Daddy's hands—

large, long fingers, well formed with rather flat but always well-groomed nails, the freckles and blond hairs, the way his hands seemed to lay across the octaves on the piano; the way his moustache seemed to protrude as he studied the music while he played. I never recorded either Daddy of Mother playing. Why? Because I didn't think of it. I never recorded the family singing Irish songs or Christmas carols. Why? Perhaps I was too busy participating or enjoying the moment, not thinking ahead that I would want to hold those moments for the rest of my life.

1115 hours. Don and Al headed back in the dinghy. Judy Westhaver waves from the top of the hill. The minute Don and Al get back, Don says we're invited to visit the Coast Guard ship *Narhwal.* It's an ice breaker, built in 1962 to support stevedores supplying eastern Arctic; now it's used as supply ship and buoy tender. In 1991, it rejoined the Western Region fleet. Originally it carried a crew of 128, but now under the Coast Guard it carries only twenty-eight, so each crew member has his or her own cabin. A Narwhal tusk hangs in the gangway of the second deck on the way to the galley.

Narwhal brought a change of assistant light-keepers to Egg Island, along with all the supplies. These were offloaded by helicopter (fourteen-passenger) by longline to the shore.

Passed *Nawitka* across Queen Charlotte Sound. The water was still as a pond. We're anchored now in the Walker Group, between Staples and Kent Islands. There's Old Growth in here—mostly cedar, some Sitka and/or blue spruce. Small islets with trees. Heard one loon in the late afternoon. Don calls this "Quiet Cove." It is!

Saw Canada geese heading north in formation, also a grebe, Arctic loons by the hundreds, and a river otter in the cove.

August 30: Sighted a mama black bear and cub on the beach, west hook of Shushartie Bay, where ruins are marked. We approached within an eighth of a mile. The mother watched, then sent the little one "packing." She headed toward the trees, stopped and watched us. The cub stood on his hind legs and grabbed a cedar branch in his mouth.

Into Port Hardy at 0800 hours to let Al off and refuel. Nothing open before 9 a.m. except the H&W store on Market Street. The Giant Food Market opened at 6 a.m. during the summer, up till August 29 (yesterday). Now it's open at 9 a.m. Most stores open at 10 a.m. or noon.

71

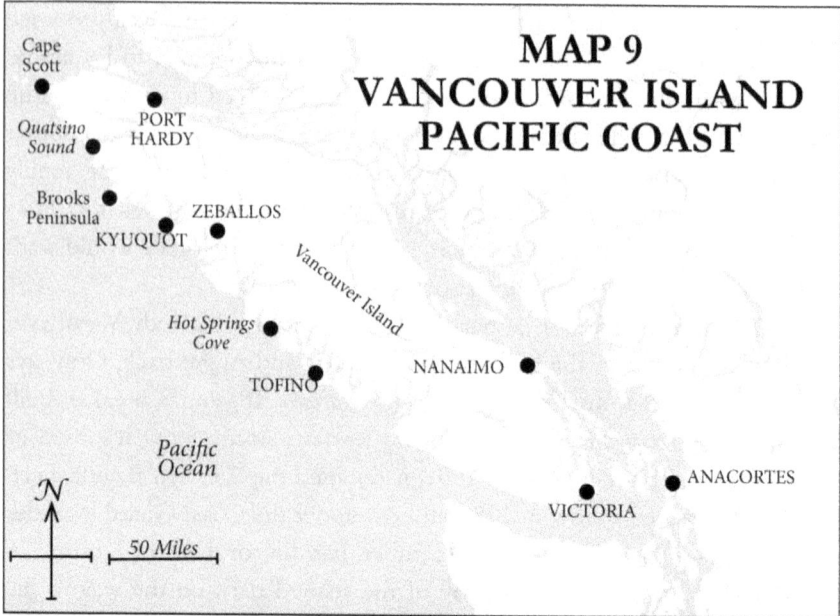

MAP 9
VANCOUVER ISLAND
PACIFIC COAST

Cape Scott
Quatsino Sound
PORT HARDY
Brooks Peninsula
KYUQUOT
ZEBALLOS
Vancouver Island
Hot Springs Cove
TOFINO
NANAIMO
Pacific Ocean
VICTORIA
ANACORTES
N
50 Miles

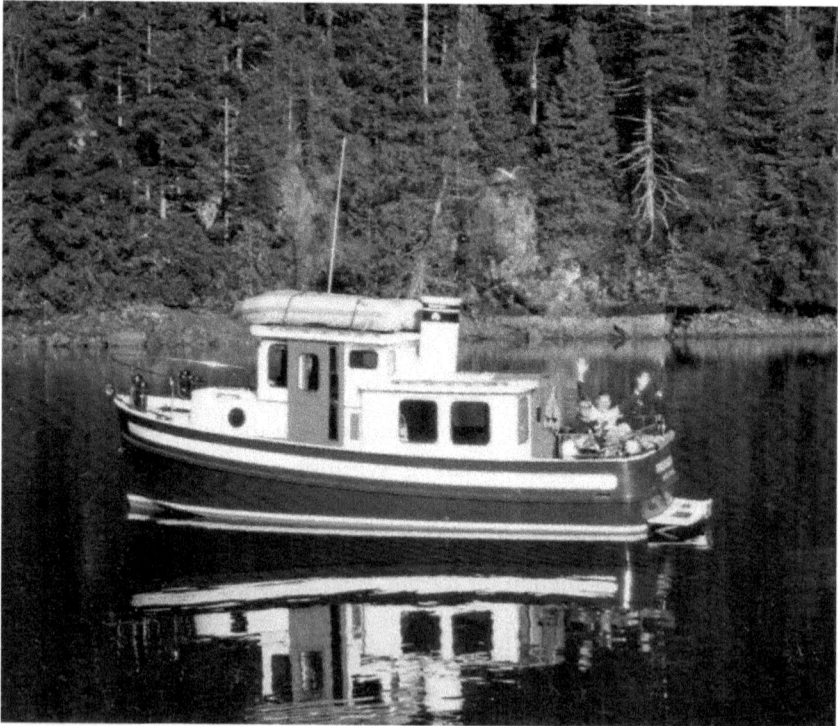

Forevergreen.

Al's bus to Campbell River and Victoria leaves at 8:45 a.m.

Left Port Hardy at 0930 hours, came via Cape Sutil and inside Tahall reefs. The beach at Sutil was lovely—sand along the waterline; grey pebbles higher up. Anchored in Bull Harbour by 1443 hours. No other boat here. A sign on the government dock says all non-government boats must stay off. One of the four or five houses at the northwest end of harbor has a light on and smoke coming from its chimney. We walked to Roller Bay along an old road. A 1960s red truck sits abandoned on the road. A freshwater pond fed the water tank for the former lighthouse station. The path to the beach leaves the road at the water tower and cuts through old growth forest, soft spongy moss, ferns, and an odd assortment of mushrooms—huge black ones, white and brown, small brown. The slugs seem to like the mushrooms. A quarter-mile walk through the forest and you come out onto the beach at Roller Bay. The beach is covered with round, smooth pebbles, difficult to walk through. Lower down, there's grey sand. Huge drift logs line the west side of the beach where the shore is steep, the logs tossed there by huge waves, obviously.

The berry bushes are dried and berry-less, probably due to the dry summer. We saw the last of the foxglove in bloom, fireweed, yarrow, dandelions. In the pond, yellow pond lilies were not quite open.

Forevergreen was anchored in the harbor when we returned from our walk. Rod Nash has two guys aboard, Kevin and Ron. Kevin is thirty-six, a Continental Airlines pilot, just promoted to full captain. Rod will drop him in Coal Harbour in a couple of days.

August 31, 1994. Passed Cape Scott and came round to Guise Bay to anchor at 0943 hours. The beach is at least a half-mile wide and covered with silver driftwood and drift logs. Vertical posts are remnants of an old road to Hanson's Lagoon.

Anchored in Julian Cove, Quatsino Sound. Last time (Fall '93) we were here with the Botleys and the engine kept quitting. Julian Cove is surrounded by high wooded hills and the sun didn't enter it until after 1830 hours.

September 1: Felt quite under the weather yesterday and slept most of the afternoon while Don took us down from Cape Scott into Quatsino Sound.

Today we pulled up anchor in Julian Cove at 1100 hours and motored over to Tom Cook's house. No one there. Tomatoes are ripe and full in their green house—I looked longingly at them. Motored across to the Quatsino boatyard.

Don to Chris Bradley, owner of the boatyard: "Do you know where Tom Cook might be?"

"California." Chris is a man of few words. "Lots of business," he tells us. "Had to put on six men." There's only one other worker there at the moment and they take a sixty-minute lunch break.

They're "the only boatyard north of Uclulet," according to Chris. I asked about other facilities.

"Post office. Pay phone. No store."

Called home, A-OK there. My *Cape Horn* book is selling to friends, but not to bookstores.

After we left Quatsino, weather reports were forecasting gales for the West Coast. As we exited, waves began to build up. We made radio communication with *Forevergreen*. Rod and Don were talking about whether Brooks Peninsula might give us some lee as we rounded Kwakiutl Point. As the two of them signed off, a fishing boat came on frequency and said, "There's a gale warning." Don said he knew but we were heading for Klashine, and wouldn't we be getting some protection from Brooks Peninsula? In an understated, monotone voice, the fisherman said, "Brooks is where the winds are born," and laughed slightly.

A while later, we heard a May Day on Channel 16. *Little Bonanza*, a forty-one foot fishing boat. "Our cockpit's filled and we're sinking. I see an American boat nearby." After the May Day "siren" alerting all boats in area to proceed with haste and stand by to give assistance, Rod came on the radio and said he would proceed. Then a fishing boat—perhaps the same one who'd contacted us about the gale warning (he had the same monotone voice without the slightest register of emotion)—came on and said he was nearby and would give assistance.

After about five minutes the fishing boat in danger called Comox Coast Guard back and said they'd got the pumps going and the stern had started to raise. The May Day was cancelled.

We poked into an unnamed cove—the second to the east of Kwakuitl Point—to wait until we heard from Rod. Don wants to name the cove

"Forevergreen" and has written a couple of paragraphs about it and why he's named it so.

Anchored in Klaskino Anchorage. We had Rod and his friend Ron Hayes over for veal stew. Rod brought the salad.

September 2: Checked out Klaskino Basin. It seemed clear at the head, but a man camping with his wife a quarter mile away came racing out to us in his skiff to warn us of rocks.

This noon we ran out of propane. I should have trusted my nose more. Since dinner last night the odor was becoming more offensive. I will have to use the microwave now to cook or boil water.

Klaskish Anchorage. We picked up one of the eight buoys. Don brought us in, in pouring rain, and as he slowed the engine, I awoke. I'd slept through the entire mess of the outside rollers, *soundly*.

September 3: Rounded Cape Cook—Brooks Peninsula, Solander Island. Nasty offshore, with three meter seas, confused and breaking.

Lunch in Columbia Cove, where we picked up one of three buoys. Then on to "Baidarka" Cove, which was still getting some roll from the southeast.

Left Baidarka Cove at 1615 hours and motored round Acous Peninsula. A wide half-rainbow hung over Acous, fluffy dark clouds rolled in and out over the coves along shore, and everything looking exquisitely green from the heavy rains of the previous night and day.

We checked out a cove behind Izard Point, but it was full of kelp, and a long rock underwater prevented our being able to continue. Rod could possibly have entered in his smaller boat.

As we headed back south toward Gay Passage, a shuddering in the engine—which made us suspect something was hooked around propeller—worsened. Rod noticed the sound and asked if we had problem. Immediately after we anchored Don stripped, got in the dinghy and with mask and snorkel looked underwater, hanging from side of dink.

"There's something wrapped around the prop… I think it's a net."

I handed him the boat hook and after several minutes he extracted a meter-long piece of kelp.

Ron called over from *Forevergreen*, "If you'll let me use the mask and snorkel, I'll go in for you." So Don rowed over wearing only his jockey shorts and waited for ten minutes while Ron changed out of his clothes. We promised him a hot shower in trade. He came in his jockey shorts with backpack, handed it to me, put on the mask and snorkel and dove in with the fish knife. Two dives and two more meter-long pieces of kelp came loose.

Ron took his shower, then visited for a while. He was an actor who appeared in *Bonanza, Everglades, Lassie.* "I did well with TV," he said, but he continued to trim tall trees—an outgrowth of his early (1940s) climbing days, because "it keeps me grounded." He told of doing a job for the USFS or Park Service in the redwoods and how thrilled he was when he got to the top of a tree that looked dead but turned out to have a live "bush" crown at the very top.

We had dinner on *Forevergreen.* Rod cooked ling cod and prepared a salad. I took rice, done in the microwave.

September 4, Sunday: Rod and Ron took off earlier than we did from Scow Bay and went ahead to Watters Cove in Kyuquot Sound. We arrived there around noon.

Rod wanted a cheeseburger and had learned from a young man who was out rowing that a café in the Indian settlement had "everything" to eat and "is open all the time." Ron rowed our dink across the bay, against wind and tide. The restaurant was closed. Rod said, "I should have suspected when the kid said that it had everything and they were always open."

Got our ice chest filled with ice ($5) and bought a Chinook salmon ($15) from a fish buyer and a halibut ($10) from an Indian family.

Anchored in "Petroglyph Cove," which apparently does not have petroglyphs, just lichen deposits on overhanging rocks at entrance that look very much like animals and other small figures. There are also some orange markings that look like pictographs. Don says, "Well, people will wonder, and they'll use their imaginations."

Spotted a twenty-four inch blue sunray star and an equally large five-legged pink starfish. Minimum size sunray we saw was three inches in diameter and bright orange. Many large oysters, six to eight inches in diameter. A cedar tree that's probably a thousand years old is at the head of the cove. A cable "graveyard" indicates heavy logging activity years ago.

Water is quite clean and clear in here compared to Scow Bay.

Weather today was beautiful! Scattered clouds with sun most of day.

September 5, Monday: Labor Day. Kyuquot Channel to Yellow Bluff. Seas of four meters. Can't help comparing motion to horseback riding—you have to flex your knees, lean forward, tip back, right, left; up down; up down. Exhausting after two or three hours.

We rendezvous with *Forevergreen* in Rolling Roadstead, north of Catala Island, part company, then head to Nuchatlity to see if Dan DeVault is at his cabin.

As usual, I'm "kif-kif" about taking the side-trip. I want to get to Zeballos to buy propane, but say to Don, "I'll do what you want to do." And the boat turns southeast.

Two fishing trawlers at DeVault's dock. We pull alongside for "just a minute," ask if Dan is home, and Dan appears, along with his wife, Fyffe (Fife) and kids, Janine (five, first grade) and Evan (three, in playschool). Fyffe is pretty, brown, straight hair to the nape of her neck, blue eyes—irises the blue of a Siberian husky—and nicely shaped. No make-up. None needed. Kids are well disciplined and enunciate well. Janine seems older than her five years. I remark about it to Fyffe and she replies it's probably because they spend so much time "out here."

We have coffee and a sandwich of home-canned sockeye.

They have a five-acre parcel and are building a slightly larger house. They would like to rent out their cabin. We're interested. They asked if we had a computer. Twelve-volt, no problem.

We stand on the porch waiting for a deluge to lessen, then head for the boat. Evan is dressed in a fisherman's green slicker that comes down to his little yellow boots. Don snaps a photo of him. He hopped into a skiff with the guy from *La Perouse* and the gal from the boat we tied to—they were going to look for "gooey ducks." In pouring rain, they go beachcombing.

We take off at 1230 hours and head to Zeballos.

Fuel up at Nootka Mission, where Kevin Hills asks if we would like to stay for supper. We do, and it's a rather touching evening. Natives came from various places, others come from Zeballos or Tahsis. We meet Anna and Gordon Lang; she is the librarian in Zeballos. Also Earl Johnson whose wife Louise wrote a cookbook and a book on the Esperanza Mission.

September 6: Sighted two bear north of Tsowwin Narrows, another three in Heron Bay, two more south of that, then one on the east side of Tahsis

Inlet. They paw and overturn a ten to fifteen pound rock as if it's a pebble, then poke their noses into the sand and munch on clams or oysters.

September 7: Kyuquot—where the winds blow. Ray Williams showed us works by his son Sanford, a carver. Sanford was chosen among ten master carvers to appear in a gallery in Victoria.

We rowed the dinghy up the "waterfall" that leads into the lake. The current was going in at the time, and two cascading creeks flowed into the lake, instead of into the sea. The current began to change as we floated in to the lake, and we floated back out. We had gone ashore to look for the house that had belonged to Cougar Annie, a pioneer woman who lived here into her nineties. We found two shacks with telephone lines to the north side of the creek. A path from the shacks leads up to a logging road where the noise of logging trucks startled us at first. The rain forest is beautiful along the path. Later we learned that Annie's house was in Boat Basin, not Rae Basin, and we could see a substantial house along the north shore of the basin.

September 8: Hot Springs Cove from 0915 to 1300 hours. At 2220 We're anchored in what Don named "Friendly Dolphin Cove"—a little bombproof bay on the east side of Obstruction Island. It has poured rain almost all day. This was especially hard as we soaked in the hot springs and walked back on the boardwalk. Then again through Shelter Inlet, and here after we anchored. Now it's quiet and the only sounds, other than the ticking of the ship's clock, are the creeks and small waterfalls draining into the cove. The boat is absolutely motionless, as if we're stuck on the bottom. There's no wind, no rain now. An occasional flash of lightning—rare in these parts.

When we motored into the cove, it was high tide, and the lowest branches of the trees dipped into the salt water, as they do in so many of the coves. There wasn't an inch of ground showing where you could go ashore.

September 10-16: Tofino. Victoria. Home.

**

October 23, Sunday: A stop in Friday Harbor so I could lunch with Barbara Marrett. Then we came on to Matia Island, a favorite of Frank and Margie Fletcher. Have worked all day on the *Exploring Southeast Alaska* book. Now I'm reading one of the books the Fletchers lent us for the weekend—*Going North*, by Jess Webb, self-published, La Conner, WA. The author has a good sense of humor and has an eye for nature. It's an easy read, a narrative of his and his wife Carroll's trip north in their forty-two foot Krogan. He compares the different types of cruising navigators—careful ones, versus the determined ones who end up on rocks and call May Day on VHF.

We watched a blue heron along the shore – moving in slow motion like a ballerina doing an intricate slow dance, or a kabuki player. It moved from a rock into the water till its legs were invisible, then paused, stretched its neck as far as it would reach, its eyes rolling around to search for a fish. Then its head darted under and instantly it had a fingerling in its beak. The fingerling glistened and wriggled as the heron waited and shook it, then swallowed it, its whole throat expanding as it raised its head to "shake it" down. I wonder if the fingerling swims around in the heron's stomach. Not long after, the heron steps carefully—always in slow motion—and catches another fingerling.

An adolescent gull—as large as its mother, but without her mature squawk—pulls his head into his body, rocks forward till he almost tips, makes himself appear small, then pecks and squeaks at his mama. She's totally oblivious to him, ignores him. I think of a few children who need to be treated this way.

Victoria, BC.

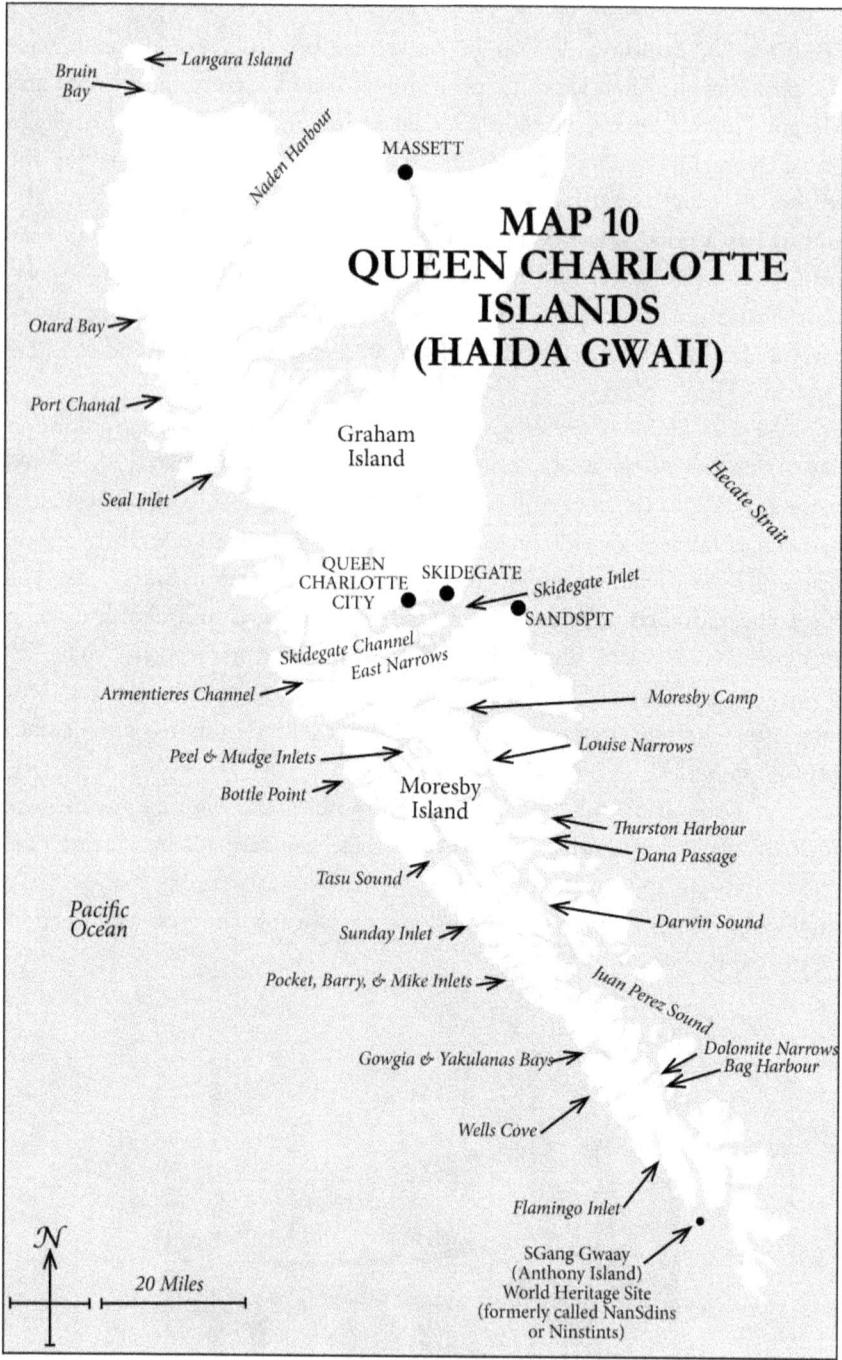

MAP 10
QUEEN CHARLOTTE ISLANDS (HAIDA GWAII)

Bruin Bay

← Langara Island

Naden Harbour

MASSETT

Otard Bay →

Port Chanal →

Graham Island

Hecate Strait

Seal Inlet →

QUEEN CHARLOTTE CITY   SKIDEGATE   Skidegate Inlet
SANDSPIT

Skidegate Channel
East Narrows

Armentieres Channel →   Moresby Camp

Peel & Mudge Inlets →   ← Louise Narrows

Bottle Point →   Moresby Island

Thurston Harbour
Dana Passage

Tasu Sound →

Pacific Ocean   Darwin Sound

Sunday Inlet →

Pocket, Barry, & Mike Inlets →

Juan Perez Sound

Gowgia & Yakulanas Bays →   Dolomite Narrows
Bag Harbour

Wells Cove

Flamingo Inlet

SGang Gwaay
(Anthony Island)
World Heritage Site
(formerly called NanSdins
or Ninstints)

N

20 Miles

QUEEN CHARLOTTE ISLANDS, 1995

August 12, 1995: Prince Rupert. Provisioned at Safeway, $500 Canadian. Took all afternoon to stow stuff.

A young man waiting at the PR fuel dock struck up a conversation with me about fishing—boats coming in because of bad weather and staying put for a few days. Trollers can take fish all year, he said, when I asked him if they were going out for the opening today.

Women in Prince Rupert can't worry so much about their hair because of the weather and they tend to look much more natural.

Dinner aboard the *Neuron II*, a thirty-two foot Grand Banks, owners Harry and Barb Patton from Seattle. Barb is seventy-seven and gets around like she's younger than I am.

August 14, Monday: Left Prince Rupert at 0615 hours, came fifty miles southwest to Larsen Harbour, the jumping off point for the Queen Charlottes. On the way we checked out two anchorages, unnamed, in Principe Channel. Keswar Inlet is great—it appears sheltered in all weather—and the *Coast Pilot* doesn't mention it.

We've seen very little sea or land life: two seals, one porpoise, one river otter; very few birds, other than petrels, gulls, Canada geese and sand pipers.

In Ogden Channel we encountered a group of twelve young people in six covered canoes. They were from the Calgary YMCA. They'd been out for two months already and seemed enthusiastic about their trip. Amazing, since Calgary's on the eastern slope and these kids had been camping in rain like they've never seen, I'm sure, in Calgary.

August 15, Tuesday: Approaching Skidegate Inlet on the five-fathom curve. The ferry boat, *Queen of Prince Rupert*, is just heading back to Prince Rupert at 1215 hours.

The Queen Charlottes, Gwai Haanas in Haida language, consist of 150 or more islands, of which Graham and Moresby are the largest. Neil Carey says in *A Guide to the Queen Charlotte Islands* that for hikers and motorists Graham Island has more to offer. Moresby has only thirty-two kilometers of public road, although some logging roads may be usable.

August 16: On CBC radio, Greg Smith, of Health Canada, says the amount of dioxin in crabs and shellfish has decreased by over ninety percent since the late 1980s, due to a decrease in effluents from pulp mills. (Health Canada has monitored the pancreas in crabs since late 1980s.) The use of chlorine has also decreased. Pulp mills apparently did this voluntarily following a memo from the government saying, in effect, "find a better way."

Flocks of surf scoters in Maude Channel.

August 17: Going back through the East Narrows from the west end is much easier than east to west. The ranges are easier to follow. So many of the navigational aids seem to be set up to help vessels going west to east.

Visited the Queen Charlotte museum at Skidegate. Left the boat at a small float west of the ferry dock and walked the half-mile east. This was not like our sortie into Queen Charlotte, two days ago, when we walked three miles round trip to the Information Centre only to discover this was not the place to get our passports for the Gwai Haanas Park. Arrived at Gwai Haanas headquarters just twenty minutes before closing time.

The young man at the fuel dock in Skidegate today grew up in Queen Charlotte. He's a student at UBC (University of British Columbia), in Vancouver; he comes home for the summers because there are good paying jobs here, but it's a strictly male-dominated society and market, he says. Females have hard time getting good paying jobs, other than at the hospital. His parents "cut him off" after twelfth grade—i.e., he has to pay his way through university, but he says he can make $2K a month easily here. Not so his sister, who must get help from their parents.

At the museum we saw a war canoe built for an expedition from Vancouver to Bella Bella and the Queen Charlottes. It's fifty feet long, carries twenty-one persons, and was carved from *one* log. A totem outside the longhouse, with a canoe, is also being carved from a single log. It's difficult to find large enough, straight enough trees to use these days.

The paths and roads are lined with thickets of black berries and salmon berries; the latter have already borne fruit; the former aren't quite ripe yet.

Field-grown tomatoes in the Queen Charlotte city center market were 99 cents a pound—the same price we pay at Vonn's in Bishop. The lettuce was $1.29 a head. Three weeks ago it was $1.99 in Bishop.

> **Chicken thighs browned in oven:** ½ cup wine; 1 large clove garlic sliced; pepper. Add ½ cup of golden raisins, 4 chopped green onions; 4 large pieces of crystallized ginger, chopped; soy sauce. Bake 15 minutes then add Chinese noodles Szechuan style for another 15 minutes.

August 18: Going down through Louise Narrows is like sailing through Savoie. High, forested mountains with triangular peaks, rounded peaks whose sides plunge down to the water.

Louise Narrows has a dredged channel only about twenty to twenty-five feet wide. The sides of the Narrows are lined with cobbles. There are starfish, jellyfish, sea nettles, and long black fish that are eel-like in appearance.

Lagoon Inlet: Don wants to attempt Tidal Rapids at high water slack (now, 0805 hours). The entrance is covered with kelp. I look at it through the binoculars and say, "No! No! It would be foolish, out here, away from help."

Don says reluctantly, "I guess it would be." He looks again and groans. The groan is half sigh of resignation, half groan of disappointment. Or, maybe it means, "Well, we can try!"

I say, "Okay, Vancouver, lower the long boats."

We turn around and leave. A boat like ours lies aground about an eighth of a mile from the tidal rapids, its hull wide open from stern to center. A sign has been tacked to its starboard side: "Danger. Blasting Area." Someone's sense of humor!

Selwyn Inlet. Bouncy, choppy. White caps. Weather from southeast. Visibility only about one mile. We head east along the south shore to get some lee from waves. A fishing boat, *Haida Crest*, with its flopper-stoppers out, and trolling, approaches going west. Don calls them on the radio and asks what it looks like. The skipper speaks slowly, deliberately but with the usual native understatement: "Oh, it's blowing up about ten footers." Don asks about Thurston Harbor. Reply: "It may be a bit breezy in there." He recommends anchoring just at the north entrance to Dana Passage if we want to turn around.

The sailboat *Ocean Light* is coming west from Hecate Strait. He calls us on Channel 16, tells us it's pretty nasty "out there." Don tells him we're heading for a buoy in Thurston. The other guy says Dana Passage has good protection. Don tells him we're heading on in. The other guy seems to have local knowledge—just my intuition from what he said—and doesn't reply about Thurston.

We head in and as we reach the buoys and round up the gusts and squalls increase. It takes us six go-rounds to pick up a buoy. I try four times and just miss each time. Then Don tries twice. The first time he's calling to me, but I can't hear a thing above the wind and the engine. On his second try, I get a line around the buoy and we manage to tie up. I think now we know why locals avoid this harbor under like conditions. Too difficult to pick up a buoy! The white caps continue to head down the harbor, making our tie-up bouncy. Once in a while we get an eighteen-incher. Some of the waves look like surf.

I was extremely angry with Don for bringing us this far. "We've got to see what it's like to be able to write about it," he says. No-one with any sense puts his wife and boat in jeopardy in these conditions, but Don's "fine edge" (pushing everything to the limit) never gives up!

At one point when we were rolling and pitching quite badly, I put my life jacket on to avoid being smashed against the chart table. I put it on again to go out and get a line around the buoy.

If this is a summer storm, thank God I'll never be here on a boat in a winter storm.

A young harbor seal pokes his nose up every so often about seventy-five feet from the boat. Once he had to put his nose straight up because the waves were covering his eyes.

When Don was out maneuvering the buoy line, he had left the aft doors open. The wind caught the hatch cover, blew it forward, and the hinges broke. The port side knob sheared off and the starboard hinge broke.

The port-side port light leaks; the carpet is filthy; likewise the upholstery, particularly the pilot berth. *Baidarka* needs some attention and renovation.

There is a huge lodge located in Pacofi Bay. As we cruised past the lights were on inside and a curl of smoke rose above its chimney. "I'd like to be curled up inside right now with a good book," I told Don.

1950 hours. It's rained almost continuously like it did two or three years ago in Bishop Bay. Weather forecast has been upgraded to storm force winds of forty to fifty knots. *We* knew, before *they* did. Could have told them!

August 20: The engine water temperature rose to 230°F and kept rising when we were in Darwin Sound. The water just north of Shuttle Island was calm and flat, and Don thought maybe we could tow *Baidarka* to Water Hole Cove, a few miles away. We got the dinghy and outboard down off the cabin, but the outboard wouldn't start. We sat barely moving while engine cooled. Then Don decided to motor slowly to Water Hole Cove. We made it and tied up at the float—a nice cement float about fifty feet long—and filled the water tanks and had a bite to eat. Then we attacked the water system. Took apart the impeller and found it had no blades remaining—it was badly chewed up. Fortunately we had a replacement kit. It took us about an hour and a half to do the repair, lifting stuff out of the engine compartment, changing, checking, rechecking, flushing.

August 22, Tuesday: Juan Perez Sound this morning and heading for Burnaby Strait.

Endeavour calls on the radio to see if we can patch them to Harbor Air. Their single side band is "down." They sight orcas off Ramsey Island.

Two groups of kayakers in upper Burnaby, one of four boats, the second of seven. More kayaks than pleasure vessels!

Meet *Clavella* anchored in the north end Burnaby. A sailing vessel with three divers exploring below the water along the shoreline.

I like Bag Harbor!

August 23: Overnight in Ikeda Cove. There was a mining operation here from the early 1900s to WWI. Then, from 1960-68, iron ore was again extracted for export to Japan. This is a beautiful little inlet—calm, quiet, and like a pond last night. Although the sight of trees fallen along east shore suggests the winds must whip at the entry with frightful force. We hung our small Danforth from the stern.

The changes in weather from minute to minute remind me of Patagonia. Rain squalls, sun for moments briefly, then rainbows, then calm, then another squall. The difference, however, is that (during summer, at least) there aren't the extremes in temperature. When Kathy Wells and I were cycling across Tierra del Fuego[3] we had snow and hail one hour, then sun with 60°F temperatures. Here, it's quite mild.

We're heading for Anthony Island now, and Ninstints [now NanSdins], the Haida World Heritage Site.

Sara, a twenty-eight foot Bristol cutter sailboat, with Elizabeth (Lizzie) and John Herchenrider, from Granville, OH. We meet them in S'Gaang Gwai (Red Cod Village), the Haida village site on Anthony Island.

August 26: In Shearwater, we met Silveci and Del D'Ancangelo, of Black Creek, B.C . Their dreams and visions: he wanted to see a child born, build a house; run his own business and have his own employees; read the Bible; sail around the world. They sailed with their twelve-year-old daughter on a twenty-eight foot sailboat down the west coast of the US and Mexico, then to Nuku Hiva in French Polynesia. Del is studying to become a nurse. Then maybe they'll take off again in slightly larger boat. At present Silveci, who is a pilot, flies excursions into lakes for fishing etc.

Bullock Channel has 65°F water, but no jellyfish. The water is muskeg or tea-colored. Must research if this discourages jellyfish.

Anchor in Neekas Cove, eastern arm of Neekas Inlet, off the west side of Spiller Channel. A mile and a half wide, Spiller lies north-south, and winds funnel up in the afternoon. Weather forecast said winds southwestly, six kilometers per hour, at Ivory Island, whereas Spiller has near-gale force now.

We had dinner ashore at the Shearwater Pub with John and Lizzie Herchenrider, then went back to *Sara* for gingerbread and tea. Their boat is not only a Bristol cutter, it's Bristol polished! They spent all winter in Warm Springs Bay house sitting and working on the boat. Last week, they holed up in Hoya Passage at the Water Hole float and varnished the teak. Thirteen coats! The interior of the boat is spotless and tastefully appointed with three or four slim oil lamps and one gimballed lamp.

John is forty-five, a sound engineer who sold his own company to buy the *Sara*. He worked two summers as engineer for the San Diego Symphony. Lizzie comes from a fairly well-off family; her father owns an art publishing company. Lizzie majored in English, then did graduate studies in art. She's a talented young woman—she showed us her illustrated recipe book and the *Sara* journal. I feel instant affinity with Lizzie as an

---

[3] An adventure described in my book, *Two Women Against the Wind.*

equal—not as a mother or grandmother figure—and it's wonderful to me when friendship can cross that many years—she is thirty-one, I am sixty-two.

Cruising or boating among *serious* boaters seems to be an equalizer. And I certainly don't include among serious boaters the owners and crew of *South Shore*, from Newport, Oregon, who pulled in to Shearwater Dock in front of us last night and ran their generator *all night* long. They also talk on Channel 16, instead of switching to another channel. Their boat is sixty-five feet long with two winding staircases, one up from the stern, the other to the fly deck. John and Lizzie call that sort of boat a "penis extender."

The weather is lovely—sunny, warm during the day; cool at night. Then foggy in the morning. What a change from the Queen Charlottes!

We are still slogging away with research and documentation. There's very little time to do anything else and I get discouraged and long for a rest and vacation.

August 28: *Sundowner*, a boat from Blaine, WA. Owners live in Kennewick. They were headed into Goldstream Harbour and called us on Channel 16 to say they enjoy our *Exploring* book.

We spent last night in a cove east of Watt Bay, in Queen Sound. It's unnamed so Don called it "Domestic Tranquility," because we had fought earlier, when we were going through some of the narrows and over to Goose Island. I lay down to nap and Don woke me just as we were going through Spitfire Channel. I nearly freaked. Later he gave me a flower as a "peace offering."

Anchored tonight in Fury Cove, where we first became acquainted with Kathy Gallizio and Bill Lowe of *Brigadoon*, when there was a horrible gale outside and calm in here. Tonight there are five boats anchored here: *Sabi, Sunshine Patriot, Alicia Marie, Baidarka,* and a fifth which we can't see. The people on *Sabi* cruised the rivers and canals of Europe for fifteen summers before shipping the boat back to the States.

We hear on CBC that three airports are closed because of bomb threats—New York is one of them. Don says, "And you think it's dangerous out here!"

Last night, in Domestic Tranquility, we saw crimson sea urchins that turn inside out when disturbed and shoot water out; also green sea urchins, kelp crabs, purple stars (which are also orange, brown, pink, and yellow), sunflower stars, mottled stars, nudibranchs; and tiny rockfish no more than four to six inches long which swim sideways like a flounder or halibut.

August 29, Tuesday: Off Smith Inlet, Queen Charlotte Sound. Just saw a pod of dolphins that charged toward us, then dove and leapt off the bow for about twenty minutes. A murre flew by and landed, sunk as if he were a dead weight, resurfaced and flapped along the top of the water as if he couldn't get airborne.

Talked to Stan Westhaver as we passed by Egg Island.

Anchored in the Walker Group, listening to CBC. Joan Scoggins reads a letter about "God's Ocean"—an appreciation of the ocean off B.C.'s Pacific Coast. She expresses what Don feels about the ocean but can't put as well into words. Hearing her piece sends chills through me. I say, "she appreciates what I fear."

Don says, "Why don't you write about your fear?"

How do you write about your lack of appreciation for the depths of water that draw their heavings from thousands of miles away, that build up to such momentous heights that they upend freighters, knock down oil platforms, and pitchpole a forty-two foot sailboat? Scoggins' piece sounds so cold, forbidding, overpowering—her ocean is a place I wouldn't choose to go. As we motored south today from Fury Cove, the breeze from the west, the heaving waters, the smell of salt air, the humidity, the lack of warmth from the sun now made me think, "I don't like this part." So Scoggins' piece came on the bow of my thoughts.

Now we're anchored surrounded by three islands with low-growing cedars, hemlocks, blue spruce loaded with cones, salal, alders—all growing out of vertical granite slabs where not a slice of sun or light enters. The water is green, translucent to depths of eighteen feet. Earlier we watched a river otter diving for fish. He climbed up on the tethered log 200 feet off our bow, shook the fish, tipped his neck straight up, swallowed, shook his head, licked his whiskers, rubbed his cheek against the log. His chestnut brown body glistened with water. He dove off the log again, resurfaced five minutes later, climbed up on what appears to be vertical rock, repeated his meal tactics, turned around and again. Don filmed for fifteen minutes as he dove, resurfaced, climbed on a rock or the log; then when he'd had enough, he swam to the right "shore"—vertical rocks, found a hold, climbed on some drift logs and disappeared behind them. Siesta time.

Water temperature is 52°F, and we're seeing moon jellyfish again. So, the low temperatures have no effect on jellyfish. The only place they seemed to be absent was in very muskeggy water—although the way the water flows in and out may have more to do with their presence than the temperature. It's too bad that in the places where the water is clear enough to swim, the temperature is either too cold or there are too many jellyfish.

1550 hours. High tide. The river otter comes out again. He swims eight to ten feet behind the stern, dives down and comes down with a sanddab in his jaw, jiggles the fish until it's in the right position so he can swallow it, takes a half dozen chews before he gets the whole thing down. Then he swims toward the swim step again as he did with the fish in his mouth. I say, "Hello, there," gently. He looks up at me without fear, perhaps with curiosity. You can tell he's never been threatened by humans. After fifteen minutes he swims to shore, climbs on a vertical rock and rubs himself in a mossy depression.

A flock of starlings flies overhead, noisy and scolding.

About the river otter, I say: "He doesn't seem to observe our mealtimes."

Don says, "No, he's not French."[4]

Mustelids (weasels, wolverine, mink, sea otter, river otter): most species mate in summer. As a result gestation takes more time than the rapidly growing embryos actually need. The fertilized ova remain dormant, floating freely in the uterus until the last month or so of pregnancy.

The river otter has a muscular tail, one-third of its total body length. Its fur is dark brown with some grey on the chin and throat. It can dive to depths of sixty feet.

August 30: After waking early, we go back to sleep till 1030. Between then and noon there's no wind, and the detritus floats around in patterns, circulating slowly around the boat.

I do Don's hair and beard on the foredeck. Halfway through, a dive boat comes in and anchors. Don is nude and quickly puts on his underpants.

---

[4] I have a strong affinity for all things French. I spent a year in France as a college student, and Don and I have made numerous trips to that country in our five decades together.

August 31: Thursday. Arrived Port Hardy about noon, "gassed" up, and filled the water tank. As we frequently do, we over-filled the diesel tank and had a spill in the cockpit.

September 1: Port McNeill. Sointula Docks in Port McNeill Harbour are in better condition than those in Port Hardy, and are well maintained. Many more cruising boats are moored here than in Port Hardy. Slips are available on a first come, first serve basis. The cruising fleet begins arriving in April and keeps coming through September. "From June to August, it's crazy," says Harbour Manager, Hiltje Binner. "They raft three deep." In winter the harbor is half-full, mostly with commercial boats.

September 2, Saturday: Anchored in Double Bay (Hanson Island), thirty miles south of Port Hardy, ten miles beyond Port McNeill. There are two "settlements" in here—one for commercial fishermen; one for sportfishing, the Double Bay Resort. This morning I spotted a man heading out in a skiff loaded with garbage bags. He stopped at a rock islet. I thought, "Oh, how nice, he's picking up trash and hauling it to town." Then he began to offload the bags. It was high tide so I was a little perplexed. We all looked through the binoculars and suspected him of dumping trash.

Kathy (Wells) said, "Let's shout at him."

Don and I said, "No, we're accusing him before we know. We'll go by and take a photo later."

Within fifteen minutes he poured something over the pile and a few minutes later the trash went up in flames.

September 3, 1995. Channel 16: "Has this damn fog lifted anywhere in Johnstone Strait?"

A low deep voice: "In Port Harvey."

"Well, there may be salvation yet."

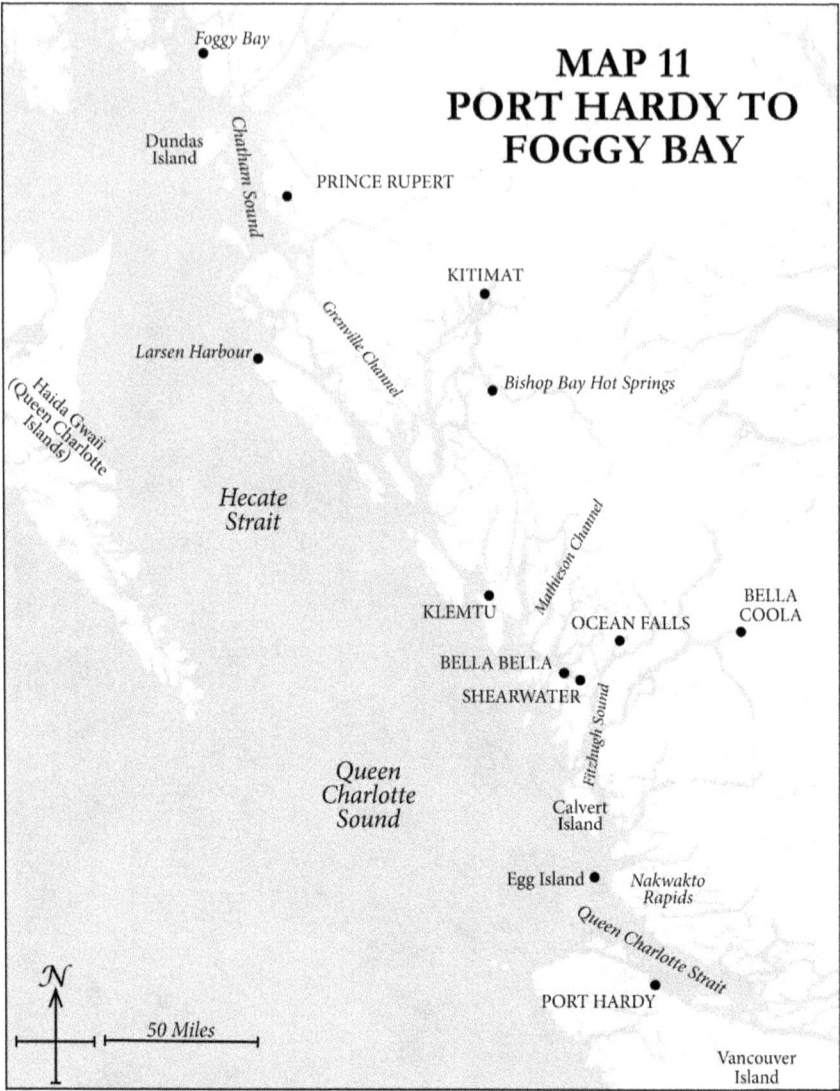

MAP 11
PORT HARDY TO
FOGGY BAY

Foggy Bay

Dundas
Island

Chatham Sound

PRINCE RUPERT

KITIMAT

Granville Channel

Larsen Harbour

Bishop Bay Hot Springs

Haida Gwaii
(Queen Charlotte
Islands)

Hecate
Strait

Mathieson Channel

KLEMTU

OCEAN FALLS

BELLA
COOLA

BELLA BELLA

SHEARWATER

Fitzhugh Sound

Queen
Charlotte
Sound

Calvert
Island

Egg Island

Nakwakto
Rapids

Queen Charlotte Strait

N

50 Miles

PORT HARDY

Vancouver
Island

BRITISH COLUMBIA NORTH COAST, 1996

June 25, 1996. Port Neville. Ole Hansen is in failing health. He had an operation for cancer of the testes and prostate. Went in with back problems; they did a scan and discovered the cancer. He's eighty-seven this year (came here when he was seven). Lorna and Erica want to stay here, though Lorna has a romantic interest and would have to leave if she married. Erica is like an untamed animal. She rears up like one who's had its way all the time. Doesn't want her mom to remarry. Doesn't want to leave Port Neville.

June 26: Port McNeill. Met Cara and Bob Barringer, aboard *Metolius*, from Hailey, ID. They did a circumnavigation, cruised for three years with *Summer Wind*, which is also here in Port McNeill. On board *Summer Wind*: Bob and Dolores Rolfe, with friends Mary Louise and Herb Stewart.

We found petroglyphs east of Collingwood Point and a huge hemlock.

June 27: Alert Bay. Tom Stringfield and Vickie Nissen, from Portland, OR. His business card says "Somewhat retired. No work. No prospects. No worries. No money." They came to the dock to meet us and say how much they like our books. We had beer aboard their thirty-six foot sailboat, *Vixen*.

June 29: Echo Bay. *SacaLaurie* from Orcas Island, WA. Laurie and Warren Miller. We pulled in behind them at the Windsong Gallery barge, in Echo Bay. Don introduced himself, Warren likewise.

Don: "Not *the* Warren Miller?"

"Yes."

I hopped off and introduced myself and said, "After all these years we finally meet!"

Then we had lunch with them. Laurie and Warren have been married since 1988. Laurie ran the Ski Shack in Seattle and used to carry our Alpenlite backpacks[5]. Warren is seventy-two. We agreed to meet them again in Viner Sound. We went ahead and found a float house with a houseboat tied up to it and four or five crab pots around the bay with polypro lines

---

[5] Don and I were the founders and owners, from 1970 to 1988, of Wilderness Group International, a California-based company that manufactured Alpenlite backpacks, Kangaroo Baggs bicycle accessories, and other outdoor gear.

out. The house itself was tied to the shore with lines, so we didn't stay. We caught the Millers coming in as we were going out and decided to return to Echo Bay. They did the same and invited us to dinner—chicken teriyaki, zucchini with sesame seeds, salad (my contribution), ice cream for dessert. Warren is a Type A personality and is taking medication to decrease his adrenalin, as he began suffering from ventricular fibrillations. They live on Orcas Island in a 900-square-foot house. "Come stay with us!"

June 30, Sunday: Sullivan Bay, with Tom and Gloria Burke on *Carousel*, Bill Swain on *High Flight III*, and Laurie and Warren Miller, on *SacaLaurie*.

Tom and Gloria caught a twenty-four pound red snapper. They have the head in a bucket; it has two ivory pieces, very delicate and leaf-like, with natural etchings along the edge. The eyes are two inches in diameter.

Pat Finnerty and Lynn Whitehead have lived here for twenty years, though they spend the winters on Cortes Island. They own foreshore and a water lease in Sullivan Bay. People lease water rights according to their frontage. Houses are owned by people from Port McNeill to Florida. There are no phones, but you can get gas and diesel. No "really uncomfortable" storms hit here in summer.

July 1: Up at 0330 hours. Anchored in Rivers Inlet at 2040 hours, soup and to bed by 2200. Horrible seas in Queen Charlotte Sound. Anchored for two and a half hours in Jones Cove, Smith Inlet, then headed back out. We both slept like logs while we were anchored. The rest of the crossing was *miserable*.

Duncanby Landing: Open all year; more floats going in. Diesel and gas, propane, showers and laundry; store, clean and simple; liquor. It was a commercial camp until 1992 and pleasure craft were discouraged. Now they're encouraged. Ken Gillis and partner Judy are the owners. This is their fourth summer. They're helpful and friendly.

John and Randi Sanger pulled in behind us at Duncanby. We had a good visit for over an hour. They left Port McNeill early this morning and made it all the way, despite rough seas, especially off Slingsby Channel and Smith Inlet. Del and Inez from *Sundowner* are also docked at Duncanby. They have our book. We crossed from Duncanby to Bilton Island. Explored north end of Bilton, then Ripon Island: Sunshine Bay, Magee Channel, Big Frypan.

We anchored within the islands north of Goose Bay, with a stern tie to shore.

July 2: Minus tide last night. At 0630 hours the sonar alarm went off. Don got up to check, looked over the stern and said, "Let's get outta here, we got twenty-four inches to go!"

Breakfast in Goose Bay. Green mud flats full of eagles, gulls and blue heron. Birds singing in trees along shore.

The gracefulness of the hemlock with their brilliant light green tips makes me want to cry—they're so beautiful—perhaps my favorite tree.

The area we explored today is an archipelago—island after island with narrow passageways leading from one bay to another, or to a hidden lagoon. We're working our way north so we'll come out in Fitz Hugh Sound instead of back into Queen Charlotte Sound. Don is absolutely delighted, happy when he can explore. He's born to explore and in his element now that he's (we're) receiving so much good feedback from people who use our *Exploring* guidebook.

1645 hours. We're anchored with the Danforth in the south end of Big Frypan Bay. It's perfectly quiet except for the drone of an occasional small plane. Spring tides this week. At high tide the limbs of the trees drop into the water.

Heard *Sagebrush Sailor* being called on Channel 16 for traffic. Betty and Bob Lynch, whom we met three or four years ago.

July 3, Wednesday: Rain, rain, rain. Mostly pouring, despite weather report of light rain. We reconnoitered Frypan Bay after we raised the Danforth at 0600 hours. Then we headed out to Fitz Hugh Sound and north. Checked out Kwakume Inlet, then coves to the north.

Don flares at me for not knowing how to go "wing 'n wing" with *Illahee*, a thirty-six foot ketch that resembles our William Garden ketch, *Le Dauphin Amical*. He continues to growl; I get tired of listening and go stand on aft deck in my Goretex, which soaks through after fifteen minutes. Not much fun today. Grey, wet, captain angry.

July 4, Thursday: Bella Coola. The harbormaster's office is at the head of gangway. It's closed during lunch hour. The fuel dock is on the east side by an ice plant. Also closed during lunch. No water on fuel dock, good water on some floats, and water available at the landing zone. Some power. Phones behind the office sometimes work. There's a tidal grid for hauling boats out.

Kevin O'Neill , the Assistant Harbourmaster, has been here six years. He's seen the number of visiting pleasure boats increase from six in 1990 to forty in 1996. A few boats winter over; there's no ice in the bay.

The Co-op in town has groceries, hardware, a liquor store. They accept Visa and Mastercard and offer free delivery to the dock for more than $70 of groceries.

There's a ferry dock on the west side of the ice plant dock. The "Discovery Coast" ferry—"too expensive for locals"—serves mostly tourists, runs from end of May to end of September.

July 7: Ellerslie Lagoon and Falls—fantastic! With *Evergreen, Starlite* and *Charisma.* Also *Lucky Girl,* a thirty-eight foot Davis motor vessel, owned by George and Evelyn Rasmussen, of Bremerton, WA. They have been married for fifty-two years, and cruising since 1958 in B.C. and Alaska. They were anchored in Ellerslie Bay with a shore tie, just southeast of a small islet against a granite bluff. They have been anchored there for six days. They waited three days for torrential rains to stop before going in to the Lagoon. They got information ahead of time from locals in Bella Bella, and caught a 29-inch bottom fish right off the narrows.

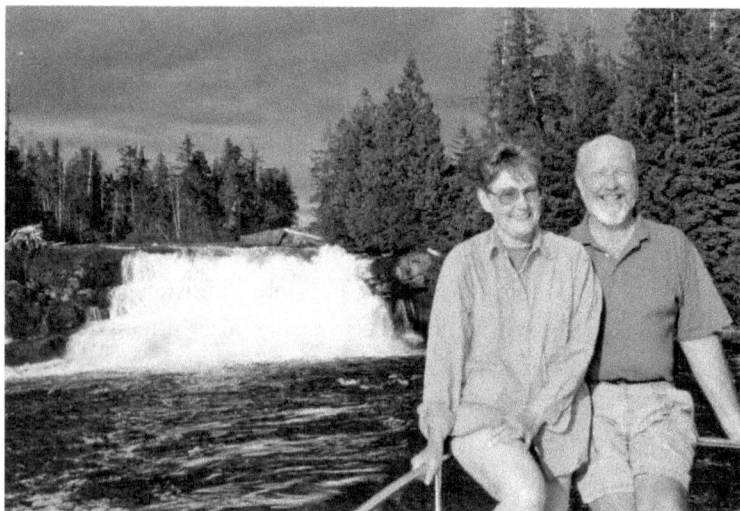

Ellerslie Falls

July 18: "Sovereignty Patrol"—the Canadian warship HMCS *Mermashee*, calling vessels that pass through Grenville Channel: "Investigating all vessels intruding our waters…":

- What is (or spell) the name of your vessel?
- What is the port of registry and the documentation/registration number?
- What was your last port of call?
- What is your next port of call?
- Where did you clear Canadian Customs?
- What is the number of your Canadian clearance?
- What is the make of your radar?
- Do you have any weapons aboard?
- Any cargo aboard?
- Name of your owner or master?

July 19: Lawson Harbour. A twenty-one foot sailboat, *Sage Hen*, from Fargo, ND, registered in Minnesota. Sandy and Alan Rawson. She is a pianist, he a violinist and professor of music at University of North Dakota.

Sandy, about Alan: "He's an animal… he's obsessed!"

Alan: "Your book paid for itself just for telling us about Lawson." They just bought the book yesterday at Seasport Marine, Prince Rupert.

Surf scoters facing into the squally wind, paddling, but their heads are hunkered down, turned sideways to protect themselves from the wind.

Welcome Harbor: "This recreational site has been created and maintained by the B.C. Forest Service (North Coast District Office), the Boy Scouts of Prince Rupert, and the North Coast Sailing Association. Please take care of this site, and use it at your own risk. A sign-in book has been provided for you to comment in. Please take your garbage with you."

A trail from Welcome Harbor to Secret Cove leads to a rope on top of a beach bluff. It's steep-to—you must use the rope for safety.

July 20: Prince Rupert. At Cow Bay Marina: Frank Kelly and Liz Cochien, *Diamond Sea*, from Vancouver, B.C. They bought our book.

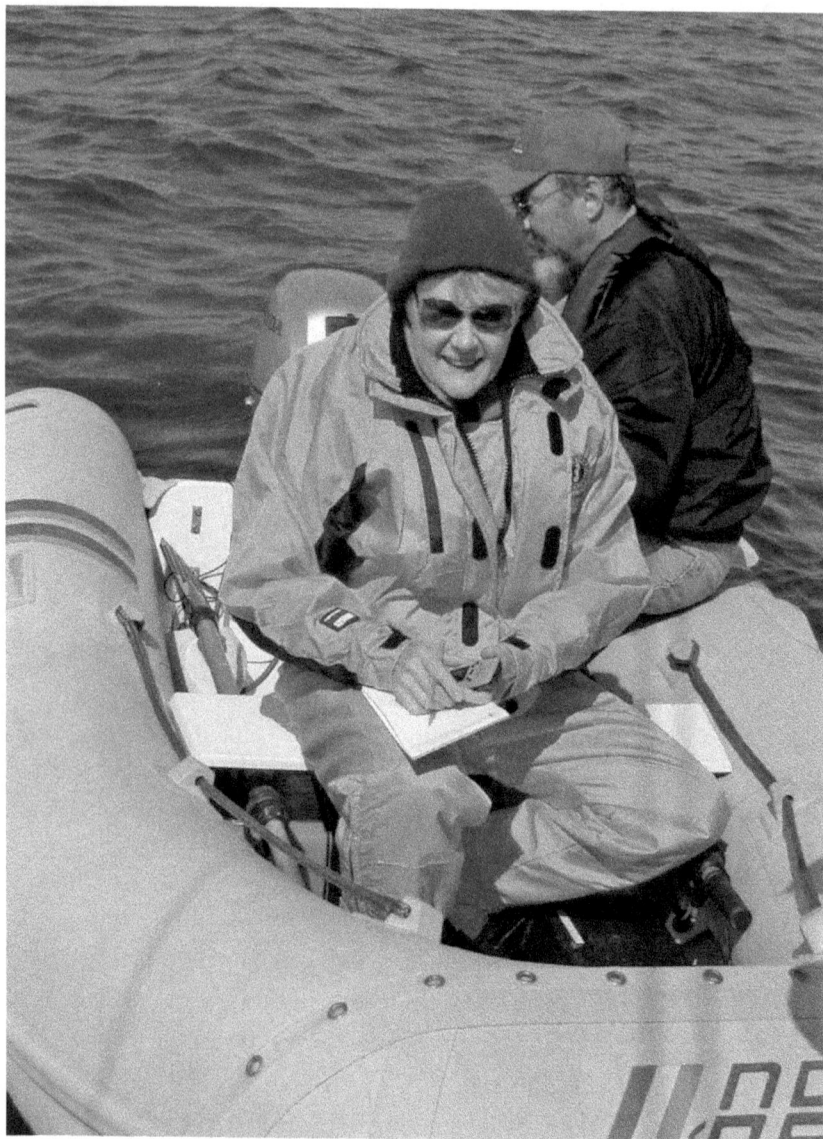

Data gathering with John Leone.

'BIG'
BAIDARKA

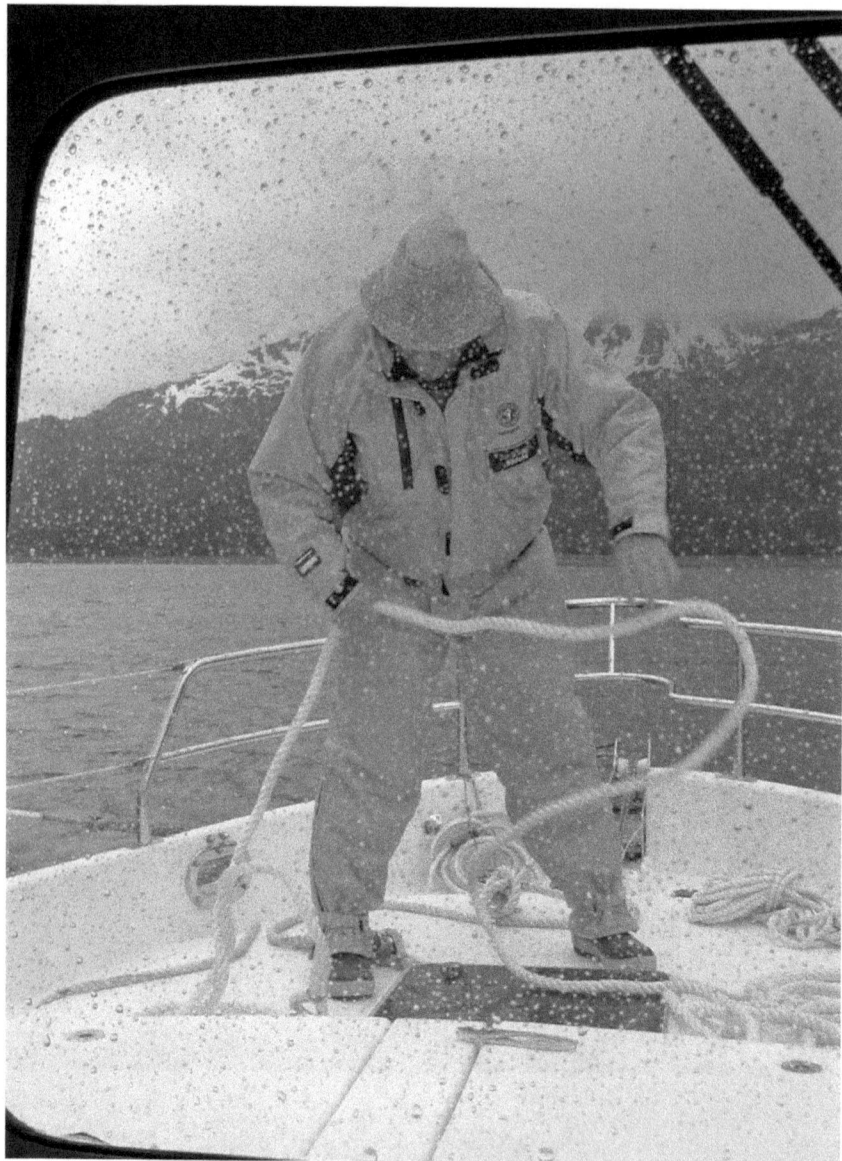

'BIG' *BAIDARKA*

By 1999, it no longer made sense to base ourselves in California when we were spending so much time in the Pacific Northwest aboard *Baidarka*, so Don and I sold our house in Bishop and bought another in Anacortes. We ran Fine Edge Productions out of an office above our new garage. Half a dozen staff members, including manager Mark Bunzel (who later bought the company from us) kept the business going during the summer months while Don and I went off on our research trips.

By this time we had explored pretty much every nook and cranny in the waters between Seattle and Skagway. We were now looking to explore further afield, including the Gulf of Alaska and the west coast of the Queen Charlotte Islands. For this we needed a larger boat, so we upgraded the Nordic Tug to a forty-foot Nordhavn trawler. This boat, which we also named *Baidarka*, gave us a much greater cruising range and greater blue water potential, without being so big that it would take more crew than the two of us to handle it.

The Nordhavn was built in another of Don's youthful stomping grounds—Fullerton, California—and her first voyage was a twenty-six day shakedown cruise up the west coast from Dana Point, via Catalina, to Anacortes. This was more like "jumping in the fire" than a pleasant summer cruise. We were also doing research for a proposed new *Exploring* book. Our son-in-law Jeff Mach and grandson Josh Douglass were aboard with us, but for me it was a white-knuckle trip. I was working until almost the day we left, and when I arrived there was still a crew of contractors doing last minute installations on the boat. When we set forth, bad weather— gales and lumpy seas—plagued us almost the entire way. Fortunately the boat proved to be exceptionally stable and seaworthy. We tried whenever possible to tie up at a dock overnight, but we spent one uncomfortable night at sea in a gale off Cape Mendocino. I summed up this experience as "To Be Endured," and TBE became part of our vocabulary thereafter.

Aboard the new *Baidarka*, Don and I continued to spend four to five months every summer doing our research, producing updated editions of our existing guidebooks and writing a new one, *Exploring the Pacific Coast – San Diego to Seattle* (2003; second edition, 2009). We also ventured into new waters, exploring the west coast of the Queen Charlotte Islands (Haida Gwaii) and incorporating our research into a new (second) edition of *Exploring the North Coast of British Columbia* (2002; a third edition was published in 2017). Much of this information was entirely new at the time, as no detailed charts existed for this part of the Queen Charlottes, and the shoreline features along an eighty mile stretch of coast had yet to be documented.

BRITISH COLUMBIA "OUTSIDE PASSAGE," 2000

July 20, 2000. Tenakee Hot Springs. Don wakes up at 0315 hours. Says, "We should go." The alarm is set for 0415. I pee and go back to bed.

"The alarm hasn't gone off yet," I say.

"Yeah, but…" He hops back in bed and cuddles up, wide awake, and starts talking.

We have a large damp spot on the comforter every morning, as if the hatch leaks each night.

"I think I know what happened," he says. "It got salt water on it last week and with the condensation every night the spot reoccurs. It never dries."

"Um." I'm trying to sneak another five-minute snooze.

"Let's get going. The tide is right." He starts to sing a military march.

"Okay, but don't be too cheery at this hour," I say grumpily.

I have to admit as we got underway that this hour is lovely.

There's no fog today. A patch of blue sky shows itself to the west from where clouds are spilling over the mountains. Spots of green appear under cloud holes; tinges of pink and yellow. Today there's definition to the sky. Yesterday all was grey mist with no more than a mile of visibility. Yesterday was TBE (To Be Endured). Today the morale rises.

Potluck dinner with crab aboard *Northern Trawler*, with Carlene and Keith, from Port Townsend, WA. Two other couples from the Sacramento area are traveling with them and had dinner with us also.

July 21: Strange reaction to the crab. Chills, swollen glands, flu-like symptoms. Perhaps an allergy?

August 3: Port Alexander is clean looking. The town is incorporated, everyone on the city council has a job to do to keep up the community. Firehose outfits are placed strategically along the boardwalk, which is well maintained. A city ordinance limits the size of the lodges.

August 5: A tour through El Capitan Cave, led by Ranger Kevin Casey. We went 600 feet into the cave, about 400 feet from the top. We wore hard hats and carried flashlights. The cave has 12,000 feet of mapped area to date.

Since Joel and Jean Gillingwaters came aboard this segment has been the most fun of all this summer's run. They're both extremely observant, helpful, and catch on quickly. Jean's done most of the cooking—great low-calorie salads. Great crew.

August 23: Prince Rupert.

August 27: Leaving Larsen Harbor I go to the bow and direct us through the kelp. At the end of the "forests" Don goes back to check the prop.

"Neutral. We've got kelp in the prop."

I pull the throttle back to idle and put the gear into neutral.

I look out the aft windows and see Don on the swim step poking with the boat hook.

"Reverse," he yells.

"Reverse." I respond pulling the gear shift handle back.

"Okay, we got it off," he yells.

I put the gear into forward and up the throttle to 1400 r.p.m.s. Don comes up to the pilothouse and stands beside me, letting me take the helm. I suspect his motive. Will I turn to port—out into the swells and down the outside of Banks Island in Hecate Strait? Or will I turn to starboard and head to Principe Channel?

He already decided this morning, listening to the weather report, that the lows coming across the Queen Charlotte Islands are too frequent. We've been in Larsen Harbor for three days waiting for better weather to cross the Strait and time is getting short.

I take us out to the ten-fathom line and turn left. Don looks at me, surprised.

"I figure I've had two nice days; now it's your turn."

"How sweet."

We head on toward Hecate Strait into an increasingly heavy westerly swell.

"Things aren't shipshape below," I say. "Turn the helm while I go stow everything."

I go below and stow the water purifier, plastic refrigerator jars, diaries and papers I was using last night to input in the computer. I fill the teakettle with water and turn on the stove. When it boils I fill the thermos.

We're now ready for rough weather.

I go up the three steps to the pilothouse. "Okay, everything's shipshape."

Don gives me a funny smile and turns the wheel to starboard. "We're going down Principe," he says. "I want you to be comfortable."

"Wow… I just filled the thermos because I thought I'd be eating potato soup all day."

"I figure you gave me eight weeks, now it's your turn," Don says and gives me a squeeze.

Out here in Principe Channel, there's not another boat. Except for the four or five fishing boats that came in to moor every night and left before dawn, we haven't seen another vessel since we turned west off the beaten track. All the others are heading south along the marine highway.

Don notes that when kelp is attached the leaves are visible on top of the water and follow the current. When kelp is detached the leaves hang underwater and the stems float on top.

"You're so observant of natural phenomena," I say.

"I'm glad you notice that. Do you appreciate that?"

"I do, I do."

He gives me a kiss. "I'm so observant of natural phenomena and you're so observant of people."

Banks Island: Grief Point, Survey Inlet, Wreck Point, Foul Bay, Terror Point, Calamity Bay, Gung Ho Bay, Despair Point, Deadman Islet, Gale Point. No wonder not many pleasure boats come out here!

I'm awakened from a twenty minute nap, south of Anger Island in Principe Channel. We've taken this route to escape ships in Grenville Channel. Slowly, layers of deck come out of the horizon, then a dark hull. Don calls to explain that we'll be reaching our waypoint and will turn, port to port. The captain of the northbound *Westerdam* says, "Roger, red to red."

We're piqued. Our space has been violated. Not another boat in three days and suddenly a cruise ship rears its head.

We move ten degrees to the right; he moves ten degrees to the right and we pass about 200 yards from each other.

We had seen a tug or two using this less crowded route but this is our first encounter with a cruise ship on the "Outer Passage."

After anchoring in Geodetic Cove another cruise ship passes going north, then a freighter with no freight, and a log transporter sans logs.

Don notices the foam from the creek flowing outward on an inflowing flood—freshwater on top of saltwater. He sees a kingfisher darting from its hiding place while I listen, teary-eyed, to Kiri TeKanawa sing Jerome Kern and feel sorry for the young generation who know only explicitly sexy, cars crashing, loud, electronic music and who despise the soft, romantic music and lyrics of "My Bill," "The Last Time I Saw Paris," "Can't Help Lovin' That Man of Mine." I sigh and am thankful I grew up when I did, and that I married a man who is so observant of nature.

It's at times like these—when we can relax and when I can write—that I appreciate Don the most. Heading up the Pacific Coast, between Dana Point (California) and Cape Flattery (Washington)—"out there"—I couldn't.

2000 hours. Balls of foam float down the cove toward the channel. Each one is like a puff of meringue. What is it that creates these balls from the creek that surges into the cove?

August 28: Monday. Geodetic Cove. Rain hits the deck. Below we snuggle and watch the Rorschach patterns on the glass of the hatch, unwilling to hop up and be on our way.

Gusts of winds knock the boat and there's a strange moan. Strain on the anchor snubber? We imagine it's an elephant seal making love under our bow, as it continues alternating between a low and high frequency.

Don gets up, goes out on the bow, naked, and stands there, listening.. "You'll freeze," I shout to him from below. He comes back in, dries himself, and crawls back into bed. "I can't figure it."

It's now 0730 hours. "Could we be in Meyers Passage by high tide?" I ask.

"Hmm. Probably not. But we might be able to anchor outside the narrows."

Neither of us makes a move. "Let's listen to the weather forecast," I suggest.

Don gets up and goes above to retrieve one of the handheld VHF radios. There's a lot of static, but we manage to decipher what we've already noticed visually: a southeasterly is blowing straight up Estevan Sound. White caps curl and roll north like surf at the edge of a sandy beach.

"Well, maybe we should head south and get a little taste of misery… It's been a while," I say. A dark purple cloud passes over the hatch. Rain pelts the glass again.

"I'm losing my ambition," I tell Don.

"Do you mean you have no goal?"

"Yeah, exactly. Once I get up I have plenty of drive to accomplish the small details but I'm so comfortable here, I don't really want to get up."

"Then let's not."

The wind went down, the Sound flattened, and a steady rain began around 1800 hours. We studied the charts and looked for an anchor site that's only a few hours away. Evinrude Inlet is too deep, Commando Inlet on Princess Royal Island is too difficult to enter. Others are too far, making an after-dark approach necessary. We decide to stay here in Geodetic Cove till morning and the boat is the calmest it's been all day. The rain hasn't let up—just steady and pouring.

August 29: Heading for Meyers Passage. There's a thin, long sabre of silver to the east; elsewhere, it's grey everywhere we look. Ripples on the water indicate a breeze from the northwest. There's a 200-foot ceiling and gradual clearing. Now I see a point of land on Compania Island, three islets off its tip. The world opens up.

Leaving Geodetic Cove, with visibility of a hundred feet, all we could see were patches of floating kelp. I was on the bow. Don hollered to me, "What can you see?"

I turned toward the pilothouse windows and, with my thumb and index finger, made an "O".

The radio calls out automatic buoy and lighthouse reports: Bonilla Island, visibility ten miles; Triple Island, zero; Tryad, zero. We turn on the radar and set it on the shortest range to be able to see the maximum definition of objects close at hand.

Sun! Visibility. Granite hummocks gleam. The world ahead is green and silver and grey and blue. Astern, it's nothing.

Meyers Narrows and Passage in sun is spectacular.

Klemtu. I spend $71 on groceries. The place has gone downhill. The entry to the store needs sweeping and trash pickup. The choice of frozen vegetables is limited to French fries and corn. The fresh vegetables and fruit are mostly moldy. Not many smiles or a welcoming attitude, although one client was quite nice to me and helped me bag the heaviest of my three bags. Don feels it's like going to a mental institution. "They're not in the here-and-now." I was happy to be out of there!

Shearwater overnight. Dinner at the restaurant. $30 moorage.

At 2330 hours there's a knock on the boat. We had gone to bed at 2230 after two hours of visiting with Don and JoAnne Kumpula, of Ocean Falls, and Kathy and Serge, of S/V *Raison d'Etre*, a forty-two foot ketch from Hileah, Hawaii.

Don went to the stern door, naked. It was Kathy, with Serge standing behind her on the dock. "Can you help me…?" she said, and began to cry.

On their way back from the pub, on bikes, Serge had lost his balance and gone into a ditch. Kathy rode by and heard him moaning and calling, helped him up and brought him back to the dock. How did she do this with two bikes? We never got the details.

Don got on Channel 6 to see if any locals could help. The guy who answered contacted Rick Andrews (of B.C. Electric), Fiona (a district nurse who happened to be on her once-monthly trip to Ocean Falls), and Jim Nyland, Ocean Falls Administrator, who all came to the boat. Rick and Fiona examined Serge, thought he'd broken his clavicle, recommended he go to Bella Bella hospital. Serge wanted to leave at once and go through Lama Passage—an eight-hour trip. We suggested Gunboat Passage in the morning and we'd either give them our chart or lead them through. Rick seconded our suggestion. Serge kept insisting but Fiona, Rick and Jim kept countering and finally convinced them to wait. We all helped get Serge on board *Raison d'Etre* and loaded the bikes and went back to bed. I was so wired I couldn't go to sleep.

September 4: Labor Day, and our first day of resumed coverage for cell phone since Prince Rupert; we're now in "extended area."

Twenty-seven gulls ride on a log thirty feet long. Further on, an animal bobs its way north, its white face skimming along the surface then dipping its nose for fish perhaps. It has white spots along its flank. Is it a dolphin injured, or a seal lazily basking in the channel? Come this way so I can see you, I say to myself. Does it move in relation to our progress?

We pass abeam. The animal leads with its chin, snout pointed up, its tail bearing a white gull, its white spots are now brown, its back is wearing a sprout of green cedar...

September 5: Off Kelsey Bay, *Panasea* passed us going about twenty knots just a hundred yards to our starboard. He did not slow down to overtake us. I rushed down to grab pots that were on the stove, cooking. As I tried to hang on to everything I watched the wake from his boat come toward our stern quarter and rise four to six feet, sending books, cups, etc. flying across the saloon.

"What a jerk... What a jerk!" turned into more rustic expletives.

We heard him called the "Harbormaster" in Kelsey Bay.

"He doesn't have our book... What would he have that's so outdated?" I wondered. "*The Sailing Directions*, perhaps."

I suspected he was a "professional" skipper, but not a northwest skipper. My suspicions proved true when we heard him on the radio a second time. "... Marina del Rey, California." That fits.

He didn't even know the name of Helmcken Island, where they anchored last night just south of North Cove, where we anchored. Did he not have a chart? It blows my mind.

1700 hours. *Panasea* calls in to the Nanaimo Harbormaster on Channel 16—again, he doesn't know that they monitor Channel 67. Does he not have any reference books on board, or does he just not read them?

September 7: Dodd Narrows. Behind us are three power boats, one sailing vessel; in front, seven boats, of which four are sailboats.

We hear a May Day from *Beverly K*. They're off Lasqueti Island, but we can't hear the details enough to know their problem except that he was in three meters of water and "could the vessel assist hurry!" Vessel Assist responded that seas were rougher than expected and that it was taking twice as long.

**

December 23: Anacortes to Victoria. Rough ride all the way, particularly at Trial Island where we rolled violently despite having the stabilizers deployed.

After we had docked the skipper of *Sheer Folly* came over and asked Don if we were associated with the Douglasses. "We *are* the Douglasses," Don said.

"So you're the bad guy," the man countered.

"You must have read *Cape Horn*," Don said, and called me out to meet him.

"Yes, and my wife told me about you." To me he said, "Has this guy changed at all?"

"Yup, he's mellowed quite a bit but he still has his moments," I laughed.

GLACIER BAY, "OUTSIDE PASSAGE," AND QUEEN CHARLOTTE ISLANDS, 2001

May 18, 2001. Leave Nanaimo at dawn, 0515 hours. Two, then three other boats follow us out. After Newcastle Channel and into Departure Bay, two of them zoom past and make an uncomfortable wake. One is still following.

Two Canada geese cross over our bow with two tiny goslings in between, protected by the parents.

Lenticular clouds hang over Texada Island as the sun comes above the clouds to the east.

May 19, 2001. Port Neville. Came into the dock at dark last night, 2245 hours. It was scary, with intermittent rain, no navigation lights, our electronic chart just small scale. We tried to use radar and searchlight. Don managed well. John (Leone) hopped off the stern as we arrived, tied us off, then ran to the bow as I tossed him the bow line. Captain was not happy with me for not being able to tell what I was seeing. I went to bed angry. Don and John stayed up and had a drink and talked.

Dinner at Lily Hansen's. Pot roast, potatoes, carrots, peas, salad; cheesecake with rhubarb in it; brownies—dessert courtesy of Erica. Lily is eighty-eight. Lovely. Her short term memory is going but she's alert and her long-term memory is fine. We gave them an Inside Passage South Coast map and she followed all the places she knew, tracing the route with her finger.

Fruit Compote:
5-6 apples peeled, cored and sliced.
Juice of 2 oranges squeezed over fruit.
½ cup apricot juice.
¼ cup honey
1 stick cinnamon
¼ cup dried cranberries
¼ cup yellow raisins
Grated rind of one orange
1 tsp of mulling spices.
Use as compote or top with pastry.

May 20, Sunday: Underway at 0545 hours. I fix orange French toast for breakfast.

Anchor for the night in Blunden Harbour. Also here: Lou and Geoff Thompson, of Sunnyvale, CA. Their boat is *Pacific High*, a forty-two foot Krogen motor vessel. Geoff and Don are two of a kind. They have much in common in their approach and are also ex-sailboaters. Geoff keeps filling up Don's glass. Soon Don is slurring his words and can't keep his boots on. Thank goodness John is able to drive us back to *Baidarka*, though it takes him three tries to get to the swim slip. We're all giggling so hard we can hardly grab hold of the boat.

May 21, Monday: Blunden Harbour. Don and John left in the dinghy at 0900 hours to go explore Bradley Lagoon, armed with the new "Humminbird" depth sounder, GPS, VHF radio. ("We'll call you on Channel 69 when we get to the narrows," Don said. They didn't.) Don had his waterproof notebook and pens; he borrowed my inflatable suspenders, since I insisted both guys wear them. I washed clothes and hung them out. The high fog dissipated around noon, then the sun came out and it was beautiful! All the other boats had taken off before 1000 hours. Just *Pacific High* and *Baidarka* remained.

I had a problem with the DC power. We had run the Genset (generator) earlier and, apparently, afterward you have to turn on the inverter at the panel. I panicked when I noticed the refrigerator wasn't on. We have lost several cartons of milk because of power loss in the fridge. I forgot to buy lettuce in Nanaimo, so we just have cucumber to use with sandwiches. The guys came back at 1400 hours ("We'll leave at noon..." Don had said.) We finally got underway at 1430, with *Pacific High* following inside Jeanette Island and others. With this route we have exposure to Queen Charlotte Sound for just a few minutes.

Now time for supper: 6 chicken thighs, a cup water, ½ cup sherry, carrots, peas, potatoes, celery, herbs de Provence, pepper, salt.

May 22: Belize Inlet, Echo Rock. The mussels attach themselves in black lines along the waterline for one to two feet; above that are miniscule silver-grey barnacles. Below the mussels, underwater, are organisms that look like either frilled anemone or red soft coral. When Don used the bow thruster to move us away from the overhanging rock, the creatures turned cream-colored—a feature of the frilled anemone, which discharges "long, white threads of stinging cells when... disturbed" (*Audubon Guide to the Pacific Coast*, page 488). We also observed sunflower starfish and smaller five-armed beige stars.

As we came into Nakwakto Rapids and were photographing "Tremble Island" with its boat signs, a couple in an inflatable approached us and told us they love our books. They had a correction to Shelter Cove (in *Exploring the North Coast of British Columbia*), so Don invited them aboard—Tilly and Anton from *Pacific Sunrise*, a thirty-four foot Hunter sailing vessel, out of Ladner, B.C. They're from Holland originally and have the lovely manners so typical of Europeans. We asked if they'd submit a sidebar or two for the next edition of the *North Coast* book. They are headed to Gwai Haanas to spend the month of July. They paid $200 for permits and registration for the season. This seems a bit steep for no services, no water.

May 23: Strachan Channel. Charlie Chilson has lived here since 1943, when he was twelve years old. He went only to third grade in school; he was too busy working. He's a rigger for a timber company, lives in an A-frame, constructed from local woods. Talking to him about how to take Nakwakto Rapids, Charlie says "Looking at the cover of the book, you guys have tooled around a lot."

1120 hours. At Nakwakto. *Inlet Charger*, inbound, does not reduce speed west of Tremble Island; we go rolling and turning. He stops at Tremble and goes behind. To watch us or read the signs? Who knows.

1900 hours. Finn Bay Retreat. Owner Peter has been here for twenty years, his partner Renée for eight years. Peter grew up on Lasquati Island. He and Renée own ten acres of land and a shore lease to the end of the inlet. They rent out rooms in a four-bedroom boatel. There's a picnic house with a fireplace in the center, hand hewn tables. Eight or nine years ago they had 755 seiners and gillnetters in here—wall to wall boats. In the past thirty years Peter has saved thirty-eight lives in his 500 h.p. tug.

Peter "kidnapped" Renée, then went into Scottie Bay and phoned Renée's dad. He spent a day at their house and asked the question. "Renée said, 'I need a year.'" Pete said, "okay." But she showed up a month later. She came in on a Grumman Goose. The pilot saw Peter and said to her, "He's shaved! ... How long were you planning to stay?"

She said, "Oh, probably the rest of my life."

May 24: 1520 Tie up in Ocean Falls. I bring us in—it takes me two tries. A woman, Judy, from *Cyndyn* helped us tie up. She asked what sort of "research" we do. Don told her. "Oh, you must be Don," she said.

"How did you know?" Don asked.

"I've been going to bed with you every night for the last week!"

B.C. Fisheries "runs" the dock, but the locals are in charge of the harbor. Only the maintenance guys are paid. Everyone else is volunteer help. The Harbormaster is Herb Carpenter. He and his wife Lena have been here twelve years. He said, "We're desperately short of thieves around here." He leaves his keys in his truck ignition, "in case someone wants to borrow it," and locks his home with the window unlocked and the key just inside.

May 26, Saturday: 1435 hours. We're waiting to enter Culpepper Lagoon, at the end of Kynoch Inlet. Don wants to go through even though the rapids look like Green Point or Whirlpool Rapids. "No!" I say, "It's foolish." Risk ruining a boat just to say "it can be done" is the height of folly. But Don wants to prove *Waggoner's* correspondent wrong[6]. We circle around for forty minutes. High slack is another two and a half hours from now. John readies the dinghy.

Don asks, "Do you want us to take the dinghy through first?"

"Yes," I say, "but wear your life vests."

I go down to the saloon to get out a third life vest, then go forward to our stateroom to stow some stuff. I hear the sonar alarm and rush up to the pilothouse. The Furino reads 1.1 fathoms. I jam the throttle in forward and rev up the r.p.m. We had been over the sand bar of the delta—now covered with water.

1453 hours. The drop in water appears less drastic now, but the guys have the dinghy ready. Two minutes of writing in my journal and we're back to five fathoms. We kept getting swept toward the creek. I take us back to over ten fathoms and put it in neutral.

The guys take off at 1500 hours and go through the rapids twice. Now they're headed back. We take *Baidarka* through the rapids at about six knots, with a two-foot height difference. They were probably running at eight to nine knots when the difference in height was three to four feet.

---

[6] *Waggoner Cruising Guide*

Once we're through the rapids and whirlpools, the depths drop dramatically to over forty-five fathoms.

We spoil the quiet of three common mergansers.

Looking back from the head of Culpepper you can see an unnamed peak 4160 feet high with snow patches all over its dark granite summit. Trees line the crevices. To the south and above the lagoon, another massif with snowfields rises. The entire Fiordland Park is shrouded with mist today. We haven't seen a single boat since we left Ivory Island – not a soul in here. Fiordland is much more intimate than Misty Fiords. I LIKE IT!

I'm "stuck in the mud" at twenty-eight fathoms—just very gently drifting around, so I turn off the engine.

We leave Culpepper at 1758 on the beginning of the ebb. I take us through and, just outside, the current jerks us around a tad.

Anchor in Windy Bay. I go to bed at 2000 exhausted.

May 28: Memorial Day. Prince Rupert. Arrived at noon. Lobster fisherman to Don: "Your book got us here."

June 2: Left Ketchikan after half a day and a night. I spent the afternoon in the Ketchikan hospital emergency room waiting to be treated for an infection. I walked from hospital back to the boat—at least a mile—and then to town. The dime store was closed, as were all the other stores I wanted to catch including the pharmacy. But I did have a visit with Holly Churchill, Haida basket-maker. Her mother was born in Masset, then moved to Ketchikan. Holly goes back and forth. Her uncles are Chief Skidegate and Chief Reynolds.[7]

Meyers Chuck. Cassie and Steve Peavey. They have lived here for forty years. Their two boys grew up here; one now lives in Kasaan, the other in Craig.

Anchored in Kindergarten Bay. We entered on the north side—horribly irregular—after having come around the point, where we discovered an underwater rock, uncharted. The echo sounder went to four fathoms in a second. Don jammed the gear into reverse and I went flying in the saloon.

---

[7] A week later, on June 9, we saw some of Holly's baskets in Juneau. They were high priced, $600 or more!

Kindergarten Cove Halibut: Saute halibut in olive oil. Add 1-2 Tbsp chopped candied ginger, 1 lime – juice only OR 1 orange with rind grated, dash of Worcestershire sauce, chopped parsley, 4-6 brown mushrooms – sliced, 2 Tbsp or ¼ cup mango salsa. When halibut is almost done pour sauce over and serve.

June 3, Sunday: 0900 to 0910 hours. A dozen dolphins follow us off the bow as we round Steamer Point. We also see two groups of orcas and over a dozen loons.

Wrangell. We tied to the "summer dock" in Wrangell, just north of the ferry dock, did our errands for several hours; bought rocks with garnets on the wharf; tried to sell some Inside Passage maps (no deal— practically everything in town is closed, including the pharmacy). I interviewed the two assistant harbormasters while Don and John filled up on water. I docked and undocked. I'm getting a little more confident.

Entrance to Wrangell Narrows. We anchor in Deception Point Cove and I cook dinner. The Alaska ferry enters while we're eating. A tug towing a log barge exits soon after. Vic on *Galaxy* is anchored here. His "hand" left in Ketchikan, so he's now solo.

Deception Point Cove Lamb and Eggplant Casserole: Saute ground lamb (1 lb) with ¼ to ½ onion and 3 Tbsp chopped parsley, ½ lb mushrooms, ½ lemon, 3 Japanese eggplants sliced thin, carrots (if desired). Peel and slice thin 1 large potato. Line 8 x 8 pan with potato slices and add lamb mixture to which I added several dashes of Italian herbs, garlic powder, sprinkled with about 1/3 cup sherry. Bake in moderate oven for 35-45 minutes covered with foil.

June 4, 2001. Petersburg. We hit the dock with the stern as we come in and I get the usual lecture from Don. It's my lack of ability to conceptualize the current's effect and what the boat will do.

A crusty old fisherman, Ron, who's cleaning and polishing his forty foot gillnet trawler, *Caron* (a Lindell Boat made on Camano island, WA), helps as we tie up next to him. He laughs all over our spring lines and says, "Pardon me, but I see all the yachts come in with expensive lines and all you need is a stern and bow line... With the stern line you're not going anywhere."

Ron calls sportfishing men "pukers."

Ron on marriage certificates: "A piece of paper doesn't guarantee you any happiness."

Ron on yachties: "Why do you [D&R] have to write a book? Don't the yachties have a fathometer?"

"Why can't the yachties figure out how not to run out of gas?"

"They rely too much on their computers. They don't have paper charts. Then they get lost and we have to go find them."

Don: "Do you want to come aboard and take a look at our latest Nobeltec electronic charts?"

Ron: "Oh, no. I hate computers."

June 5: Up at 0730 hours. Shower, breakfast, clean up, listen to weather report.

0900 hours. I call the office from a phone on the dock. Talk for twenty minutes, giving orders etc. Mailed a letter. John went to buy prawns. I spent ten minutes taking photos.

1000 hours. Leave Petersburg. I back out. "Oh, a woman driver," Ron grins.

I shake my finger at him and say, "Yeah and you'll be criticizing me all the way out, won't you?"

1030 hours. Passed the first icebergs. John shucks shrimp. Don and I are in the pilothouse.

1100 hours. Off the bar at Le Conte Bay. I cook shrimp—boil water, dump shrimp in for three minutes till cooked through, dump out the water in colander. I rush back up for photos as we approach the bar and head through grounded bergs. The current is running about four knots in the opposite direction near a big blue berg. It's like running a river for us.

At 1233 hours we leave the east side of Le Conte Bar and head back up. Eat lunch: shrimp in caper sauce, bread and vegetables. Then all afternoon up Frederick Sound to Cape Fanshaw. We take turns at the helm. I wash my hair in the early afternoon, hang my socks to dry in the engine room.

Don prepares popcorn after we anchor at 1900 hours. We're eating shrimp salad and bread for supper as two guys in *Shemya* cruise by. Don says, "They're probably mad that we have their anchor spot." They kept heading toward our stern, with smiles.

Don to guys aboard *Shemya*: "It's a beautiful evening."

They: "Yes it is."

Don: "How's fishing?"

They: "Great. We just caught a three hundred pounder."

Don: "I'd like to see it and take a photo."

They: "Okay. We'll come alongside."

They do this and raft for a while. They're Brooks Hollern, the captain/owner, from Carlsborg, WA, and Aaron Cummins, of Petersburg, AK. Brooks told us he uses our books and wouldn't go anywhere without them. ("Been reading your book since before I bought my new boat.") His boat is named after the third-to-last island of the Aleutians. Brooks has been up there on another boat. It hit a reef and they had to dive to see the damage. He comes up for two months in summer to fish, makes enough to pay for his boat. His wife raises horses in Carlsborg, doesn't want to go to the Aleutians or fishing with him. His fish hold converts into an aft cabin which he uses in the winter. His boat is about thirty-eight feet long.

Aaron is married, has lived in Petersburg since he was two years old. He owns a boat called *Fairlead*.

After we'd taken our photos, they offered us a small halibut. "Only if we can trade," we said. So we gave them a bottle of beer and my *Cape Horn* book. "I almost bought your book at Captain's Nautical," Brooks told me.

By the time we've visited, finished supper, cleaned up and prepared halibut for the fridge it's almost 2300 hours and twilight. I read about six pages of a novel today!

June 6, Wednesday: Anchor up at 0800 hours and underway from Cleveland Passage, where we anchored in eight fathoms. Don and John took off in the dinghy to explore the westernmost of the Roberts Islets. I stood off in *Baidarka* with the engine running, while they disappeared into the woods.

About forty-five minutes later I see them come over the hill and down to the beach—a wide shell-grey shale beach about 200 yards wide. Suddenly I see the dinghy floating away. They start running toward it. "Those stupid guys," I say aloud to myself. John takes off his boots and runs toward the water, stops short, obviously realizing the dink's too far away now, drifting eastward.

A few seconds later I get a call on Channel 69. "The dinghy's loose."

"Yeah, I know. What do you want me to do?"

"Bring the boat in on the east side of the dink... It's pretty deep in close... Then pick it up."

I imagine the two of them on the island without food, two shipwrecked sailors. As they stand on the beach looking toward the dinghy

119

I think of a drawing from A.A. Milne—a sailor (Christopher Robin) in cut-offs staring out from a lone island, looking forlorn.

I run to the bow, to the stern, back to pilothouse, put the boat in gear, watch the depth sounder. I drive it to the east of the dink, run back to the stern. I'm too short—the current took it immediately away. I jam the throttle into forward, give it 1500 r.p.m. and do a 360-degree turn. Depth okay, so far. Then, slowly, in neutral, I draw near the dink, run back to the stern, untie the long heavy boat hook, grab the stern of the dink and pull it in.

All this time Don's trying to give me instructions via VHF Channel 69. Finally I holler, "Stop talking. I don't have time to listen."

I maneuver the dink around to the stern of *Baidarka*, turn it around and catch the painter, tie it off at the stern, run back up to the pilothouse. The echo sounder reads fifteen fathoms. Still okay.

I pick up the mike and say, "Now what?"

"Drive the boat over there." Don points to a spot about 150 yards to the west, and fifty yards off the beach. "Then get in the dinghy, start the motor and come get us. The boat will drift east… but hurry."

I grab the second portable VHF, turn it to 69 and hop in the dink, retie the painter through the hawser hole so I can release it from the dink, and set the VHF on the seat. I haven't run the dinghy this season yet. Don's talking non-stop. "Pull the motor forward to push it back in the water, then pull the starter. The throttle should be in neutral." It is.

The motor starts on the first pull. I release the painter, turn the dink toward shore.

"Hurry," Don yells. I turn the throttle to slow forward. I want to be sure I start cautiously.

"Hurry up!" Don yells again. "Fast forward!"

I jam it into fast forward and roar toward the beach. The current is taking *Baidarka* rapidly to the east. This whole area is uncharted.

I drive the boat toward the beach, slow as I come to shore, and the guys hop in like they're running from a bear.

"We're sworn to secrecy," John says.

"Oh, yeah," I say. "I plan to tell all."

We get back aboard *Baidarka* and I break out the shortbread cookies. "I really should withhold rations from you guys," I say.

Later, at the end of Port Houghton, I circle around in twenty-four-plus fathoms while the guys go to explore a south inlet, then the back (chuck). The current is strong—a good three knots on a rising flood, along with wind that's coming down the port, and I keep getting swept toward the shallows. I have to move the boat every five to ten minutes. Finally the guys head back out of the salt chuck and toward the boat. Don motions me to come toward them. It's raining and windy and they look soaked. John huddles at the bow of the dink. I wonder if he's injured or just trying to avoid the spray and wind.

I head in to meet them and, when I'm a couple hundred yards away from them, I take a look at the echo sounder. Seconds before, it read eighteen fathoms. Now it reads 2.2 fathoms. I jam the throttle full speed ahead, open the door and shout "Two point two!"

So what if they have another couple hundred yards to endure?

We leave the end of Houghton and motor back to Sandborn Channel, anchor in seven fathoms. Sunny and Bob Johnson from *Raven* come over for popcorn and port.

It's 1930 hours when I begin dinner: fresh halibut from the *Shemya*, mashed garlic potatoes, salad, ice cream for dessert.

June 7, Thursday: Anchored inside Thistle Ledge. This is a beautiful bay with grassy shores alternating with dinosaur-back slate formations, vertical and thin, that resemble decaying wood frames of a boat. Both John and I thought the stone was wood when we first saw it from a distance.

Ground dogwood is still in bloom and there are flowers resembling Indian paint brush but more crimson with almost purple leaves.

The guys spent several hours exploring after an initial hour-long exploration. In between I gave Don a haircut and beard trim—badly needed. He stripped down in the sun; then, before I'd finished, it began to sprinkle—all while the sun still shone.

June 8, Friday: Up anchor at 0500 hours. En route to Tracy Arm where we rendezvous with *Raven*. Then we spend all day in Tracy Arm. Also with Lowell and Sue Marsh, of Cathlamet, WA, aboard *Ghost Rider*. Sue says the perfume in the air is from the alder flowers.

We arrived in front of North Sawyer Glacier around 1130 after thinking we'd probably not be able to get through the bergs. Don maneuvered brilliantly. *Raven* and *Ghost Rider* followed not too far behind. We all sat with our boats in neutral just watching the glacier—a beautiful deep translucent blue along the base. It was so quiet and peaceful, with hardly a ripple on the water. Then the glacier would calve, sending waves and rocking our boats.

Seals with their pups lay on icebergs and usually gave just a glance without stirring. We came too close to one large one, however, and he dove into the water.

Headed out of Tracy Arm around 1300. I napped for thirty minutes, then Don woke me to help with the helm. John and I brought the boat across the bar and on up Stevens Passage. Don woke up at 1530 and I took another nap. (John had gone down earlier.)

Headed into Taku and were tied up by 1810, along with *Ghost Rider* and other boats. *Raven* came in soon afterward, along with *Sanctuary*, from Portland Yacht Club—Sue and Dave Kjome, of Rancho Murieta, CA. By 2000 hours the dock was full of boats.

We toured *Ghost Rider*, visited with Sue and Dave from *Sanctuary*, then had drinks aboard *Raven* and a long talk with Sunny. 2100 hours before we came back to *Baidarka*, another hour before we ate dinner.

It's now 2330 hours. The guys went to bed an hour ago and I'm headed there now. Tomorrow, on to Juneau.

June 9: Male voice heard over Channel 16: *"Cat's Paw,* if you come any closer you'll have to stay for breakfast."

Five minutes later, *Cat's Paw* (from Kennewick, WA) passes us going full speed—a little runabout that creates a wake for three minutes

Docked at 1100 hours in Auke Bay. Our son-in-law Jeff Mach came down around 1300 hours, lent me his truck to do shopping. I spent an hour in town at Annie Kaile's, Raven's Journey and Hearthside Books, then to Fred Meyer—two hours to provision, two hours to stow.

John, Don, Jeff and I all went to supper at a Tex-Mex restaurant in town.

June 11: Monday. 1200 hours. Swanson Harbor. I brought the boat in and docked it. Spent the rest of day at the float.

Judy and Allan Reese, S/V *Amorosa,* Seattle, WA. Judy wrote in my notebook, "Thanks so much for publishing your AK research. I have experts mark all their anchor recommendations on our chart book with a red dot, then I look up and write the Douglass book page number beside each for handy reference as we head north."

June 12: Hoonah. Buy salmon at the fish plant, fifteen pounds at $3 a pound. Anchor in Flynn Cove.

June 13: Head for Glacier Bay in the morning. A twenty minute orientation at the Park Headquarters. We visit the Interpretive Center, then head back to the boat for lunch—salmon salad. Don heads to the Alaska Natural History Association store in the lodge while I telephone Ray Majeski, Harbormaster in Sitka. Don leaves an Inside Passage folded map with Karen Platt (ANHA branch manager) at the lodge store and then meets with Chuck Young, Chief Ranger. A good meeting but Don learns the park is being sued by an organization that thinks there are too many boats in Glacier Bay. A judge has taken it under study.

Rainy day today. I docked the boat and took it back out from Bartlett Cove.

Anchor in South Fingers Cove, northwest side. Saw one black bear grazing along the shore around dinner time. We had baked salmon marinated in a sauce I invented but didn't write down. As I remember, it had rice vinegar, sherry, Worcestershire sauce, garlic, chopped ginger, soy sauce, juice of one orange, juice of half a lime, white balsamic vinegar, ½ tsp salt, pepper. Bake salmon till done on the outside, still red on the inside.

June 14: Salmon salad sandwiches "on the run," with cucumber slices and lettuce. Beautiful weather today. Puffy clouds all around with blue sky. We're able to see Mt Fairweather peaking above the other mountains. We dodge icebergs. There are kayakers on the shore west of Reid Inlet. *Northern Exposure* gives Don a call on Channel 16/68 and they have a long chat. Larry Edgerton and Charleen Folly. Their boat is a forty-nine foot De Fever. They saw a grizzly and some mountain goats in Tidal Inlet about noon. Quote: "Sure glad we have your book to guide us along."

We visit Lamplugh Glacier for an hour or so, then head back to Reid Inlet where we take photos at the snout, then anchor off in ten fathoms. While we're sitting, talking on the saloon settee, the glacier calves twice. Jean (Doudeau) goes out to try and photograph more, but catches just one, then abandons the effort after an hour.

We had wanted to enter Johns Hopkins Inlet but it was choked with ice.

Anchored by 1640, then we can relax with an aperitif. The sun is still at about forty-five degrees above the horizon.

June 15: Late start. Much ice outside in the main west arm. We finally cross to the north shore where there's less ice. I sight a grizzly on shore and we go in to about fifty feet from shore to film him. He's a beauty—chestnut brown with a full coat. He looks up once or twice but ignores us totally. Don whistles once or twice but the bear keeps on grazing.

Four boats at Grand Pacific/Margerie Glaciers. We head toward Margerie, turn off the engine to have lunch. The tour boat *Spirit of Adventure* calls us to say they have friends aboard who'd like to talk to us: Gloria and Tom Burke. Don has a chat with Tom over the VHF.

Additional conversation from *Spirit of Adventure:* "Well, our passengers are kind of lethargic today. We saw whales off the bow coming from Juneau and some of the passengers were inside watching a video on whales."

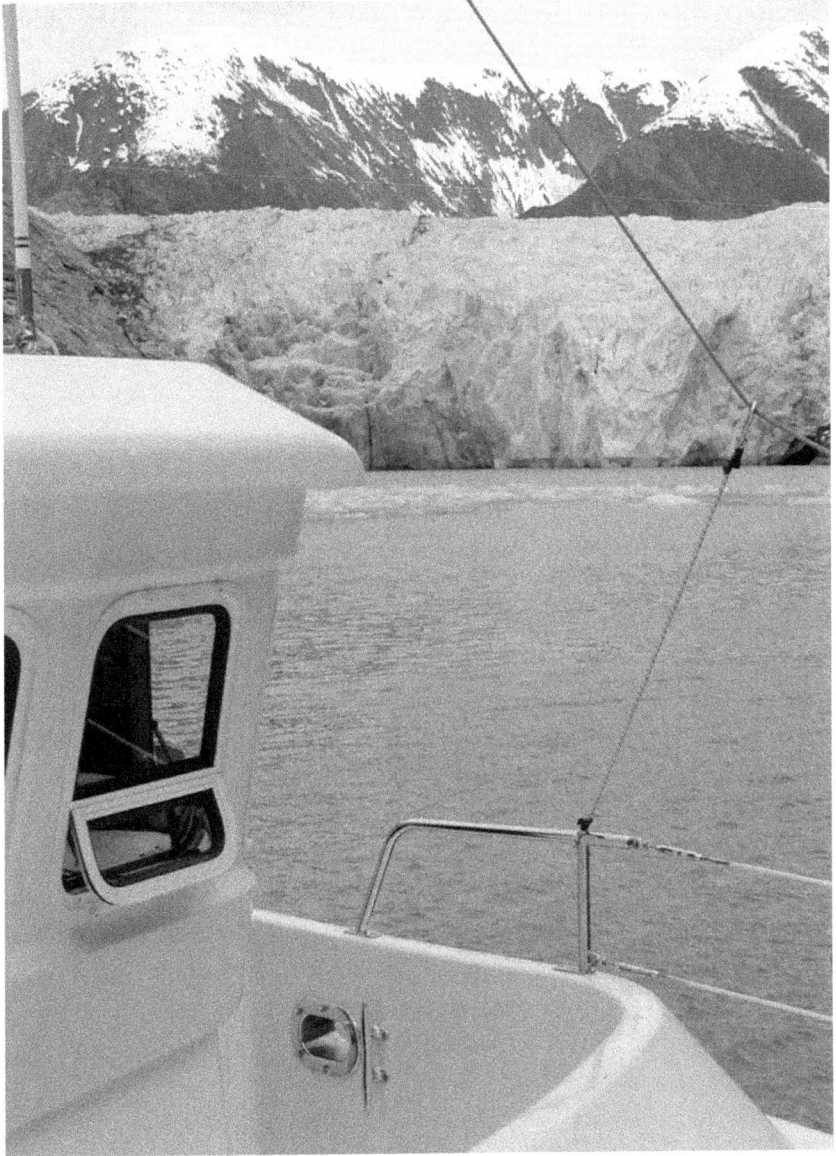

Grand Pacific Glacier.

Anchor in North Sandy Cove at 1905 hours. Bright sun. Two other boats are here: *Cat's Paw* and S/V *Winddancer*.

To the big white boat running its radar in bright sun and blue skies that enters North Sandy at full five knots—enough to rock us so things began to fall off the galley counter—I would say: "Did you think we wanted you to rock us to sleep?" Or, "We thought you'd like to know that your wake was the topic of conversation of our quiet hour this evening." Or, "We were impressed by your big white boat but not by your habit of shaking up your neighbors." Or, "Your arrival was announced by a pronounced rocking as you entered 'our harbor.'"

June 16, Saturday: Leave North Sandy at 0615. Pass *Norma Jean* from Reno, NV. This was the boat that created yesterday's big wake. A jerk.

Visit Berg Bay at about 1000 hours. Lovely, spacious bay that we need to enter on high tide. Anchor in Fern Harbor. Slightly rolly.

June 17: Elfin Cove. Arrived 1975 hours. The inner float is not for general use but reserved for resident fishing boats. The outermost float is for transients like us. Far inner harbor: okay to anchor but you must have local knowledge. No garbage facilities in Elfin Cove. No electricity or water available at floats. Water is available at the fuel dock; it is *not* for washing boats. Harbormaster is Dave Walton; he's been here twenty-five years. Worked for United Airlines on the East Coast before that.

A seiner, *Home Shore,* passes us in Liskianski Strait and calls on Channel 16. I'm on watch and answer. Jim Kyle, who uses his boat for adventure tours outside of the seining season, tells me he has a book that was written by some people who had a boat with the same name, *Baidarka.* "That's us," I tell him. "Réanne and Don Douglass."

"I'd pay several times the fare for the information in your book."

We go through our "special" route to avoid the outside. Gentle rolling seas. Jean, Genevieve and I stand watch on the bow. Enter Imperial Passage and anchor by 1830 hours inside Maud Island in seven fathoms. Good discussion during dinner about democracy, the US Constitution, etc. It got quite heated for a while.

June 18: Ogden Passage. At least fifty sea otters in total in the passage. Wonderful! We slide past them with the throttle in neutral.

0920 hours. A gale is expected tonight so we head on south. At the south side of Ogden Passage Don says, "The south wind has already begun."

"You are so observant," I say. "You are micro observant. You have an innate talent, as well as a trained eye for these details."

He laughs and shrugs his shoulders.

"I can never learn all this even though you've taught me a lot since we started boating. And you can't expect other people who haven't had the same experience to understand."

"I suppose you're right," he says.

Anchor in Kalinin Bay.

June 19: Layover day in Kalinin Bay. Lots of boats in here, including *Miniship, White Star* with Gloria and Tom, and *Locassos*, a fifty-two foot Nordhavn, with two other boats rafted alongside—thirteen in all—last night. I work all afternoon on the computer. My gut hurts from bending and sitting yesterday and today.

June 20: Neva Strait was fogged over so we ran with radar for about an hour. Crossing Salisbury Sound was bouncy. We listened all the way to a Pan Pan and rescue—a charter boat with five passengers from a tour ship lost its raw water filter, so the engine pumped raw water into the engine room. The passengers were finally off-loaded to a fishing boat and then to a Coast Guard boat. The entire incident took about three hours from start to completion. A Coast Guard helicopter was launched and hovered while the passengers were transferred from *Kunamatata* to *Black and Blue*. They even sent a diver down into the water in case anyone fell into the water during transfer.

June 21: Sitka. Sheet' ka Kwaan Naa Kahidi Tlingit native dancers—a mix of Siberian, Asian, Russian and white folks like us. From two years old to our age. Kids were adorable, costumes colorful.

**

Mt. Edgecumbe.

July 18, 2001: Sitka. Arrived at New Thompson dock at 1430 after the flight from Seattle.

Supper with Bob and Sunny Johnson, of *Raven*, at Van Winkles. Nice food—fresh Halibut Florentine for three of us, sockeye salmon for Don. Walked back to the boat with Sunny and Bob, had a nightcap and showed them charts for the west coast of Baranof Island. Sunny looks forty-five; Bob is Don's age. I haven't asked how old Sunny is but they've been together since 1975; married in 1992 ("Didn't want to spoil a good thing."). Bob read my *Cape Horn* book, raved about it.

July 19: Provisioned at Lakeview Market—two hours—then to True Value Hardware, where I bought a flower box to use as a "book box" and inserted it with industrial strength Velcro. Groceries were delivered at 1430 hours; it took me over an hour to stow them.

At 1800 hours we went to *Hawkeye II* for dinner with Clark and Maggie Oster, who flew in for a vacation with Thad Wardell, owner of *Hawkeye*, and Leo Nigg, of S/V *Moonlight*. Leo, who is Swiss, built the superstructure on *Moonlight*'s Dutch steel hull; it took him sixteen years, working weekends and holidays. He has now been circumnavigating for years, came around Cape Horn exactly two years ago to the day, had a terrible rounding—very rough. Stopped in Puerto Williams, Valdivia, Juan Fernando, Isla de Pascua, Pitcairn (couldn't get ashore), Rapa Nui, other Polynesian islands, then Hawaii and up to Kodiak, Prince William Sound and down to Sitka. Lovely person—unassuming, gentle and intelligent!

July 20: Left Sitka two hours after our planned time because Don forgot to pick up our laundry yesterday; so, while he readied the boat for takeoff, I went up the hill at 0700 hours to the laundromat. We decided not to go to Goddard Hot Springs, and came outside Baranof Island. Rough trip. We deployed stabilizers and still rocked quite a bit. I don't have my sea legs yet and was nauseated all day. Don took watch all morning, till 1400 hours, when I got up, and we decided to head to "Réanne's Relief" instead of continuing for six to eight more hours to Coronation Island. Réanne's Relief is lovely; super quiet and calm. One other boat, F/V *Star* (a small troller) is in here, with one man aboard. We both slept again after setting anchor; got up at 1900 hours, made spinach salad, and now to bed at 2130.

July 21: Left Réanne's Relief at 0515 hours. Down Baranof in fog, then clear weather. Past Cape Ommaney to Coronation Island. Windy Bay at noon. Set the lunch hook for lunch and three hours' sleep. Now it's 1500 hours and foggy, foggy. We're leaving under radar. There were sea otters in kelp on the north side where we anchored. I was seasick all morning and I'm still feeling the effects.

Navigated under radar to Noyes Island, Ulitka Bay. Anchored at 2010 hours, omelet for supper, then to bed and slept for eleven hours.

July 22: Did washing in machine. Fog finally cleared at noon and we hauled anchor, explored Steamboat Bay, took in stabilizers, and headed for Craig. As the waters calmed I felt better and better. Mike Kampich helped us tie up as we docked in Craig at 1600 hours. Then we attended a potlatch for Ethel Elizabeth Yates, a village elder who died last year. This was a one-year memorial service with:

• Feast—potato salad, coleslaw, Chinese slaw, seaweed slaw, rice balls, shrimp and prawns, roast turkey, chicken, beef, ham, blueberry and salmonberry punch with pears, desserts. (No alcohol.)

• Flute player (one of the sons); solo singing, Haida songs and dances: Announcement song, Entrance song, Songs of death and happiness, Men's and Women's songs.

• Presentation of gifts: a) oldest elders—otter skins; b) elders—some otter skins; c) friends and family—blankets; d) all guests—baskets with jam, candle, soap, seaweed, candies, mug, cotton scarf, gold and silver dollars, pillows, hot mitts, photo cards and trinkets, pins, bead necklaces, etc.

At the potlatch we met Julius ("Doug") and Georgie Douglas, of Ketchikan, AK. Doug is a Haida descendent, born in Hydaburg. His father is from Forrester Island. Doug brought up their son and daughter in Bellingham, then moved back to Ketchikan. He was in the Navy for years. Daughter Diane Douglas Willard is the manager of an art gallery on Creek Street in Ketchikan.

July 23, Monday: Spent three hours downloading digital photos. My computer kept crashing, which put me in a foul humor because I had so much to do. We didn't get up to Thompson's Market until 1500 hours, after having dropped off the laundry. Provisioned, then Don went with the groceries in the truck while I went to Voyageur Bookstore to visit with Gail (owner), then to a clothing store to buy t-shirts. I ordered pizza for 1800 hour delivery to the dock, picked up the laundry, and headed back to the boat where three other couples were bringing pizza to *Baidarka*. Pizza had been delivered ninety minutes early to *Raven* (Don and Red McVittie, Seattle) and they refused it. Crew from *Jazz* and *Gairloch* came aboard for a riotous evening of pizza and good conversation, then we were joined by Derek Ingram of *Sea Web II*, from North Vancouver. Derek calls himself "retired" (from publishing international trade directories), though he only seems to be in his late thirties.

July 24: Tuesday. Left Craig 0600 hours. Headed down Bucareli Bay to Dall Island. Explored Bob's Bay for about an hour. (Test anchor didn't hold.) Then down to Sea Otter Harbor, Hook Arm. Dead calm, no swells, full of islands and shoreline reefs, grey sand beaches. Shores are absolutely clear of windblown logs. A great place to explore by kayak and canoe.

I worked on Chapters 1-4 of *Exploring the North Coast of British Columbia*, copy-editing and yellowing for Don's attention.

Craig.

I do not like the rolling out in the Gulf!! Don is still fascinated by the Aleutians. "Listen to this: Adak is the most southerly of Alaska's cities." City? Who are they kidding! Plus, it's 1300 miles from Anchorage and only 1000 miles from Kamchatka Peninsula.

We were wiped out this afternoon. Slept from 1430 to 1730 hours. It's now 2100 and we're hitting the sack.

The women last night who said they "love" the West Coast probably have no idea what our schedules are like. Maybe it is fun but we don't have time to spend doing *fun* exploring.

July 25: Wednesday. Left Hook Arm at 0630 hours. Explored Fisherman Cove. Passed up Sakie Bay because of tide rips; also, it is unsurveyed. Passed up Camp Cove—full of rocks—but studied the drainage of Devil Lake, to the north of Devil Island; it looks like a good place for dinghy exploration. Into Welcome Cove to test the bottom; I said "Get me out of here"—too shallow! Passed up Augustine Bay, then in to Waterfall Bay for lunch; there's a lovely high waterfall on the north side of the bay, then another at the head, hidden until you're practically on it. The little bight mentioned in *Coast Pilot* is too small for anything but one boat of less than thirty-two feet. We test anchored for lunch off the south side, then continued to Gooseneck Harbor where we had planned to spend the night. This is a "bay of islands" and rocks topped with tufts of shrubs and small trees. Harrowing going in; then we couldn't get the anchor to set; also the depths were not as shown on the chart. We found three fathoms where it's marked seven on the chart. We pulled the anchor—a really hard pull—and found a twenty-pound rock wedged inside the flukes of the Bruce anchor. It took about thirty minutes to extricate the rock, then we tried again. No hold. "Let's go on to Port Bazan," I said. "I don't like this!"

By this time (1500 hours) the prevailing wind had come up and was blowing us toward the rocks. We looked at the chart. Port Bazan was only about three miles southeast, so we headed down and into Bazan, where we now have a calm, lovely anchor site on the northeast side behind an unnamed islet. There's good visibility here. The only disadvantage is that the southeast side has been clear-cut.

We anchored in Port Bazan at 1608 hours after ten hours of work. Amazing how much mental energy we expend in a day like this. To bed at 2100 hours.

July 26: Don lets me sleep until 0700 hours, then brings me breakfast. We exit Port Bazan through the southeast (east side of Dolgoi Island)—there's a minimum depth of five fathoms in the fairway. The chart where we anchored shows "STKY" (sticky). It was, and it was also STKY for stinky. As I laid the chain in the locker I suddenly noticed the brown on the chain, then an outpouring stench of organic matter. "Pull the last twenty-five feet of chain up and wash it off again," I shouted. It really needed a scrub brush but with just the two of us aboard it was impossible for one person to haul, wash and scrub at the same time.

Coming out in the narrows, we spotted a great blue heron walking along the top of kelp about a hundred yards from shore, as if he were walking along shore. At the entrance, dozens of auklets were feeding. This morning there was high fog with the promise of clearing above the mountains.

From Point Cornwallis south are beautiful, stunning white rock formations, like giant molars. At the point, there's a high rock with a hole through it.

Liscombe Bay, on its southwest side, has stunted small trees and grass amongst grey rocky knobs, calling to mind the terrain of the Patagonian Channels. At first I thought terrain had been clear-cut, but then I realized this side would be exposed to full southeasterly storms. The east shore cliffs are not windblasted. Raw land! This is by far the most dramatic scenery we've seen to date on Dall Island.

An eagle swoops down from a tree at the head of the cove and grabs a strand of kelp in his talons, flies to a log on shore and eats whatever was clinging to the kelp.

Came on around Cape Muzon, at the end of Dall Island, into McLeod Bay where the wind was howling. It was not picturesque and we decided to tuck in north of Datzkoo Harbor, where we're protected by a line of small islets. Gentle rocking from waters of Kaigani Strait, but not uncomfortable.

More auklets—cute little birds with white mustaches. They dive for about thirty seconds, then pop up again.

This has been another exhausting day—we both slept for almost two hours, then got up and organized for B.C. Stowed Alaska charts and data, and got out B.C. charts and data for the Queen Charlotte Islands. Ready for early morning crossing of Dixon Entrance. Goodbye to Alaska!

July 27, Friday: Entering Refuge Island I expended more energy than in one entire day at home. Through a "hole" in the kelp, past a storm-damage concrete pillar that once held a light. Into gear at 800 r.p.m., then into neutral. The depth alarm goes off—3.1 fathoms, 2.8 fathoms, 2.1! I turn left. Don finally has the poles up. The inlet is an L-shape; the floats are built into the "L." I point the boat into the V of the float and go into reverse to stop forward movement. Then I use the bow thruster to turn left and aim toward the dock. "Head left on the rudder," Don says. He jumps off the stern, takes one wrap around the board, and runs to the bow. "Give me some help," he says. I use the bow thruster to turn right.

Massett, Queen Charlotte Islands. The Dixon Entrance Maritime Museum, a half mile north of the harbor, mainly emphasizes the boat building "industry." Government money was used to renovate the building, which was once a hospital and school.

July 28: Spent the night in Naden Harbour on a buoy. Then on to Langara Island, testing Bruin Bay, Marchand Reef, and across to Beal and Henslung Coves. Lunch on the five-pound test anchor in Beal Cove in front of North Island Lodge, a floating fishing lodge. Henslung Cove looks like a town with all its floating lodges and a huge complex uphill via log rail. Then to Hazardous Cove. Beautiful rock formations along the Langara and Cox Island shores—cones and pinnacles, some of which looked like they'd been extruded from a pastry tube. Fury Cove N.F.G. (no f***ing good). Contact with Langara Light Station on Channel 22 (they monitor 16 and 82). The little cove northeast of the lighthouse looked too tight for us to tie up, much less to enter, so we didn't. We photographed sea lions on the north end of Langara Rocks—huge males that trumpeted our arrival with angry barks. We approached too close and they all began to bellow and some dove into the water. After circumnavigating the island we are now anchored facing west in Egeria Bay where the wind howls across a low spot. The rigging is ringing. Astern we can see Rose Spit to the east.

To bed at 2015 hours, exhausted.

July 30: Monday. Egeria Bay, 0700 hours. A sunny morning. Three does are directly in front of the bow and munching along rocks of foreshore, one large one to the north. At least a dozen eagles are sitting on the foreshore.

Tian Head—beautiful! We anchor in the east "cove" at 53°48.05'N, 133°04.02'W. Frank (Caldwell) and Don go ashore. I remain on the boat, which begins to roll just after they leave. Swells are now coming in from south. At 1740 hours the guys pick up a big red fender from the rocky beach.

July 31: Anchored in Otard Bay. We took the dink up Otard River about half a mile to where it became too shallow to proceed further. A marvelous experience through primitive rain forest. On shore in the sand were prints of river otter and deer. Frank counted at least ten different mosses, including pine gauze moss and palm moss. Also Sitka spruce, red alder and hemlock—some as tall as 200 feet, and obviously old-growths—and several types of fungus, including huge white ones. We saw no stumps, no sign of logging at all. The ground was easy to walk on—soft and spongy, not mushy. Along the beach onshore to the south Frank sighted a huge cedar which had been scraped off years ago, probably by Haida. On the top of the beach Don found a midden, the only place along a half mile of beach. Lots of jetsam—fenders, plastic bottles, and two or three brand new tennis shoes from the Japanese freighter that went aground a few years ago.

Left Otard at about 1600 hours and headed out into southeasterly conditions—choppy and rolly, but we only had a few miles to go to come into Port Louis, Tingley Cove. A resident loon was swimming back and forth off the head of the cove.

It starts to pour rain as we go to bed at 2200 hours. I love the sound of the rain when we're well anchored and cozy inside.

August 1: The guys spent three hours exploring the bitter end of Port Louis. At 1455 hours we left and came down to Port Chanal and checked out "Cave Cove" and Goose Cove, where we found the three buoys mentioned in *Sailing Directions* lashed together. Found Neal Frazer (author of *Boat Camping Haida Gwaii*) to be in error; he said there was only one buoy, so obviously he looked through binoculars, wasn't in the cove. Entering was harrowing—lots of underwater rocks. We didn't like it. Checked out the center of Empire Anchorage, then came on down to the head of Port Chanal, off Mace Creek, where we anchored in six fathoms at 1805 hours. A long, hard-working day. Supper: stew of cabbage, red potatoes, carrots, onions, red wine, paprika, herbs, etc.

Getting the dink up is a pain in the butt. Don caught the shackle for one of the stabilizers and Frank had to spend twenty minutes remedying the situation. The hammer came to the rescue, then again when the anchor shackle got caught.

August 2: Up anchor and head west out of Port Chanal in partial sun. Shores bright with golden rockweed. Once in a while there's a small sandy beach at the outlet of a creek. Between 53°35.15'N, 132°51.17'W and 53° 35.61'N, 132°52.952'W, the south hillside is denuded of trees—the terrain is alpine-like, with low grasses and mosses perhaps an indication of the paucity of soil. Elsewhere the trees are of medium height. Behind Empire Anchorage, the same conditions. Were these areas clear-cut at some time or are these natural conditions? There's a waterfall high up at 132°53.74'W

Skelu Point. Tiny trees with spindly trunks have sprung up since 1958 earthquake. The point looks quite volcanic. There's a large cave and many smaller caves, particularly along Hippa Island. One double cave looks like a pair of eyes peering out.

1740 hours. Anchored at the head of Seal Inlet; scoped out the cove behind Lauder Island.

August 4, 2001. 1500 hours. Three Canadian Fisheries & Oceans guys come by in a little red inflatable checking on us to see if we're okay: Gordie Usher, Fisheries Officer based in Queen Charlotte City, Ron Paziac, skipper of the fishery patrol vessel *Arrow Post*, and Darrell Robertson, also of the *Arrow Post*.

Overnight at Armentieres Channel with one other vessel, S/V *Mithrandir*, from the British Virgin Islands. Rick and Elke Cunningham. No wind.

August 5, 2001. Sunday. Layover day in Armentieres Channel. Good thing we came around from Buck Channel yesterday afternoon. It's now blowing a full gale (thirty-seven knots at 1400 hours) at Kindakun Rocks and Langara Island. From time to time a strong gust comes through the Channel, kicking up white caps and blowing us from side to side.

August 8, 2001. A meeting with Gwaii Haanas National Park/Haida Heritage Site officials in Queen Charlotte City.

August 9, 2001. Sunny and warm. Walked to the post office in Sandspit—a good three miles round trip. About a dozen kids were swimming without wetsuits in 65°F water. A father and his wife and baby came down to sunbathe and he dove in, then took his baby in. Vegetation: wild roses, clover, wild strawberries, salmonberries, blueberries, lilies of the valley, salal. A raven with hiccups!

A crow flew up to the railing of the pub where we ate. "They're really stupid," the waitress said, pointing at her head. "They're not like the ravens who find plenty of foods along the beach. These ones have to come up here and beg."

August 11, 2001. Left the dock last night at 1930 hours with Kevin (Monahan) aboard. Tied to a mooring buoy at east end of Skidegate Narrows. Up and underway at first light. Beautiful clear day and warm. Explored Trounce Inlet, then headed out and around to Buck Channel where we've spent the whole day.

We anchored at Nesi Cove for the afternoon. Had naps, then Kevin and Don went ashore at Chaatl Island so Kevin could see the totems. By the time they finished exploring it was 1800 hours. We headed down to the end of the channel, intending to anchor there for the night, but it was so steep-to and the wind howled straight down the inlet so we came back to Nesi to anchor. Lovely sunset.

Supper: turkey sausage "stew:" cabbage, potatoes, carrots, onions, chicken broth, paprika, red wine, garlic, zip, herbes de Provence, pepper.

August 12, 2001. Kitgoro Inlet—unsurveyed. Kevin does the drawings and watches the radar. Don does the electronic navigation. I watch with binoculars for hazards and kelp, or do bow watch. We head due east into the sun in Kitgoro, through kelp. At three fathoms I can see the bottom clearly—rocks and boulders. We get to the narrowest part and decide to turn around—it's a forest of kelp and we decide to be prudent.

We're now anchored in Peel Inlet.

Masses of mating moon jellyfish make the water look like shoal and gave us a start the first time we came upon such an area. Moon jellyfish with pink reproductive organs means they are mature and ripe, probably females. White centers means immature.

Haven't seen any animals in here—just guillemots.

Queen Charlotte Islands.

August 13: 0645 hours. Up and lay chain in aft chain locker till 0735.

0800: I prepare eggs-in-blankets.

0830: End of Mudge Inlet. Do two anchor tests (first won't hold)—kelpy bottom with mud and rocks. Grotesque, beautiful silver spruce snag that looks just like a totem at the head between two avalanche scars. Several creeks enter head of inlet.

0900: Heading back out of Mudge.

1000-1030: Mitchell Inlet—has a power plant at the head.

1030-1100: Do a grid off Una Point. Notice the expanse of light green water—a hundred feet long at least—which is the Thorn Rock that's noted on the chart with a small cross. Don calls this "putting your boat at risk."

1130: Heading into Douglas Inlet, which has zero soundings. We find several good anchor sites; beautiful scenery; also a water hose.

1330: Lunch—halibut salad

1600: Bottle Inlet. The entrance has extraordinary geological formations—basalt rock columns with a cave. Sides are high and so rocky and angular that nothing grows. Rock is grey and orangey and yellow. Waterfalls drop off the peaks. On south side, one "double falls" comes from a bowl halfway up. One of the most dramatic and stunning sights we've seen to date.

A 2000-foot ridge comes into view from the head as the sun comes out. A large grassy flat at the head is a hundred yards wide. A creek comes out at the south side.

We felt a brisk wind at the head of the inlet, while outside again it's almost flat calm—one- to two-foot seas.

Bottle Point has a basalt column on south side. The point is remarkably rugged. The area south of the point is highly vertical, forested, and with yellowish earth exposed in some places.

It's now 1740 hours and the sky is clearing to the east. 3010-foot Mt Ross shows its head behind the massif on the south side of the entrance. A lake drains into the north shore through a cleft due north of Kootenay Point. The falls have pierced a cleft through the rock. To the southeast along the shore, about 200 yards south, there appears to be an ancient beach about sixty feet up from the shore.

The south entrance shore has a "haystack" close in.

The north arm entrance has islets that come two-thirds of the way across—Don describes them as "exquisitely intricate." There are pines on the islets, also spruce, cedar, hemlock, alders. An island to north center has numerous silver snags. No chop, no driftwood, no stress.

We cruise through a rocky channel through narrows to the south arm of Kootenay Inlet; it's a hundred feet wide for three-quarters of a mile. Cruising through it is like floating down a river on either side of which is thick primeval forest of spruce, yellow and red cedar, hemlock, pines, alders, maidenhair ferns.

A view of Mt Ross from the Creation Coast—it's riddled with caves. Extruded, layered, swirled, poured, tumbled, chiseled, slashed, carved; thick lava flows, chunks, slabs.

From the north, the entrance to Portland Bay looks like a low ridge that walls off a hanging basin behind a waterfall. Off the entrance is another sea cave, this one rounded. There's a log-littered, stony beach on the north side.

The west coast of Moresby Island has to be the most spectacular coastline of the northwest. The geological formations are stunning. To appreciate it, you must follow it about a fifth of a mile offshore, particularly the stretch between Kootenay Inlet and Tasu Sound.

There's a perfect sharp cone at the base of a green avalanche chute. A series of cones between Portland Bay and the south are volcanic, then faulting. This entire coast is fissured and faulted.

Tasu Sound. This is bounded on the south by 2625-foot vertical Tasu Head. The entrance is much more impressive than the view of the inner sound, which is thoroughly logged. Upon entering, tailings from the old mine are immediately evident. It makes me wonder how companies can do this without any thought to the ugliness and lack of reseeding etc. Otherwise, this coasts looks as if it might have appeared just after its creation.

Finger Inlet—exquisite! High walls, a *narrow* inlet, with an echo off the walls. It's every bit as beautiful as Yosemite Valley. The walls almost overhang in places. Basalt and conglomerate. Evidence of earthquake or storm damage. There's a big blowdown area on the north side as well as an avalanche chute.

Anchored at 1600 hours in Sunday Inlet. Nap for an hour and a half. Download digital photos, prepare dinner—salmon and rock fish, peas, salad, frozen yogurt.

August 16, Thursday: Left Sunday Inlet this morning at 0730 hours. We've always admired what Neil and Betty Carey did exploring the coast, but as we explore it ourselves with radar, a depth sounder, GPS and electronic charting our amazement increases. They missed a few critical rocks here and there, but they were exploring without all these electronic aids.

Kwoon Cove, on the south side of Sunday Inlet, has the most beautiful white sand beach we've seen yet. It's littered with drift logs and is a good beachcombing beach. It would be beautiful camp site for kayakers in good weather. For boaters like us, it's open to the northwest and has a hard bottom with poor holding.

Pocket Inlet, 0840 hours. "Four Fangs" at the north side. Outer rocks at the narrows show evidence of heavy seas into winter even through the narrows. There's a waterfall on the south shore.

Barry Inlet has a stunning headwall 3000 feet high at the head. The south side is particularly impressive—sub and alpine with shrubs over which a cascade falls. In the water, mating moon jellyfish.

Mike Inlet—one and a half miles to the north is a deep valley of tall, vertical granite slabs with trees that fall directly into the ocean from a tortuous rock path. The lake above is about a mile and a third long. The entrance to the inlet is steep-walled and choked with kelp. Walls are white and black granite with overhanging roofs, such as those found in Yosemite Valley. Inside it's lovely, though we fouled our anchor.

Two Buck Bay—pretty!

Iron Balls Bay—didn't like it very much.

Gowgaia Bay—After much impressive scenery between here and Tasu, this bay is rather a let-down—wide, forested and pretty, but without any distinguishing geological features.

August 17: Layover in Yakulanas/Gowgaia Bay.

August 18: Leave Yakulanas and head into Tcuga (Cooga) Cove, which is tiny. As we're leaving, the Parks Canada vessel *Gwaii Haanas II*, which is also in the cove, radios us to ask if we saw the wreck inside. We hadn't sighted it, so they asked if we'd like to raft aside and go with them in their tender. We tied up to their starboard side, toured the boat, met the crew— Ken Brillon, the skipper-engineer, and his deckhand Wally Pelton; also Heather Toews, Richard Scott, Richelle Leonard (the retiring park Superintendent), and Ernie Gladstone, the new Superintendent. Wally is Haida, grew up mainly in Skidegate with his grandmother. (His parents live in Alberta.) Ken is an affable chap who's interested in everything along this coast. Heather Toews is from the University of British Columbia, doing research for a Masters degree on phytoplankton ecology.

First we visited the wreck, then the village inside the narrows above a sandy beach. There were shells of all kinds—red abalone, turban shells, clams, scallops, sea urchins, and all sizes from exquisitely small to eight inches wide. The abalone was well-weathered, polished to a pearly, thin surface. The shells were attached to little mosses—exquisite little gardens.

There were also masses of all kinds of fungus, the backbone of some kind of coral. Heather named these as we walked together. "Do you know mushrooms?" I asked.

"Not very well, but I have to teach a class in September so I have some studying to do."

Richard and Richelle are both Quebecois. We speak French for a few minutes. Great group!

We head north to Puffin Cove to take route soundings. The *Gwaii Haanas II* is headed there too. Inside the outer cove Ken and Don talk by radio. Ken says the entrance is pretty narrow.

We turn and head back south. Yesterday's southeasterly weather has produced some "nice"-sized southwesterly swells—the most seas we've had to date. But we're running without poles. Don asked earlier if I wanted to put them down, but I told him we should have done it *before* we came out here, not when we're rolling around in slop. The weather forecast was favorable, but dark clouds are building to the southwest. What's in store for tonight?

Coast south to Flamingo Inlet. Rolly. We deploy stabilizers in Wells Bay. Anchor at 1930 hours in Sperm Bay.

August 19: A half-day layover. I rearrange the galley lockers so heavier items are below, then prepare a salmon omelet for brunch (1230 hours). We decide to move on because there's an "aggressive" low coming through with gale- to storm-force winds expected. We go up to Staki Bay to do soundings, then head south out of Flamingo as Kevin and Don do their chart adjustments.

August 20: The gusts begin. A flock of gulls flies in to bathe in the stream along shore. They dip, then shake their wings of water. Others feed in the rock weed of the mud flats. Every fifteen minutes or so, a dozen or so take off, circle around the cove, then land again. A gust comes through and the entire flock of perhaps 200 takes off while four only remain on shore feeding. A gust of thirty knots blows through the cove. Gradually the rest of the gulls return.

August 22, Wednesday: Three days of waiting out full gales. Squall after squall. "It just never quits, does it?" Kevin says as he goes out on deck for a smoke. A patch of blue appears. Then, just as quickly, the clouds lower and visibility decreases and another squall moves through—dark purplish clouds blow through in billowed layers. Then there's a lull of five minutes before the howling starts again. 2125 hours and it's nearly dark.

We hope to make it up to Bag Harbor by tomorrow evening (Thursday). This requires a transit of Dolomite Narrows. Will the seas have decreased in Hecate Strait? I hope so.

August 23, Thursday: Bag Harbor by early afternoon. Transited Dolomite Narrows without a problem after Don and Kevin scouted it out by dinghy. S/V *Tasman* (Alan Brown) came south through the narrows and anchored in Bag Harbor. Alan was using our book—an upper after a "No comment" from a boater in Anvil Cove. Picked up a buoy in Section Cove for the night.

August 24, Friday: "Gales" to "storms" (Canadian Coast Guard) continue. We leave 0900 hours. Check out Hot Springs Island, Ramsey Island, and Murchison Island, which has a *dicey* entrance with buoys in terrible shape. Then to Hoya Passage, where the tour boat *Island Roamer*, a sixty-eight foot sailing vessel, is moored. Their waterline broke so they are sending shore crew to repair it—two young crew members who have obviously done this before. It takes them about three hours to repair the line. They have to saw through a section of pipe and reinstall a new section. Water starts to flow at a good rate, but they had to put the line directly into the creek instead of reinstalling it into the "box" (probably a filter box) and there was too much suspension in the water for us to use, so we didn't fill up on water.

The guys who did the repair have a good attitude—"It's good to get out"—even in pouring rain. By the time they completed their repairs the creek was running out like a river, with a current of perhaps six knots. We pulled away from the water dock and picked up the inside buoy. For a couple of hours we sat just twenty feet away from *Island Roamer* and their two tenders.

On *Island Roamer* is Natalie, Director of the Skidegate Museum, who calls to our attention a bad error on our North Coast map—Marble Island, a major landmark at the west entrance to Skidegate Channel, is misnamed.

August 25, Saturday: Gales continue. Forecast: Gales to continue. Now we're concerned about getting Kevin to Sandspit in time for his flight. We leave at 0815 hours and head northward out of Hoya Passage.

Louise Narrows is like a canal in Europe, with a narrow, narrow fairway. We called security to say *Baidarka* was northbound in Louise

Narrows. Who should be waiting to head south but Mr "No Comment" from Anvil Cove. We just went right on by without waving or acknowledging him.

Moresby Camp—we go to the dock to see if we'll fit in, in case we have to drop Kevin off. Then we come over to Gordon Cove and pick up one of the seven buoys. The gale warnings continue and another low pressure of 993 millibars is expected to follow upon this one. We decide to make a run for it to Sandspit, set the alarm for 0400 hours. I go to bed at 2100. Don, all out of sorts, went to bed at 2030.

Bruce's Taxi will go to the airport: "Variable pricing—psychic returns." Unimproved logging truck roads. He lost two tires going down to Moresby. "The road was so bad and the mud was so thick that I couldn't tell that my tires were flat. But I never let anyone walk."

August 26, Sunday: As we went around from Cumshewa Inlet to Sandspit, even Kevin was eating cheddar cheese rice cakes. Last night I cut slices of cheese and put them in a Ziploc bag for snacks today. No one was hungry in the confused chop off Cumshewa Island, but once we turned north and had the seas behind us we craved something to eat.

August 27: Take off at 1230 hours for Larsen Harbour after our return from the airport.

August 28: Fog much of the day till late afternoon. After we left Larsen Harbour we had to navigate with radar most of the morning. Tried going in to Colby Bay but we couldn't see more than sixty feet, so it was no use to try.

There are shore birds in Principe Channel. We haven't sighted as many birds in the past few years as we did in the beginning.

Contrails of jets flying the Seattle-Anchorage route are reflected in the water.

August 29, Wednesday: Meyers Passage by moonlight. The almost-full moon is at a twenty-degree angle above the horizon to the south, with a scarf of voile wrapped elegantly around it. Horizontal clouds—rose, mauve, turquoise, grey—are the muted colors of high latitudes. There's the smell of earth after rain. Kelp gardens make themselves visible in the flash light.

After ten days of gales, storm-force winds, and pelting rain our adrenaline is spent. We have a shot glass of Dubonnet Gold.

"Were you scared?" Don asked me after I came in from bow watch.

"Why would I be scared?" I ask.

"Most women would be."

"It's only the big waves that frighten me."

I loved it on the bow. With the moonlight, the kelp was easy to see.

August 30 to September 1, Thursday to Saturday: To Ocean Falls. Gales overnight. Some gusts of forty to fifty knots. The storm continues through Saturday. White caps blow up Cousins Inlet, hit the elbow and make a ninety degree turn. There's sea smoke and horizontal rain.

Saturday evening. *Coastal Messenger,* a Christian missionary vessel, comes in and rafts alongside. We have herbal tea and cookies aboard with Brian, Tom and Debbie, and good discussions about First Nations problems and what's what in certain spots of the coast. Debbie sends us "home" with a plate of cookies. I gave them a copy of my *Cape Horn* book. Don tells them: "This may not appeal to ministerial types…"

Tom replies: "We're not exactly ordinary ministerial types."

September 2: Left Ocean Falls at 0650. To Frypan Bay, along with John and Midge Stapleton on *Sundown,* S/V *Cadenza,* and *Rhapsody,* a trawler.

Dugout Rocks. Crossing Queen Charlotte Sound we see a line of geese heading south. *They know* something we've been experiencing for the last two weeks! Stan at Egg Island says the geese don't usually head south until end of September, early October.

A sailing vessel gets a call from the Canadian Coast Guard saying his wife is trying to contact him from Port Hardy. "What a surprise," he tells her after they get patched in. He was planning to go to Sullivan Bay but obviously has to change his plans. He asks her if she's alone. She says, "Yes, are you?"

"Of course I am."

He tells her where to look for him when he gets to Port Hardy. Later he talks to a buddy on another boat and explains that his wife tracked him down and he's meeting her in Hardy. "Maybe she's going to serve papers," he tells his buddy.

Obviously we'd like to know the story!

145

September 4: Off at 0630 hours from Pearse Island Narrows and down into Johnstone Strait at dawn. Seiners are staking out their ground all along the Vancouver Island shore.

September 5-6: Wednesday and Thursday in Nanaimo. Dinner with Bruce and Margaret Evertz (*Tapawingo*) at Milano Café & Grill. Excellent.

Today (Thursday) shopped at Artisans' Guild; got hair cut; had laundry done and did one load on board. Worked on 35 mm camera lists. Took a thirty minute nap when Don came back from errands. Supper on board, then a walk to a mailbox with a stop for ice cream along the walkway. We're both feeling a bit let down by urban cruising and the fact we can't get into the Port Sidney marina. Too many people!

At the park by the fountain above the promenade, a tree "sang" with *hundreds* of birds. It was too dark to discern what type they were, but perhaps starlings. The leaves, large and non-serrated, were white with bird droppings.

GULF OF ALASKA, 2003

April 29, 2003. Crisis #1. This occurred at the dock in Anacortes before we took off and just after Don started the engine. Everyone was waiting for Don to come to the stern for a photo. He and John Leone were kneeling in front of the electrical panel. "Come on," I said, "They're waiting for a photo."

Don turned around and glared. "We don't have an inverter. No AC power."

I ran back to the stern and told the crowd: "A little problem... A few more minutes." Inwardly, I was thinking, "Oh, good grief, we're not even out of the slip yet."

Finally they got the inverter set up and we motored out, me at the helm. We rounded the corner and heard honking. We waved. "Who's that?" I asked.

"I don't know..."

Then we saw Gina M., pregnant and carrying her nearly-three-year-old, rushing to yell, "I've got a loaf of banana bread for you!"

"Okay, we'll come to the dock."

I handed the helm over to Don. The dock was the very last in Flounder Bay and it was too tight, too shallow for my docking skills. Don backed up to near six feet and maneuvered us in. Gina handed me the banana bread, Don and I kissed her, and we headed back out.

Crisis #2: Our Mac doesn't open the PC zip version of *Exploring the San Juans and Gulf Islands*. I'm angry at myself for not insisting that Mark (our Fine Edge Productions manager) use a Mac disk. I'm dead in the water for working on the book on my computer.

Crisis #3: As we're pulling into Warren and Laurie Miller's dock on Orcas Island, I hear the water pump cycling. I check all three faucets. They're closed. Don goes to check the water pump. The release valve is apparently kaput. We hope it's not more serious than that. We can buy a replacement in Nanaimo if we clear Customs in time tomorrow.

Crisis #4: Autopilot in Auto mode gives signals that the flux-gate compass has lost control. Also the Nobeltec navigation app on the ship's computer freezes once in a while when we hit the down arrow, then we have to reset.

Crisis #5: No Red Dot heater. Don goes down to engine room, after which I hear the Red Dot purring. It's working. I ask Don: "What did you do to get it the Red Dot going?"

"I banged on the electric motor."

"Maybe if we bang on the instruments they'll start working," I say.

Meanwhile John is reading the manufacturing manuals—and the "Leone" adjustable window opener works. John says: "All the simple, non-electronic things are operating well."

April 30: 1230 hours. Dodd Narrows. A thirty minute nap, then I'm woken by turbulence. John's taking us through. Arrive Nanaimo 1330.

May 1: Leave Nanaimo 0500 hours. By 1015 we're out in Georgia Strait. The boat is still far from shipshape. Yesterday we filled up with water up to the boat strip, so we're low in the water. John and Don loaded twelve two-litre bottles of Okanagan Port and four cases of beer.

Campbell River overnight. Dock in front of the Riptide Pub, where we eat dinner. Don was out of sorts all afternoon, because of problems with the computer, navigation, autopilot, etc. Then the GPS section in the Introduction to *San Juan and Gulf Islands* made him explode at me. The usual "You don't understand…" lecture, ad infinitum. "Why are you still working on that book? Why don't you let Mark handle it?" Because I had a responsibility to fulfil, I say. Don glares and starts lecturing again. I fight back tears.

Mark calls us to say he emailed his version and Don works on it before we go to dinner. We print out three copies so we can all read it and comment at dinner. I stay up till midnight editing and writing notes on Chapters 1-3 to send to Mark.

May 2: Leave Campbell River at 0510 hours The Dell mouse/cursor won't work, so we have to restart the computer. The second time it works, so we send two emails to Mark.

Tied up at Port Neville by noon. Lorna Hansen Chesluk helps us dock after three tries (me, first—an aborted try; then Don second and third tries). Too much wind and current. We visit with Lorna for an hour on board over Goldfish crackers, port and Dubonnet (Lorna drinks orange juice). Don, John and I all crash at 1300 hours. I stay up on the pilothouse berth to work on Chapter 3 of *Exploring the San Juans and Gulf Islands*, but fall asleep again at 1400. Sleep till 1630 hours. Get up, put on *osso bucco* to take to Lorna's for dinner.

May 3, 2003. Blackney Passage 0845 hours. Ten and a half knots at 1200 r.p.m. Nobeltec doesn't work in this turbulence.

2018 hours. Anchor in Fury Cove after a fifteen-hour, 107 nautical mile day. There are four other boats in here, including M/V *Pelorus* from Bellingham—Joe and Margy Orem—who are going to Prince William Sound, as we are.

The Captain is still out of sorts, and mad with me.

May 4, 2003. Sunday. Leave Fury Cove, head up Fitz Hugh Sound, then into Kwakshua Channel to Hahai Passage. The winds pick up to gale force; there are white caps all over. Seas are short and nasty. We have the poles down. Don asks the crew what we want to do. John points east. Don says, "I hate democracy."

Fury Cove.

We go north through Ward Channel with Don at the helm, then he says "That was just a squall. It looks beau-tee-ful now. What do you say?"

"It's obvious you want to do it," I say. "Let's go," with a little reluctance showing. We turn left into Spitfire Narrows. The guys take in the poles. Don tells John to put over the big red fenders. I take us on through, angry at Don for being so cocksure we can make it. A dead tree branch hangs about ten feet over the water at the narrowest part. I can see shoal water (light green) and rocks left and right. Don's screaming "Réanne's done it. She's taken us through twice. What a woman!"

John says, "It's a good thing you don't have guns aboard.

"A knife in the pilothouse would do," I say, poking Don in the ribs.

Having made it through, we head across Queens Sound toward the Goose Islands. Don looks at me sheepishly and asks if I know where we're going. "Of course."

May 5: Layover day at Goose Island. The guys go ashore in the morning. I stay aboard to wash and dry a small load of clothes and continue organizing. I go ashore in the afternoon and we walk the beach—nice sand with beautiful polished logs strewn all over. There are sandhill cranes here.

Went in to Rudolf Bay for the first time. The only entry directions we had to work with were those Kevin Monahan had given Don from memory, which appeared to be wrong. We enter south of a round island at idle speed. Nobeltec is working at the moment and continues to do so for the next two hours. We glide to the end of the channel, which opens up to a large basin with an extensive mud flat on its south side. Hundreds of shore birds are feeding on the mud. A loon calls, then disappears underwater.

After a lunch of tacos, we head back out into Laredo Sound. Our planned destination for the night: Ethelda Bay. John and Don take a nap, I take the helm. Just off Haig Rock, Nobeltec on the main computer goes blank. It's been reading slow (GPS) all day, and it just froze. Don tells me to look for chart 3737 which I do, and double check it. Chart 3605 (Cape Scott) opens up. Don tries to give me instructions, obviously enjoying my frustration. "This is a waste of time," I say. "Let's just turn it off and navigate visually."

"No, just play with it for another three hours and you'll see why I've been in such a foul mood these past three days," Don says.

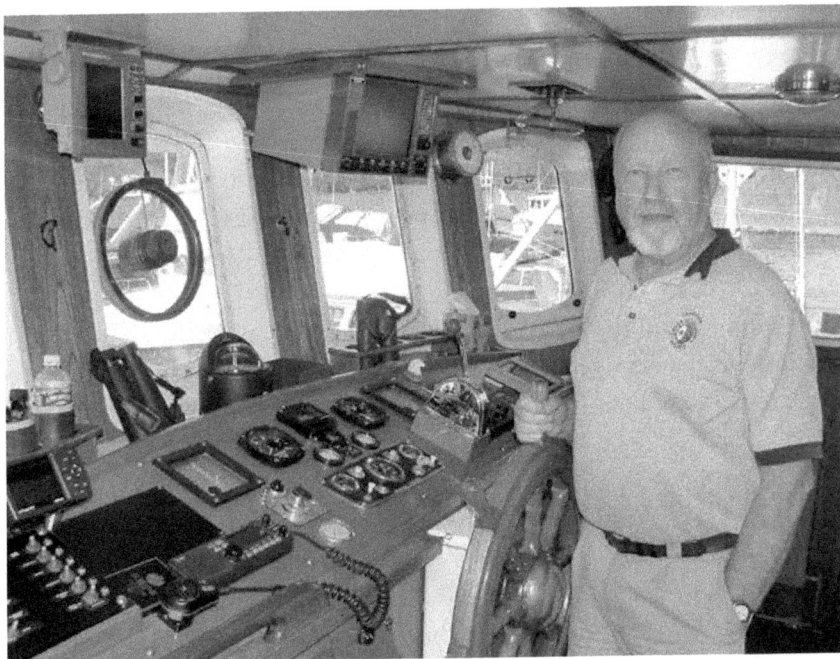

May 6: John says our pilothouse looks like a penny arcade. Don says, "Yeah, it looks like Las Vegas and it beeps like Las Vegas."

John: "Think what you accomplished before you had all this: a good depth sounder, a GPS, a paper chart..."

May 7: Reconnoitered Gillespie Channel in the dink, then I took *Baidarka* through Langley Passage to Ethelda Bay. Blew the horn at the Pollacks' dock and Danielle came down, then Dan, Mikal, Ilene and Nicole. They invited us to hike with them on Trutch Island up to the old radio towers. One and a half hours, said Danielle. We bushwhacked to the top—a thousand foot elevation gain. We had left *Baidarka* at 1430 hours, returned at 1830. Both Don and I feel our age. My legs are now like rubber. Don says about the hike, "It was like the Bataan Death March." We had to keep our hands and arms in front of us to keep from having our eyes poked out. The view on top was worth all the misery, but as John kept saying, "I think you only want to do this once in a lifetime."

Don and John took the dink to reconnoiter the west entrance to Langley. The family came down to the boat and Danielle, Mikal and I went to pick up the prawn and crab traps. No crabs but huge prawns! Then we went up to the lodge for dinner. Prawns, ribs, salad, couscous, curried lentils from me, fruit salad for dessert.

May 8, Thursday: Left the Ethelda Bay float at 0630 hours. Today Nobeltec is working on the ship's computer. Don did a "Delete Routes and Marks Database" on the diagnostic menu and the display reverted to its original view, but now, instead of *Baidarka* it reads SS *Minnow*.

May 9: Our bread from La Vie En Rose (the French Bakery in Anacortes) was vacuum packed with my "Food Saver". It compressed the bread so much I'm considering taking all the loaves to a saw-mill to have them sliced.

May 12: Leave Prince Rupert 0510 hours. S/V *Nellie Juan*—Ken and Judy Carpenter, of Seward, AK—follows us out to go through Venn Passage.

May 15: Up at 0440 hours. Leave Bushy Island anchor site at 0500 hours. From 0530 to 0730 I do a trip report to post on the website, then lie down for a nap. We've decided to take the outside route instead of Rocky Pass, since as Don says, "it's faster." It's nasty but we make great time, cruising at nine to ten knots in confused seas. We got to Réanne's Relief at 1735 instead of 2000 hours.

May 16: Ice on the roof when we get up.

May 17: Sitka. In 1999, the schooner *Merlin* (seventy-three feet, 111 years old, rebuilt by Ward Eldridge from the keel up) was rammed by a whale. Baleen from a humpback was found inside the five-foot hole in the hull. Baleen whales have good hearing but don't have systems for echo-sounding. The sailing magazine *48°North* did a story on the *Merlin*. Ward Eldridge now has a 40-foot Cal, *Blue Merlin*.

A guy passes by *Baidarka* when I'm in pilothouse. He pauses and looks at our anchor. I open up the Dutch door. He says, "We don't often see mud on anchors on this kind of a boat."

Anchor in Katlian Bay for the night. Six other boats, among them *Pelorus*.

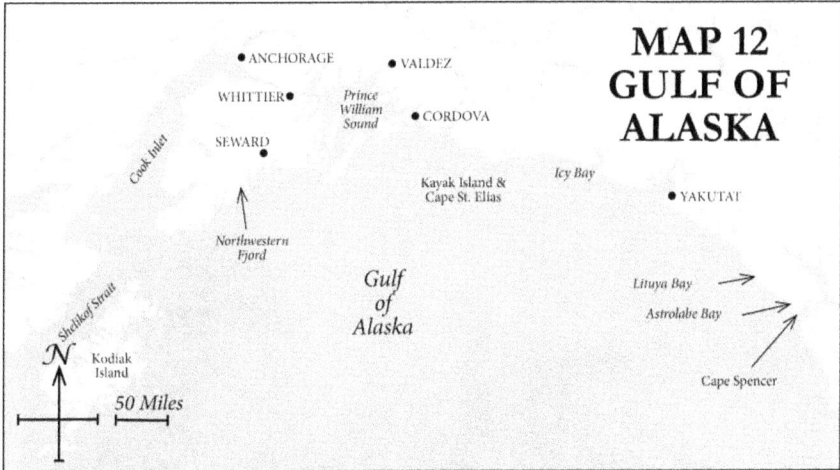

May 18, 2003.   0345-0500 hours: Up

0500-0645: Sleep

0700-0845: Watch

0900-1000: Sleep

1000-1130: Watch

1200-1400: Sleep

1400 hours: Awake; take photos

1735 hours: Anchor in Astrolabe Bay. Take off my Relief Band.

• Help guys get off in dinghy after preparing their survival suits and gear for going in dink

• Stand by on Channel 69

• Print out weather reports

• Try to receive email (six tries, no good)

• Prepare dinner—soft halibut tacos

• Help guys get out of suits

• Help guys lift dink

• Wash their float bags and put away cameras etc. Replace battery in digital camera

• Set out dinner

• Eat dinner; dessert: tapioca, rhubarb

• Do dishes (since the guys took my watches)

John was okay today with a Scopolamine patch. I wasn't nauseated, but I felt dizzy and super tired.

"The Mink Road"—the name for the 5-10 fathom line between Cape Fairweather and Yakutat.

Boussole Arch, Astrolable Bay.

May 19, Monday:. Astrolabe Bay to Lituya Bay. I could see the tide rips off Lituya from about four miles away. Don woke up and said, "What'd ya see?"

We went into Lituya Bay an hour and a half before slack on the ebb, with an estimated nine to ten knot current. As we were surfing in I was having trouble keeping the boat from yawing. "Don, you've got to take the boat over for me," I said.

"Okay, then you take the photos."

He took over the helm and had to keep it completely clear over from one side to the other to keep on the range. John kept a watch on the swells behind us. We hardly had any of these till the entrance, then wow! The swells from the southwest were the most dangerous.

"John, what's happening behind us," Don asked.

"You don't want to know. You'll know soon enough. If I were you I'd push the pedal to the metal."

May 20: Underway at 0435 hours from Cenotaph anchor site, Lituya Bay.

Lituya Bay.

Halibut Wraps á la Lituya Bay:
1 lb cooked halibut, flaked
Shredded lettuce (head or romaine)
Chopped tomatoes or 1 can drained tomatoes
½ onion, chopped
1 can black beans, drained
1 cup shredded cheese (your choice)
½ cup chopped chilies (mild)
Salsa (Trader Joe's mango salsa)
1 package whole wheat flour tortillas (heat desired quantity in oven wrapped in foil)
Combine all ingredients and add to tortilla and serve with salsa. Wrap to eat.

May 21: Yakutat. Population: 600 in winter, 900 in summer. Harbormaster is Brandt Petersen. He's been here five years here, was in Port Townsend, WA, before that. He would like the harbor to have facilities—showers, laundry, a harbor office—but there's no budget for them. He works full time and gets paid half time. The town is now thinking of eliminating his pay altogether. He is married to a native, Tina. They just got a lease to build a cabin on one of the islands. Tina does gillnets at Siku River with her seventy-eight-year-old father in the summer. Tina's parents lived in Dry Bay, and Tina did also as a baby.

They've had seven boats visit so far this season. M/V *Taz* hit a log last week; Brandt says the skipper changed name of vessel ("which brings bad luck"). S/V *Pazzo* comes in on the second day we're there.

It's 200 miles by air or boat to the nearest towns—Cordova and Sitka. People fly out or take the ferry. The ferry comes in twice a month; a barge twice in summer, once in winter but this may be dropped back due to the economy.

Geoff Widdows, of *Sea Raven*, does ocean charters and glacier tours. He has lived in Yakutat for over thirty years and fished for halibut most of that time. He has been in Lituya Bay many times. He took a B.C. crew to Hubbard Glacier to film glacier bears; these are offshoots of black bears, like the Kermode "spirit" bears. Hubbard Glacier is 800 to 900 feet wide, grows during winter then calves in summer; it's one of the few still-advancing glaciers. In 2002, Hubbard broke and raised up a hundred feet, putting seals on land. Volunteers and Fish & Game and Forest Service personnel had to go up and rescue them.

Geoff says you can drive on Cannon Beach, west of Yakutat airport. All the islands and foreshore are owned by Natives. A forty mile road goes to headwaters of Dangerous River.

We rented a car, drove out to beach, about twenty miles; got stuck in mud; took us twenty minutes to extricate ourselves, then another bumpy turn off to the cemetery. "Home" after two hours.

May 22: The ferry was due to come in Wednesday or Thursday this week, but couldn't due to the weather. I commented on the good selection of food supplies at Mallott's. The cashier replied, "You should see it after the barge comes in!" Tomatoes at Mallott's (Canadian, on the vine) were $2.49 a pound, compared to $2.99 in Anacortes when we left. Asparagus was also cheaper at Mallott's.

Drove out to Harlequin Lake. The forest along the road to Harlequin Lake has been clear-cut. It looks like a cemetery with tombstones. A bear stands up in the road. There's lupine all over the ground; also wild strawberry, pussy willows; and some most interesting rocks: granite conglomerates with green, orange, brown, quartz. The willows along the trail to the lake formed a canopy fifteen feet tall. The air is perfumed.

Took the road to Russell Fjord—the second road after the bridge with broken down metal ports, then two and half miles to a parking spot at the trailhead, then one mile to the fjord. Strong currents and ice. Forty- to fifty-foot seiners go into the fjord occasionally, but it's considered dangerous and not recommended.

Alsek River: the normal route is to approach Dry Bay from the west and look for a break in the breakers. Breakers are to starboard along the outer wall of channel. Water flow varies from tens of thousands of cubic feet to four- or five-hundred thousand. It's better to go in when less there's water, because there's less current, but there's also less depth. Recent storms appear to have opened up channel to the southwest. There's a temporary anchor site along the south shore of the channel within the bay, depth twelve to fifteen feet. What is shown as tidal land is all dry.

Dangerous River. Photo by John Leone.

Yakutat dump—cars, refrigerators, washing machines, dryers, oil drums, tires, all piled in their own areas and surrounded by forests.

Skyview B&B has a smashed Bronco in front of their door. It didn't look like somewhere we'd ever want to stay.

A visit to Park Service headquarters, where Ranger Jacqueline Lott was on duty. They had our *Exploring Southeast Alaska* book. Jacqueline told me she sold one recently to a man who was "very happy to have it." Yakutat Park (combining Wrangell-St. Elias and Glacier Bay National Parks) is 13.3 million acres, the largest national park in the U.S.—a little bigger than Switzerland, or about the size of West Virginia. Hubbard Glacier is twenty-five percent larger than Rhode Island. Malaspina Glacier, nearby, is the size of Rhode Island.

Leonard's Landing. We thought we'd made reservations for dinner at 1800 hours. When we got there they were having a wine tasting, hors d'ouevres and dinner. About ten percent of Yakutat showed up—probably mostly the movers and shakers. We sat next to Steve Estes and Josh Stachnik, seismologists from the University of Alaska, Fairbanks, who are down here to adjust and check equipment. Last night at 2010 hours, when we were driving along the road that parallels the beach, there was a 4.9 earthquake. People in town felt it, but we didn't. "Would your equipment have measured last night's quake accurately?" I asked Steve and Josh. No, they said, it's not sophisticated enough, and they don't have the budget to upgrade.

We walked to "town" and back in pouring rain. No one stopped to offer us a ride. "Maybe that's just because when they see someone walking in the rain, it's just a normal everyday occurrence," Don said.

May 24, Saturday: Memorial Day weekend. No holiday for us. Left Yakutat at 0455 hours. Sixty-one nautical miles to Icy Bay. After two hours, I went down to the head and was seasick. I slept on the salon couch for most of morning after that.

1600 hours. Wind is whipping down from the northeast at thirty-plus knots. We're anchored behind a tug in a cove east of a moraine, really a peninsula.

At 1130 hours we were following the fifteen fathom curve at two miles offshore. We had huge following seas, estimated at thirteen feet high, with eleven second intervals. Couldn't see the horizon when we were in the troughs. Don explained his plan to go to Icy Bay and asked John and me if we were up for it. I asked how wide open Icy Bay is. Six miles, so it's not like Lituya, but there's less local information on getting into it. We all decided where best anchor site might be and headed in. I read the depth sounder, John looked through binoculars, and vice versa.

Earlier I had been so frightened by waves that I began to cry. I took several deep breaths then thought, "I've got to be philosophical about this; it's like having flight fear syndrome; I just have to realize if I go, I go." Then I thought of all the things I'd forgotten to tell my sons. Where my jewelry is; what the combination to the safe is, etc. etc. Finally, I fell asleep.

When I got up and came up to the pilothouse Don brought up all our survival suits. I asked, "Do I put it on now and not be able to maneuver inside the boat, or wait until we're ready to go down?"

Off Icy Cape (a low spit) we watched the breakers at several points and thought they were bergs. Then we saw actual bergs in the distance. Not many and not huge. Most of them had been blown by the northeast wind to the opposite side of the bay. As we came round I said, "There's a car with lights on or something like a fire." It turned out to be a tug with its anchor light on. Don thinks he turned the light on just for us, because after we got in here he turned it off. Don called him on Channel 16, then switched to Channel 10. The tug captain gave us local knowledge about foul areas and shoals. Our original "pick" was too shallow and as we started toward the southwest side he came and warned us.

Before we turned across the bar Don kept saying, "Look out the window, look out the window at the seas."

"I don't want to know what the seas are like. I just want to keep my eyes on the horizon, thank you."

"I don't want to know about them either," Don said.

Log booms protect the cove and depths aren't as charted. A foul area on the southwest side is more extensive than shown. A creek comes out on the east side. There are logs on the beach, particularly on the southwest side.

Squalls kept hitting all morning. Another one hit just as we were making our turn into Icy Bay. Now, at 1640 hours, more squalls.

Earlier John said, "It's Saturday. Bacon and eggs at the bowling alley."

I said, "Just get me safely anchored and I'll fix you ham and eggs."

Don is very pleased with my observations. I spotted S.S. *Veendam* this morning and bergs etc. here in Icy Bay. He told me I'm a good helmsman. Nice to have some appreciation!

Veendam, *off Yakutat.*

May 25: Layover day. I reorganized and labeled cupboards. Don cleaned the stove—a two-hour job.

Sighted a moose at 1857 hours on the northeast point. This is the first moose I've seen since our Bowran Lakes kayaking trip in 1989.

Don talked some more to the captain of the tug, *Peril Strait*. The captain has never been north of here but has been into Lituya Bay twice, he said. They work sixty days on, sixty off, and bring in stevedores to load log ships that go directly to Japan and Korea.

Don said he regretted the weather wasn't cooperating so we could go on shore. The tug captain said, "That's brown bear territory…" He says coming into Icy Bay is far less difficult than going into Lituya, since the opening is much wider and the currents much less. The first cove is no good—it's rolly and exposed. Farther up Icy Bay, there's too much ice. He's crossed the bar in fifteen foot seas without a problem.

Icy Bay Bread Pudding

6 cups bread, tightly packed in 1½ inch squares

2 eggs, beaten

3 cups milk, or 2 cups milk & 1 cup fruit juice

Juice of 1 orange

Grated rind from ½ - 1 orange

½ tsp cinnamon or 1 stick heated with milk

¼ tsp nutmeg

½ cup yellow raisins (sultanas)

¼ cup dried cranberries or cherries

Optional: ½ cup chopped walnuts

¼ cup Turbinado or brown sugar (4 packets)

½ -1 tsp vanilla

8-9" square pan, buttered

1) Put bread squares in pan; preheat oven to 325-350°.

2) Mix milk with dried fruit and cinnamon. Add sugar and heat to scalding and let fruit plump up.

3) When cooled to warm, add to egg/orange rind/vanilla mixture

4) Pour liquid over bread and be sure all is well mixed

5) Bake in 325-350° oven for +/- 45 minutes

6) Let cool and serve with vanilla pudding, whipped cream or plain.

Cape St. Elias.

May 26: Monday. Memorial Day. "For the next thirty-five minutes, I'll be tied up 'carving' bread." (I'm cutting the vacuum-packed multi-grain bread from La Vie en Rose bakery in Anacortes.)

"That qualifies for hazard pay," John says.

"Except I wouldn't qualify. I'm an owner. No rights, no pay."

May 27: 1830 hours. Cape St. Elias, at the south end of Kayak Island—in sun! Seas are calm off the west side. There's a monolith along the shore.

2100 hours. Anchored in Entrance Bay, Kayak Island.

May 28: Up at 0600 hours so the guys can explore with the dinghy. They leave at 0740 hours and head for rocks that bare at about 305°M from our helm at anchorage. The rocks are uncharted and unmentioned in *Coast Pilot.*

A "beauteefull" day, as Don says. On Wingham Island Rock: Stellar's sea lions; gulls by the thousands; black-legged kittiwakes; murres; puffins; cormorants. The rock is about 100 feet tall by 150 feet wide.

From the north end of Wingham Island we can see Bering Glacier to the north. John and I take depth soundings in the dinghy off the north

162

shore—twenty-five to forty feet until till we're about fifty feet from the shore. After returning to *Baidarka*, we anchor in six fathoms, about 150 feet from the shore.

1430 hours. Now we're headed for Martin Islands, twelve nautical miles to the west. Wind is from the southwest. The distance from Wingham Island to Fox Island, at the southern tip of Martin Island, is ten miles. The distance from Fox Island to Cape Hinchinbrook is sixty-two nautical miles.

Garden Cove, in Port Etches, ten miles from Cape Hinchinbrook, offers good protection.

This morning when I got up the rolling, although gentle, made me extremely dizzy. I could barely take my shower without losing my balance. I put on my Relief Band and lay down for twenty minutes. Then I felt better.

The guys came back from exploring the east side of the Martin Islands. The chop had built up by then and getting the dinghy back on board was very dangerous. It swung from side to side and nearly did John in with the motor. It was an emergency. "Last time we do this in these conditions," John said. Exactly my sentiments. After it was all over, I nearly burst out in tears.

May 29: Thursday. Overcast with a medium ceiling of clouds. A "table cloth" over Cape St Elias and Wingham Island. Don got up at 0230 hours to check the anchor—the wind had changed and the motion of the boat was different. Underway at 0450 hours. We all find we don't sleep quite as well when we have to get up so early. I set the alarm for 0345 and began waking up thirty to forty-five minutes before that. As we got underway we saw a sea otter with a baby on its back.

Six miles from land, it's only eight to ten fathoms deep along the Copper River Delta. As we pass the delta, which is filled with glacier ice, I sight three fishing vessels north of us and close to shore. They probably came from Cordova.

Seas from take-off until about 0900 hours were almost flat. Now they've built to four to six feet, following off our stern quarter.

0945 hours. A little while ago while Don was sleeping I heard a noise like something chafing. Finally I figured out it was Don snoring on the pilot berth above me.

I'm wearing half of a Scopolamine patch, along with my Relief Band. So far I have been able to write a short email to Mark and write in the log and this journal without a problem.

Almost too overwhelming—mountains with solid snow at back of Prince William Sound, and all along shore are mountains that plunge into the sea.

Message from Bill Swain: "Re your computer problems, steer by the stars." Then the inverter "craps out" again, with the computer, too.

1159 hours. We sight an oil tanker leaving Prince William Sound. Also the Coast Guard cutter *Sycamore*, a buoy tender. "The buoy that becomes a boat; a boat disguised as a buoy."

1320 hours. Nearly to Cape Hinchinbrook. The island is green "velvet" with bluffs along the base, pinkish granite, evergreens in patches all over. Don talks of "designer gulls."

2045 hours. After I give Don a haircut, he says to John and me, "Shall we pull in a hundred feet on the chain, or wait until tomorrow?" The williwaws we had endured for two or three hours earlier had subsided.

John says, "Whatever you want to do, kid." Just then a williwaw starts howling through the rigging. I raise my arm and say, "And it shall be done…"

"Okay, okay," Don says. "We'll wait till morning."

Earlier, we sighted a grizzly on shore.

Supper: turkey breasts, roasted potato slices, salad; wine. A nice improvement over last night, when we just had soup cups and rye crisps at 2130 hours.

May 30: Garden Cove. A wonderful night's sleep with a few williwaws, but we hung tight on the anchor. The guys went to explore the shore, then came back to pick me up and we all crossed to Constantine Harbor, which the chart showed as having three feet of depth. We crisscrossed, checking the depths, then went in with the flood and checked two spots for anchoring. Saw a mink on the shore twice.

On the return crossing we went by a moored barge—Barge *450-1*, a rapid response oil spill recovery barge. Three guys were at the stanchions—one from New Orleans, one from Phoenix, one from Wasilla, AK. They work on/off sixty or forty-two days year-round. There are three other barges like theirs in the sound and one in Valdez.

MAP 13
KAYAK ISLAND TO SEWARD

• ANCHORAGE   *Barry Arm*   VALDEZ

WHITTIER

*Prince
William
Sound*   CORDOVA

*Hinchinbrook
Island*

SEWARD   *Montague
Island*

N

20 Miles   *Gulf
of
Alaska*   *Kayak Island*

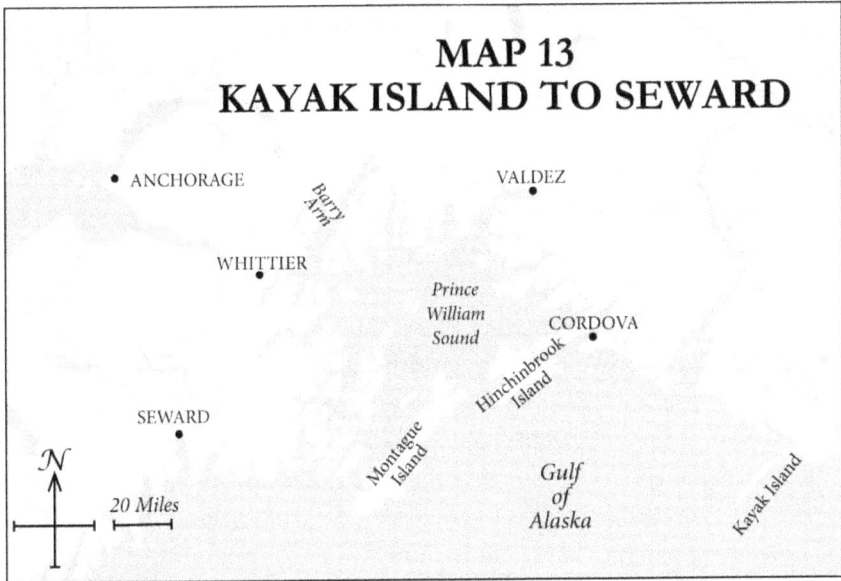

Naively, I ask, "How often do you get called out?"

"We've been here since 1989," went the reply.

After we returned, we took up the anchor and headed out of Port Etches. As we did, the tug *Alert* called us on Channel 16. He'd heard Don talking to the guys on *450-1*. He asked what kind of boat we have. "That's a beautiful boat. I've been admiring it."

"Want to trade straight across the board?"

That tug cost $20,000,000!

At the west side of Hinchinbrook Island we saw about two dozen tufted puffins, common terns, and Arctic terns.

We came around to north side of Hinchinbrook to a cove that is unnamed on the chart. Lethcoes' *Cruising Guide to Prince William Sound* calls it Double Bay, the *Alert* tug called it Davis Bay. The entrance is tricky and the bay fairly shallow. Now it's 2140 hours and blowing like hell, as we face into a southeast wind. There's a resident sea otter here but we don't sight anything else at the moment.

May 31, Saturday: 0030 hours. It's light outside as Don redoes the snubber using medium-sized line along with the thinner line, just in case the thinner one breaks. A storm started at 2200 hours. I went to bed at 2030 after having showered and checked everything. Before this I stood for about twenty minutes in the pilothouse, since there was supposed to be a solar eclipse, only visible in upper B.C. and Alaska. The sky was covered so we couldn't see the sun, but I noticed that it was darker when I went to bed than when we got up at 0030 hours. I had set the alarm for 0600 but in the middle of night I apparently turned it off mistakenly and we awoke at 0700.

We had planned to anchor inside Heather Bay, at the entrance to Columbia Glacier, but the bergs and ice are quite thick and the southeasterly wind threatened to close entry to Jade Harbor, so we came on in Valdez Arm to Sawmill Bay, which is a Marine Park. Our call on Channel 16 was answered by Dave and Evie Frisby, aboard *Enetai*. They were in the northwest corner of Long Bay and advised against Jade Harbor. They will meet us tomorrow in Sawmill Bay. There's no evidence here in the Sound of indiscriminate clear-cutting, as in B.C. and Southeast Alaska.

We're surrounded by snowy peaks. S/V *Rose* from Unalaska is anchored here and providing a nice photo op. At 2230 hours the M/V *Billie Sue* comes in and anchors after fishing all afternoon in the entrance.

I opened a jar of king salmon put up by Brandt and Tina Petersen in Yakutat and decided that would be our supper. I made chocolate pudding and we watched *A River Runs Through It* on the computer.

I'm tired of being afraid and tired of pretending I'm not afraid. How do I do what I do? How do I overcome fear?

June 1: Harlequin ducks play in the rocks north of us. I count seven in all, the first we've seen in years. They play the little back eddies around the rocks. Three sit atop a rock and survey the area.

Sawmill Bay, where we meet up with Evie and Dave Frisby, of Duncan, B.C. *Enetai* is a forty-nine foot trawler with classic lines. Dave is a "brother" to Don. Supper and evening on *Enetai*. Shrimp, salmon and potato salad.

June 2, Monday: This morning there are six boats in Sawmill Bay: *Enetai*, *Baidarka*, *Billie Sue*, S/V *Rose*, a twenty-five foot sailboat from Valdez crewed by a man and his grand-daughter from Soldatna, and a little aluminum runabout. (No one used their anchor light!)

Up anchor at 0530 hours. Dave and Evie unhooked from us fifteen minutes earlier.

Sawmill Bay "meet and greet." John Leone at right. Photo by David Frisby.

Valdez. This place is surrounded on all sides by peaks that plunge into the sea in a "bowl." It has a great museum and a Safeway store. Some locals complain about the prices, but many items cost less than in Anacortes. Milk (Matanuska) is two gallons for $5. Swiss cheese costs about the same as in Anacortes. I spent three hours at the laundry; breakfast at Totem; Safeway; sporting goods.

The "Like Home" laundry, charges $1.75 a load; it's crowded. This is tattoo country; every man and woman I've seen so far has a tattoo. The one woman I saw "up town" who was nice-looking was driving a big SUV.

June 4, Tuesday: 0800-1130 hours: prepared carrot salad; did dishes; washed hair; downloaded photos and made a CD; made a call to Aunt Lois.

1130-1230: post office; museum to buy books.

1200-1315: Safeway, $297, with ten percent off for senior day! Jim Lethcoe drives John back to the boat with the groceries. I walk and shop at a fish store to buy Copper River red salmon and halibut for dinner.

1400-1700: stow groceries.

1715: walk to museum.

1730-1800: visit museum so late they let me in free.

1800-1815: back to Safeway to buy tomatoes and to the liquor store to buy beer. Evie Frisby is there and helps carry tomatoes. I carry a twelve-pack of beer.

1830: prepare sliced tomatoes for salad; slice bread; get ready for guests; John has the salmon prepared already.

1900: Lethcoes and Frisbys arrive; dinner; conversation; heated discussion till 2200 hours.

2200-2300: clean up galley; make bed; Don helps with the bottom sheet, then the top sheet, then climbs in between them while I put the rest of the duvet and blanket on top.

June 5, Wednesday: Up at 0545 hours, leave Valdez 0600 for Jade Harbor. Anchor in Jade Harbor after test-anchoring in two other places. The bight on the south side of Heather Island is guarded by a pair of huge Canada geese.

Jade Harbor is free of ice and has a "window" looking northeast toward the Columbia Glacier. The shoreline is cut by tidal action, and has skinny trees from alpine elevations to the waterline. Trees branch down and hang over the water, as in Southeast Alaska and B.C. There are green pasture-like areas between the stands of trees. Not a ripple in Jade Harbor. The guys go hiking with Dave Frisby for two and a half hours, trying to get to the base of the Columbia. No deal, it's too far. They hiked at least four

Valdez.

miles total. In the morning I slept for three hours, then for another one and a half hours in the afternoon. I was exhausted from the day in port.

Leave Jade Harbor at 1025 hours. Follow *Enetai* west to Cedar Bay; check out Jackson Hole, in Campbell Bay; then we pass Iceberg Point and we're out into Prince William Sound with large rollers to beam. Dave leads us through a Fairmount Island shortcut to avoid the seas. We go around to Granite Bay to anchor-check. Don wants to go into the innermost cove. John and I advise against it, since the williwaws are bad, visibility is bad and it's raining heavily. We did a test anchor—bad bottom (no hold). Then to Cedar Bay, where *Enetai* was waiting to lead us in to the inner bay. A perfect alpine setting, and flat calm. Continuous rain all day. Dinner and a video on *Enetai*. Afterward, Evie and I talked for one and a half hours (woman talk).

June 6: D-Day Anniversary. At the head of Cedar Bay are four waterfalls; to the northwest, a thousand-foot alpine ridge with granite knolls, bluffs, grassy and low forests to the northwest; to the southwest, a 1540-foot peak with snow fields. It reminds me of Thousand Island Lake in the Sierra. But in the Sierra the alpine meadows start at 8000 feet. Here, they start at sea level.

John and Don say fifty years from now Prince William Sound will be the Desolation Sound of Alaska.

We see a light green spot where the chart indicates sufficient depths and suspect jellyfish. Yup. Moon jellyfish breeding grounds. A gray jay perches on the port "fish" chair for two minutes, then flies off. A new sighting.

To bed at 2230 hours. It's still light. Don wears a mask over his eyes.

June 7, Saturday: Up at 0550 hours. The guys get the dinghy down; cocoa and tea; up anchor. Blue sky. Fog in Unakwik Inlet.

0630: Underway to Jonah Bay

0650: Four sea otters

0710: John and Don take off in the dink to explore the entrance to Jonah. I stand off in *Baidarka*.

0915: Mueller Cove. A pair of mergansers, male and female.

Every day I think I'll be able to lay down what I do each hour "to write home about." Our kids and grandkids have no idea whatsoever and probably don't give a hoot. Our friends think we're on a grand "holiday."

> **Taco pie:** made from brisket of beef with a taco package. I added Greek olives, half a can of corn, topped with gruyere. Layered corn tortillas first "couche," then the meat, then half of the sauce, then more tortillas and the rest of the sauce. A big hit!

But I complain about how tired we are. Most of my creativity comes out through cooking and meal planning. There's not much time for anything else.

Olsen Cove. 60°52.06'N, 147°36.62'W. Landlocked if you get inside the bar (least depth is three feet). The cove is full of the most and largest fish we've seen on the entire trip! Eagles too. John goes out fishing for an hour or so; comes back with nothing; gets the lure Brandt Petersen gave him in Yakutat and returns fifteen minutes later with a beauty. He goes out again and comes back with another.

1500 hours. Enter Agaguat Bay, where Susie and Dave Sczawinski, of Pristine Products, have an oyster farm—850 floats, each with one or more pens. She is from Santa Barbara and Oakland, he from Seal Beach, CA. She came to Alaska twenty-four years ago and met Dave. They've been in Agaguat for twelve years. After the *Exxon Valdez* oil spill, they studied the flows of the oil and looked at aerial photos to choose this place for their oyster farm. When they applied for the permit they put in for three spots and got them all. They live here year-round in a WWII-era barge, and get deliveries via the Whittier-Cordova barge, which comes by three days a week, or by float plane. Susie has a super attitude ("Met a wonderful guy; live in a beautiful place...").

Shoup Lagoon. Cocktails and dinner. The passage into the lagoon follows an S-curve with depths in the fairway at mid-tide about twelve feet minimum. I could see the bottom the whole way through. Once we were through the narrows the fresh water flowing out on top nearly stopped the boat while the saltwater was still flooding in. We have our "happy hour" anchored with the five pound Danforth in the middle of the inside lagoon. We have the rear door open, with the sun shining through!

June 8, Sunday: Don eating his multigrain bread which had been vacuum-packed, compressed and frozen, says, "This is like eating a bucket of hay that some cow stomped on."

I said, "You could tie a line around it and drop it for anchor."

Dink to shore—all three of us. We tie to a tree and hike up the "lawn," which is a bog. Water oozes out with each step we make. Small streams meander here and there cutting into the bog. Above shore on the slopes are tiny flowers: pink lantern-shapes (3-4 millimeters) along the wetter spots; ground dogwood around the base of small hemlock or spruce bushes; buttercups; beach strawberry; blueberry.

In Cascade Bay, we meet *For Play* (Cliff and Linda Ricketts) and *Sea Alaska* (Barbara and Dick Crittenden). They're all from Eagle River.

In front of the cascade I spotted a rock fish about fourteen inches long with orange and yellow spots and butterfly-like pectoral fins.

Crossing the sound and approaching Esther Passage, we see the most boats (pleasure craft) we've seen since Kalinin Bay, north of Sitka—six of them, plus *Enetai* and *Baidarka*.

At the northwest exit of Esther Passage we meet kayaker Kip Melling, an avalanche instructor from Eagle River. We invited him aboard for cocoa. He carries a radio and GPS. Makes his own dried vegetables and fish. "I eat good!"

Barry Arm. Cascade, Barry and Coxe Glaciers fall to the sea at the head. We pull in a quarter-mile from the snout of Cascade and stand off, listening to the glacier crack and break, its sound resonating like dynamite and echoing in the bowl. John says, "This is like the Hollywood Bowl. The acoustics are fantastic!"

Don blows the horn and it echoes. The glacier cracks again.

The composition of each glacier is different. Cascade Glacier is precipitous and jumbled; its margins are black with the particles it grinds off the rock. Barry curves down to the north from the northeast and has a plateau of about 500 feet above the water, then drops squarely, its face in vertical chunks. Coxe comes in from the east, a more gradual "cascade" than its opposing glacier.

"I've never seen a glacier like Cascade," Don says. It really looks more like an avalanche field than a glacier.

John wants to know if Glacier Bay is as impressive. "NO!" Plus, it has all the cruise ships, other tony boats and pleasure craft. This sound is spectacular! I would come back here and spend a summer for pleasure if I could, but I don't want to ride these seas again.

171

Barry Arm.

Earlier today we rendezvoused with Dave and Evie and exchanged salmon (John's) and shrimp (theirs). Tonight John's preparing the salmon (chum) filets; we have mashed potatoes to go with it.

Anchor in Serpentine Cove below a black, black glacier covered in rock, dirt, gravel. Above us are three hanging glaciers.

June 9, Monday: We leave Serpentine at 0830 hours. It takes fifteen minutes to up anchor because we had 175 feet of chain out. Pass Surprise Glacier, which is distinctive for its black spine. I wonder whether up above somewhere the glacier splits across a rocky spike, then meets again bringing with it the dirt and rock to its center. Everywhere there are hanging glaciers, in addition to the tidewater glaciers. About two miles north of Harriman Glacier we sight a flock of puffins—the most in quantity we've seen so far—also a lone sea otter, sleeping. We couldn't tell if he was dead or alive, he lay so rigidly on the water with his feet crossed. But as we motored by he raised his head slightly and watched us go by. Otherwise he made no move to go under. We were so transfixed watching him we didn't think to take a telephoto shot, which I could easily have done with my 200 millimeter lens.

A float plane flies over and lands on the moraine to the east of Harriman Glacier.

Overnight in Bettles Lagoon.

June 10, Tuesday: Hummer Bay is huge—a third to half a mile across near the head, which opens into a wide valley. The margins are either grassy, looking like a tended golf course, or gravelly beaches. Dead snags line some of the beaches; their "death" appears to be from tidal wave rather than inundation, because elsewhere in the bay the trees are undisturbed. Geese occupy the western of the two islets inside the entrance. They fly around, warning us off and honking raucously.

1200 hours. Almost to Whittier harbor. Susie Sczawinski called Whittier "witless," and thinks people who live here are "part of the witness protection program."

Don tells me I've been so nice that I should go buy myself a nice dress. You have to know Whittier to catch this humor.

Whittier is a one-lane town. The harbor is tight but we get a slip for a few hours. Leonard Jones, Whittier Harbormaster, comes on board so Don can interview him. Debbie, on *Caspar*, gives me ride to and from the "market." This has basic supplies; not much in the way of vegetables, although they have broccoli, romaine, zucchini and cantaloupe. Milk from Matanuska Valley still reads 6/13/03, which is what we bought in Valdez and which went sour 6/8/03. I bought taco fixings.

Debbie tells me not to eat a Buffalo Burger: "Lots of dogs have been disappearing and the woman who owns the place cooks with a cigarette in her mouth."

I comment on the fact that almost everyone seems to smoke in Alaska. "There's not much else to do!" Debbie replies.

Anchor overnight in Culross Cove, at the north end of Culross Passage.

June 11: Encounter a French flag-bearing sailing vessel (about thirty feet; two guys) in Culross middle narrows, then a second bearing an American flag in the courtesy position (forty-five feet; three guys). I gave a call on Channel 16 in French, but got no contact from either one.

I LIKE Culross Passage.

Deep Water Bay—another favorite! Glacial polish, glacial cuts, scree and talus. John says, "This is a perfect example of land renewing itself after glacial retreat." A white sand beach at the head has a waterfall that tumbles over two consecutive rock falls, one fifty feet inland from the exit falls. There are boulder piles; sheared off rocks. Half a mile from the beach we kicked up sand from the bottom. This is the most spectacular bay we've visited to date, in my opinion.

Anchor at 1650 hours in "Nellie Juan Anchorage" in Derickson Bay. The water is an exquisite aquamarine. The surrounding shores have granite erratics and series of three 300- to 500-foot rounded granite domes. It's not as spectacular as Deep Water Bay, but I told Don I'd settle for second best.

Supper: 1 can chili refried beans layered in bottom of greased cake pan; grated onions; ½ cup grated cheddar or Monterey Jack cheese; lay 6 corn tortilla strips across in a lattice; spread a layer of taco-seasoned ground turkey and pork; pour 1 can of enchilada sauce over all; lattice 6 more tortilla strips across top; sprinkle ½ cup grated cheese on top; bake at 350° for 45-60 minutes or until cheese is bubbly.

June 12: Sunny. Check out Blue Fjord Hook inside the northeast corner of Blue Fjord, then Cannery Cove in McClure Bay.

Crossing Knight Passage, the air temperature goes down to 55°F. It's been 60 to 65°F in the inlets. Water temperature is also 55°F.

Have not seen sea otters yesterday or today, but we saw geese.

Everywhere there is evidence of the 1964 earthquake/tsunami devastation—shore features, man-made structures, or stories of lives lost.

June 13, Friday: Seven Fathom Hole, Jackpot Bay. We anchor here for lunch and see a Red-throated Loon—our first ever. There's a nice wind coming through which keeps the bugs away. First we entered Twenty-Nine Fathom Hole through a fifty-foot circle passage/narrows where the tide was still flooding.

"I don't like this!" I shouted. "You're going through it? You're crazy!" I could see light green water. John was on starboard and I was on port and we directed Don through with twenty feet maximum on either side of *Baidarka.*

"We'd better advise people to come through at slack tide," Don says, but I'm angry. John makes a joke of it. I say, "I can't keep my sense of humor like you do."

John says, "You have to have a sense of humor about Don or you'd kill him."

Friday the Thirteenth, continued:

1. Broke test anchor in Seven Fathom anchorage.

2. AC power goes off at 1445. A short somewhere? Inverter kaput, or what? The guys are trying to trouble shoot.

3. This morning when Don got up the battery was in the red so he started and ran the Gensat for an hour.

4. 1530 hours. I see the bottom in an unnamed cove on the mainland south of Otter Cove, and holler "bottom!" Within seconds we're on top of a huge rock. Don can't use the throttle because we risk damaging the prop. We have to wait while the wind blows the stern around and we pass the critical point.

5. 1600 hours. Lose AC power again.

We checked out the north end of Bainbridge Island where there's a beautiful V-shaped bay (unnamed) full of islands and rocks. The west "shore" is precipitous and treeless, but covered in bushes from the waterline to high up. Bainbridge Passage is like Grenville Channel.

The Captain is in a foul mood because of all the problems. He has a tantrum on the radio with *Enetai* trying to find their location, and is rude to John and me. "Calm down," I say. "We'll figure it out." I'm exhausted and not having fun dealing with his mood.

June 14: Day Harbor.

June 15, Sunday: A low day. Not feeling good. I'm burned out with the constant going, going, going. John is this way also. Don changes his mind about the schedule and decides not to go outside. Then he's disappointed. We anchor in Humpy Cove. Not a very good anchorage.

June 16: Into Seward by mid-morning. Visit the Sea Life Center for three hours.

June 17, Tuesday: I do three loads of washing and drying, then cut four CDs of photos—a five-hour process. I'm still beat. I do the provisioning, thinking Tuesday is seniors' day, but in Seward it's Thursday. Seward is two "towns"—downtown at the south end, with the old section of port at the north end. There's no copying service in the port area, so I have to go downtown to a drug store.

June 18: To Anchorage by rental car.

June 20, Friday: Leave Seward. Visit Mary Cove, Fox Island; Bear Glacier; also Bulldog Cove, which is guarded by triangular, sharp-pointed rocks and columnar rock. The rock is uplifted and tilted so sheer nothing grows on it. Calisto Head appears to have been cut. We see murres off the entrance to Bulldog.

The mountains on east side of Aialik Bay have no trees, just green brush—perhaps because of an avalanche?

Three Hole Bay should be named Four Hole. Rocks that sit at the north entrance point have four arches.

Two guys—kayakers—are camping on shore near South Western Glacier. It's wet!

June 21: Headed north in Harris Bay toward South Western and North Western Glaciers. We left Coleman Bay at 0645 hours and headed south out of Aialik Bay. Chose not to go through Granite Passage (big mistake), because the anchor sites are NFG, so we headed around Granite Cape. Don said, "You wonder why they didn't name it Cape Granite... because granite is the important word." And it is!

Seas which were predicted to be two feet were more than that, and they reflected off Granite Island, adding to the confusion. Add in ebbing seas, and we had ugly conditions. John was at the helm and let it get broadside. We were flung forty-five degrees to starboard, thirty degrees to port, and everything not tied down flew, including my computer table with the computer belted onto it, books not in bookcases, magazines not secured, everything under the oven. A box of Goldfish crackers under the oven flew and landed on the stairs to the lower companion way, spewing all over the stairs and into John's stateroom. I had taken half a Stugeron and didn't get seasick. Don wanted to put the "fish" down, but neither John nor I wanted to put them in while we were wallowing around. Too dangerous. Don had trouble controlling the helm but we kept going, hoping to get into Taz Basin for lunch. When we were abeam the entrance, Don said, "Okay, get ready for high performance." I put on my boots and John disappeared, then reappeared wearing his PFD. Immediately, I went in search of mine. "Bow watch time."

"I don't like the look of this," I said, as we drew closer with the depths rising.

"We'll just go have a look," Don said.

The south side of the narrow entrance was filled with kelp. We'd been warned it was "rocky!" A fifteen- to twenty-foot wide, twelve-foot-high rock blocks the entrance. North of the rock, a passageway about forty to fifty feet wide and two fathoms deep is the entry for boats. We had been warned, "Do not enter when southwest swells are running." Southwest swells *were* running and we were rolling from side to side.

David Frisby told us in a radio contact (with poor reception) earlier in the morning that they'd gone in. About all we could hear after his advice and information was, "If you do go in, be sure to go to the bathroom first." I didn't hear that, but John did and understood perfectly what David meant. Don told me to take the helm while he went out to look. We were about a hundred yards from the north entrance and could see how narrow it was.

"This is NOT good," I said. "It's too dangerous with these seas." John agreed.

Don agreed too. "Okay, we'll keep going about and heading north."

When we finally got to the end of Granite Island and into Crater Bay for a lunch break, the seas had calmed somewhat.

Later Don complimented me on being so cool about everything and so helpful. "I can handle that kind of situation," I told him. "I cannot handle your meanness and blaming others and getting so testy and nervous. All you needed to tell David when he called on the radio was, 'look, I'll call you back, we're too rolly right now,' or something like that. When you talk to me and John like that I want to leave and never set foot on this boat again."

Ten weeks of this intensity is too much! I hope Richard (Spore, who is to replace Réanne and John as crew for the return trip from Kodiak Island) hangs in there without losing his cool. Perhaps he'll be a better help to Don than John and I are, but who knows… "Anticipate, be ahead of me," ad infinitum. But you could give ninety-nine percent and it would never be enough for Don.

We met David in his inflatable off Ribbonfall Cove. He tied his tender and came aboard while we continued to Monolith Point, where *Enetai* was

177

anchored. We all talked about Taz Basin and other places to check out. David and Evie had anchored in Taz and loved it. They went through with their poles down and no problem, but they went through NOT on an ebb.

David and Evie gave us cod and silver salmon for dinner, which John prepared in his inimitable manner.

We continued on up to the head of Harris Bay where it leads to Northwest Fjord. This is separated from Harris by a two- to three-mile-wide terminal moraine. The fairway to cross the moraine is about a quarter-mile wide and shallowest depths we registered were five fathoms. Depths were shallow for about 200 to 300 yards.

At the head of Northwest Passage are six glaciers: Northeastern (nearly tidal), Redstone (not tidal), Northwestern (tidal), Ogive (the most unusual, with vertical spires like cathedrals), Anchor (where we did a test anchor), and Southwestern. All unique and impressive. We were the only boat there, and what a marvelous experience!

We tried to get in to the face of Northwestern Glacier, but there were too many icebergs blocking the way. As we were standing off Anchor Glacier it started to calve but not in the usual cracking manner. Instead, ice cascaded down in falls on either side of the center of the upper section. Anchor Glacier had "aprons" of ice—three tiers with different layered effects.

We've seen over a hundred glaciers, either close or from a distance—tidewater, hanging glaciers, receding glaciers, etc.—and all much more magnificent than what can be seen in Glacier Bay. This is "Glacier Wilderness" and I'm glad to be able to see it. But sometimes there's just too much: too much to comprehend; too much to do, write, watch electronics, take data, too far to go in a day. I was exhausted by 1700 hours and getting testy myself.

June 22, Sunday: Sunny and lovely! Granite Island, Taz Basin, 1000-1030 hours. Wonderful. Magical. Surrounded by vertical cliffs or faces on three sides. It reminded me of Ruby Lake in the Sierra.

Two Arm Bay: Paguna is longer and more easterly; Takora is to the west and shorter. Takora Head is out of the southerly swell but has very narrow swinging room. A bight on east side of Paguna was lovely—a gravel beach with subsided area behind. Possibly a lagoon inside of two waterfalls; the one to the left was substantial.

Midnight Cove, in Moonlight Bay. Tied alongside *Enetai* for the night on their anchor.

June 23, Monday: Our thirty-sixth wedding anniversary and we had the worst fight of the entire trip, after a day that began badly and continued downhill from there.

In the morning, still in Midnight Cove, the wind started up. David came aboard and said, "Not good weather news. Gale warnings for the next five days. You won't be leaving for Kodiak…"

Crisis #1. While I was downloading the digital photos (208 photos) and making CDs of them I looked out and saw we were about a hundred feet or less from *Meander*, a sailing vessel from Homer that had anchored in the cove for the night. We had to let off our lines from *Enetai*, stand off and get the dinghy aboard with the wind gusting periodically.

Crisis#2. We were running the Genset at the time we started the engine, and Don tried to set up the inverter so he could start the ship's computer. That tripped a breaker, so no AC. Don finally figured that out and told me to head out of the cove.

Crisis #3. Don kept giving me conflicting orders. I was looking at the chart on the Dell which was in small scale, so I failed to notice a rock off the northeast point of Moonlight Bay. I commented, "Evie must be at the helm; they turned left instead of going straight out…" Just after I said that the echo sounder shot up to 4 fathoms, then to 3.8. I jammed the throttle into reverse.

"No, no, neutral," Don yelled. "You're over the rock… I told you to follow *Enetai*, goddammit." He hadn't. He had said, "head on out." Which I did, unprepared. With all the panicking and unpreparedness on all our parts, and his yelling at me, I dissolved, with tears flowing down my face and my nose running.

Crisis #4. An argument about the numbering system on the Nikon camera versus the one on my computer. I had the solution: change the mode to "sequential" on the camera so they match up to numbers in the iBook. Don: "No, no, you don't understand. I want a system that works, goddammit." I tried one more time and got the same bug-eyed wall, and at that point I exploded. Then the conflagration began… Poor John was trying to stay away by going on the aft deck, etc., etc.

We finally rounded into Nuka Passage, broadside to the swells, and put the throttle in neutral and wallowed around while Don tried to send the *Baidarka Report* (our trip blog) to Mark Bunzel. Then we continued on across westerly, rounded south and into Home Cove, of which the *Coast Pilot* says only, "Home Cove, 1.5 miles south from Hardover Point, is small." It's not really; it just looks that way on Chart 16681, scale 1: 83,074.

Hardover Point is aptly named: "That's where the old sailing skippers said 'Hard over!'" Don said. We rounded in to the north side of the cove, did a "grid" sounding and anchored in about seven fathoms (200-plus feet of chain out). The southeast wind comes over a saddle of about 500 to 600 feet, but we're better protected in this section of the bay than the middle. *Enetai* went up West Arm of Nuka Bay and said gusts were forty knots. They're planning to head in here late this afternoon. Our final anchor position (resting) was 59°23.858'N, 150°42.041'W. Don turned off the GPS, so I took bearings and after two hours the bearings haven't changed.

John and I fixed an afternoon "breakfast"—potatoes done in the oven, bacon, eggs, bread, butter, jam. I woke Don for this at 1400 hours and we all were in a better mood. I still have a sore throat which was quite bad during the night.

This morning we heard Kodiak Air Station say a tsunami warning had been cancelled for Shelikof Strait. Good thing we didn't hear the original warning!

June 24, Tuesday: Layover in Home Cove, on Nuka Island. Gales, rain, poor visibility and squalls that scudded across the water and tossed the boat a bit. Patagonia weather! We all slept a good part of the day. My sore throat has gotten better but I now have a drippy nose and the crummy feeling of a real cold. Made corn meal-and-apple pancakes and pork links for breakfast.

Supper: shrimp, halibut and bread; also lemon pudding in a shortbread crumb crust, which was sort of yucky. I made the pudding because we had invited Evie and David, but I was glad they couldn't taste it. They declined the invite because they need to leave early in the morning to start on their way south.

June 25: Two hundred and fifty feet of anchor chain to raise this morning. Anchored in Tonsina Bay at 1500 hours. S/V *Perspective* is anchored in here, too—Dave and Karen Summerfeld and their two kids, Jaden and Danielle, ages seven and eleven. They live in Anchorage, leave the boat, a thirty foot Hunter, in Seward.

June 26: Up anchor and away from Tonsina at 0600 hours. Stabilisers and fish down. Seas are down substantially from yesterday, when they were ten to twelve feet. Depths are all over, from 55 to 45 to 38 to 34, 31, 22, 15 fathoms within just a fifteen-minute period. Visibility poor; the weather is dreary and dark off Gore Point.

Looking at chart 16645 Gore Point to Anchor Point—the entrance to Cook Inlet—I recall my brother's remark, "Are you going to Anchorage too?" Too bad I can't show him the chart. Shallow! Open to the south. Depths of three to six fathoms, sometimes down to ten.

John's comment re Chart 16681: "All these bears on the chart and we still haven't seen one."

Drop anchor at Port Chatham at exactly 1159 hours. Don says, "A few hours here and we can be on our way to the Barren Islands."

My cold seems to have settled in my upper neck, neck and shoulders. Now Don has a sore throat. Slept two and a half hours this afternoon. Rain all day, heavy at times. When we woke up *Meander* had picked up the Coast Guard buoy. One other small boat was anchored near the cannery shore.

June 27, Friday: Left Port Chatham 0945 hours, reached Barren Islands (Ushagat) by 1325 hours. Awesome—awe plus fearsome. Precipitous sides with folded faults, peaks that rise from sea level to a thousand feet. Stripped of everything but green carpeting. Very few trees except where protected. "Prehistoric!" John says.

This is whale territory! Twelve fathoms.

Shuyak Island—low, flat, rolling hills.

June 28: Shuyak Harbor. Sven Kelly, a trooper from Kodiak, has a cabin on the west side opposite Wonder Bay. His kayak was stolen a year and a half ago and his place was vandalized. He just recovered the kayak two days ago, on his own steam.

Kevin Murphy, at the Big Bay Ranger Station, says Shuyak Island, with three exceptions of inholdings, is all State Park. There are several Forest Service cabins, and another west of Carry Inlet across a portage.

Shuyak Harbor used to have four salteries and a barrel manufacturer. The trees here are all virgin timber. Where you see clearings, that's where the salteries and related operations were situated.

We meet Sam Barber and Fran Wilson, from Anchorage, who are paddling *Sea Eagle*, an Easy Rider kayak. Sam was a diver on the USCG cutter *Storis*, which was the flagship of the first successful transit of the Northwest Passage by U.S. Coast Guard vessels, in 1957.

Sam says of our book, "*Coast Pilot* with KOA aspirations," and that "Shuyak Narrows is a hydraulic show." Southwesterly winds are the prevailing winds in summer. "You get pounded," Sam says, "but you just have to slosh through it. One hundred and thirty knot winds are not uncommon in November. Three crabbers were circling Barren Island in a storm and all three ran their seventy-five-foot-plus boats ashore because they couldn't find a lee. Shelikof Strait is the worst weather factory." But there's good moorage on either side of Kodiak Island. On the Gulf side of Kodiak, the tide is about six feet lower than on the Strait side.

1200 hours. Port Williams. There's an old cannery here; it closed in 1979.

Weather is beautiful! Sunny and seas calm. We're able to see snow-covered mountains across Shelikof, on the Alaska Peninsula. It's imposing and rather overpowering to see what's there—and what a boat would be up against in bad weather.

1330 hours and we're cruising.

1550 hours. Heading south at six and a half knots to check out anchor sites on the east side of Afognak Island—Delfin Bay. The hills—Native lands—are highly logged here. John says, "Everyone got a new pick-up out of this."

We try to pick up the Kodiak Coast Guard station. It's a woman operator today. "She's not modulating," Don says. There's a MAYDAY, she says, but doesn't repeat or ask if any vessels heard. It's as if she doesn't know what to do.

We anchor in "West" Seal Bay by 1740 hours. When we entered we spotted about ten sea otters. After we anchored they all disappeared. Outside, they were less frightened of us, often not diving or swimming away till we were no more than a hundred feet away.

In these waters—Shelikof Strait and the Gulf—we've seen more whales, puffins (horned and tufted), storm petrels, and murres, and here on the rocky island across from us is a colony of herring gulls (probably), peeping and crying—a high-pitched call, not raucous like that of the California gull.

Don's beginning to lighten up, realizing how hard we've worked, and the fact that I'm going home has sunk in and he's beginning to miss me already. He's been telling me what a big help I've been and finally I think he believes it. Especially since the Stugeron has done its trick in preventing seasickness. What a difference sunny weather and not being seasick make! And—being appreciated.

Our Iridium satellite phone is not working. We can't send or receive emails, and then the Dell quits suddenly on its own without warning. Thank goodness we're near Kodiak! People might start to worry.

June 29, Sunday: Underway at 0840 hours to explore the east arm of Seal Bay. This isn't as pretty as the west arm but the bottom is more regular and it's easier to get into. Nothing man-made in sight other than here and there a portion of heavy poly line from a fishing vessel, or a blue tarp in shreds.

Afternoon—heading south through Marmot Strait. We sight Kodiak Island around 1400 hours and feel the swell from the peninsula that extends north from Pillar Cape. Its sides are a thousand feet high—rocky-volcanic and covered with green, Christmas tree-shaped trees, forty to sixty feet high maximum.

June 30: Left "No-Name" cove in Izhut Bay at 0600 hours. Crossed Marmot Bay with header. Lots of pitching for the first one and a half hours, then fog for twenty minutes. Now there's fog to the west and clear to the south. Depths are all over the place—162 fathoms, up to 21, then back down to 103.

Five or six fishing boats—small seiners—were all out at the entrance to No Name as we left this morning. Don remarked that they probably thought we were spies.

July 1: Saw a French flag on a sailing vessel yesterday. I called in French to the couple on board —Sylvie and Jean-François André—and learned they'd just arrived three days ago from Hawaii and plan to winter in Southwest or central Alaska. They came by in the late afternoon and had a glass of wine with us. He's a naval architect. They've been cruising, with their cat, for about sixteen years.

The ferry from Seward comes four times a week in summer; it leaves Kodiak 1655 hours, arrives Seward 0800. It goes to Dutch Harbor once a month.

The reason sea otters swim on their back with hands together is they are praying—"Don't shoot me."

July 3: Sunny but windy. We have rented a Suzuki "compact" SUV—it's more like a mini-compact—to explore Kodiak. The pavement ends at fourteen miles. There's graffiti on the rocks just after the convergence of the paved road with the gravel.

The island is a lovely green, with a few trees—spruce and alders—but mostly low bushes. There's cow parsnip, ferns, lupine, salmonberries, willows.

American River is a fishing area. The middle bay has dozens of eagles, with glacial erratics here and there along the shallows. Mesa-like rock formations at the end of a long flat spit are typical and frequent.

Kalsin Bay has a nice stand of Sitka Spruce, recognizable by the brown crowns covered with cones. There's heavy moss on the spruce trees. Cattle graze on south side of Kalsin. A couple of hippie properties are at the east end of the isthmus.

Lunch at Road's End. Halibut sandwich. Home-made strawberry rhubarb.

We drove to end of road where there are some bunkers. There are twelve of them along the Kodiak Island coast with guns, search lights—a project that began in the 1930s.

Chiniak Lake. The head is 200 to 300 feet above water, covered with lupin, wild roses, salmonberries, lavender-colored flowers, wild orchids, shooting stars. Chiniak school has eighteen students. Kids are playing in the Chiniak River.

Pasagshak River Recreation Site. It's hard not to make a comparison, but it reminds me of Tierra del Fuego or *Magallanes*. Little kids are playing in a rubber raft. The bay where the river exits has turquoise water. There's a camping area and small cabins on "stilts"—rentals or privately owned.

Back in Kodiak: Fireworks from Near Island start three minutes after midnight. We watch from the foredeck, sitting in our canvas chairs and talking with Thor and Connie Olsen, of the fishing vessel *Viking Star*. The sky is still light as the show starts, gets increasingly dark within thirty minutes. Kodiak harbormaster Marty Owen comes by during the fireworks to invite us for supper on Sunday. Unfortunately I can't go, since I leave that afternoon.

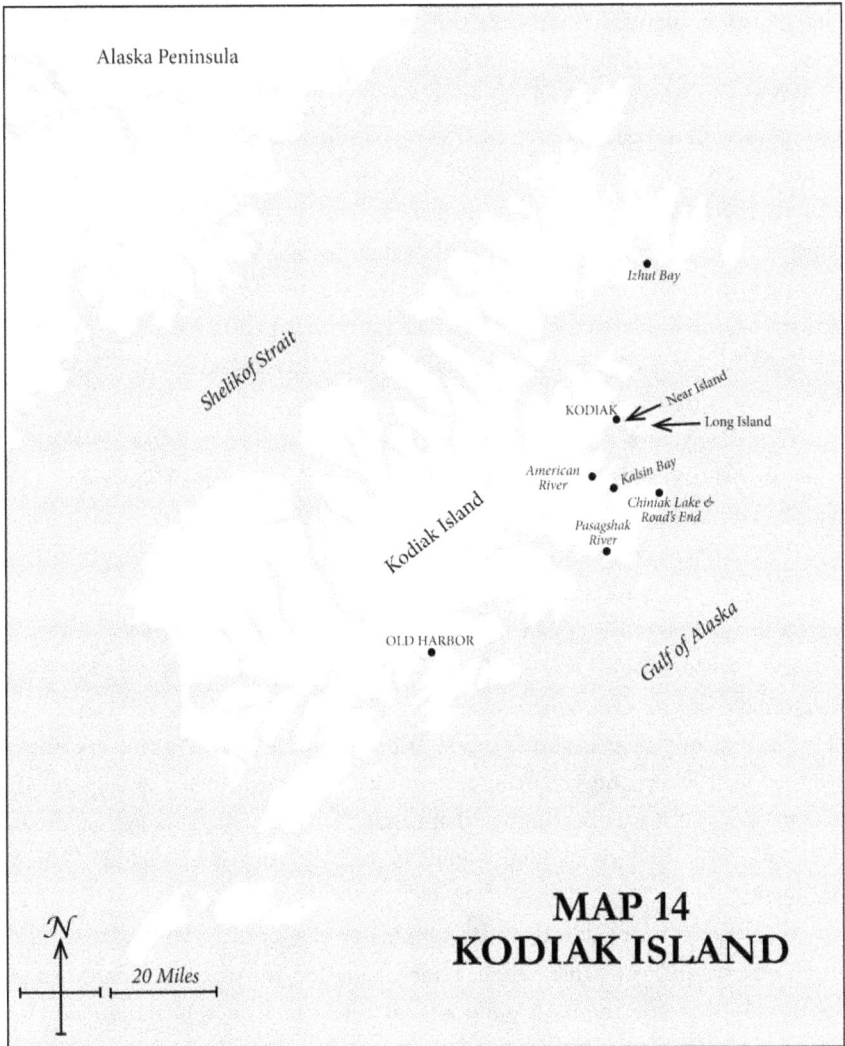

Alaska Peninsula

Izhut Bay

Shelikof Strait

KODIAK
Near Island
Long Island

American River
Kalsin Bay
Chiniak Lake & Road's End
Pasagshak River

Kodiak Island

Gulf of Alaska

OLD HARBOR

N

20 Miles

MAP 14
KODIAK ISLAND

July 4: This day has 17 hours, 54 minutes of daylight. From 1130 to 1930 hours we go out for a picnic to Long Island with the extended Olsen family on *Viking Star.*

I help Connie cut up potatoes—five to ten pounds of them (it seemed like ten!)—for potato salad, with chopped green onions, celery, etc. Connie is a general contractor, photographer and businesswoman (Amway). She's warm, exuberant, spontaneous. We take a hike for an hour to the northeast end of Long Island. Connie asks me, "What direction do you think we're going?" I tell her northeast. "You have a lot of common sense," she says.

We pass several sets of campers along the beach. Dark blue lupine en masse above the beach in places. The forest floor is spongy with moss. It's utterly quiet but for the sound of one bird's call. I see the bird flitting around the tree tops, but can't identify it. But I see a small blue eggshell lying on the path. A small dark bird that hops like a water ouzel plays on stumps and hops from shrub to shrub. The mossy floor is full of tiny pink flowers whose faces are overturned that hide their pistils and stamens from the sun. Along a tiny stream two large purple iris surprise us. "How and why are they here?"

We reach an old WWII army camp. There are rusty Quonset huts, a fallen-down cabin, the remnants of a house—perhaps officers' quarters.

"You can have that one. I'll take this one," Connie says.

"Real fixer-uppers, aren't they?" I say.

The picnic is hamburgers cooked on a foiled grill over an open fire; baked beans cooked in a can in the fire; the potato salad; pirosk—Russian fish pie with cabbage, rice, rutabaga, salmon, and a pie crust on top. Also marshmallows and Graham crackers to make "smores."

Smoke got in everyone's eyes. When Connie and I got back from another walk everyone was having "smores." Don and Thor had gone off in the skiff and it was beginning to sprinkle. We packed up, began to break down the fire, the kids hauling water up from the beach in cut-out Clorox bottles.

Five boxes, four adults and four kids in the skiff to *Viking Star.* Eric and Cecil waited on shore while Thor offloaded us and the picnic boxes and went back for them. A sailboat anchored nearby was pulling at the anchor in the wind and rain, and the hatch was open—with no one on board. Eric raced to shore in the skiff to look for the owners. They'd gone for a hike and wouldn't be back for two hours, so he let out some line for them and closed their hatch.

July 5: Foggy and rainy all day. Kodiak Safeway is touted as the biggest in Alaska, and it's the biggest I've ever seen.

Flight from Kodiak to Anchorage. One hour. We flew over the Barren Islands; the strait was covered in clouds but I could see the main island with its spit and spine. It's just as impressive from the air as from the sea. As we flew over Homer we hit a pocket and everyone was heaved upward. I commented to John, "We crossed the Gulf of Alaska without any problems and this is the most excitement we've had."

1638 hours. Taking off from Anchorage we get good view of extensive mud flats of Cook Inlet, Kenai mountains, and mountains to the southwest. The weather is clear and sunny. This country is overwhelmingly beautiful!

Flying over Northwestern Fjord and the fjord to west of it. Prince William Sound; Columbia Glacier, where the bay is still choked with ice. I see Valdez in the distance and the entrances to Cordova, then Cordova itself. Very shallow. The land looks like jungle camouflage. South of Cordova there's cloud cover for twenty-five to fifty miles along coast.

I have mixed feelings about flying home. I loved Kodiak and would have liked to spend more time there. John felt the same way. Perhaps because it's so different from every place else we'd been, and so raw, so new geologically.

As I fly south over this magnificent scenery I wonder how I can ever be content again to just cruise to B.C. Even Southeast Alaska begins to dim in comparison, although I can probably never say that in print because of our books.

After Prince William Sound, Sitka and everything south is under the clouds.

"Ladies and Gentlemen, we're beginning our descent over Puget Sound!" I wake up and look down to a brown haze, which is nothing compared to L.A. Basin, but it's depressing after having come from such pristine skies. I feel let down, disappointed. I signed on for only half the trip and now I wish I'd signed on for the entire round trip…

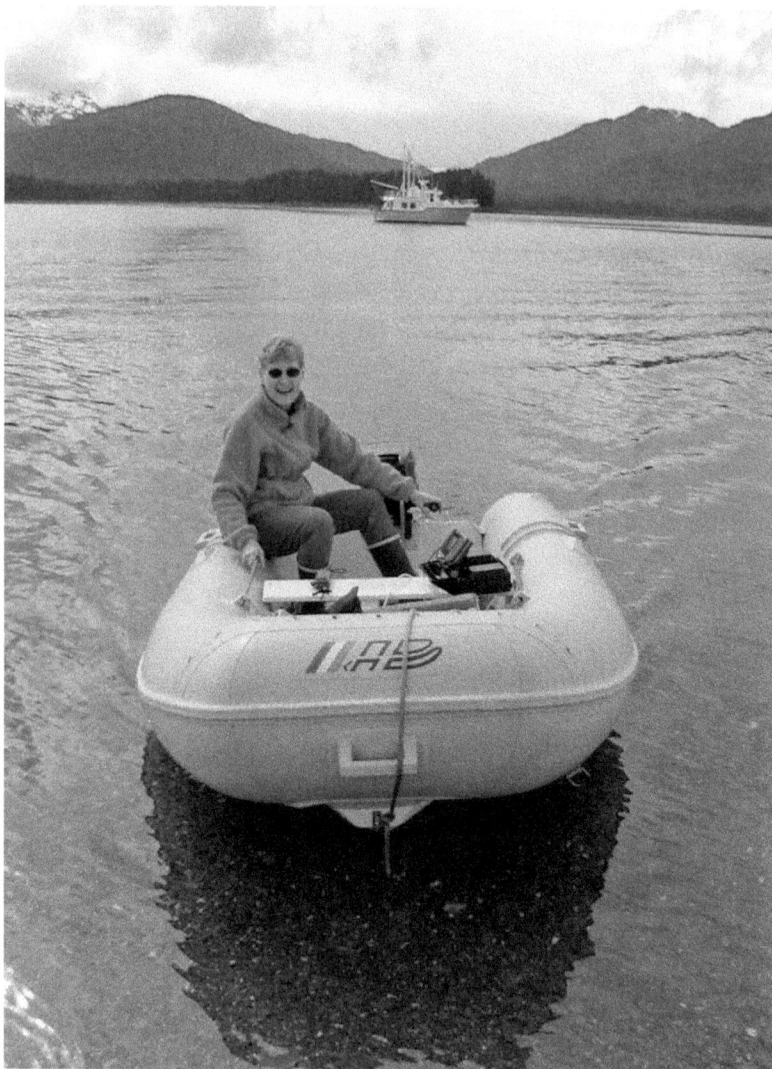

SITKA TO ANACORTES, 2003

Richard Spore, Don Odegard and Mark Bunzel crewed for Don for parts of the return trip. I rejoined Don in Sitka on August 18 for what was meant to be a "quiet and calm" final leg home to Anacortes.

August 18, 2003. Sitka. Dinner on *Home Shore,* Jim Kyle's boat, with Audrey Sutherland, who has kayaked over ten thousand miles. *Home Shore* is named for the shore east of Porpoise Islands. Jim Kyle has renovated his fishing boat as a passenger vessel, adding two full staterooms and two full heads and showers.

Audrey Sutherland was taking a week tour around Baranof to visit all the places she previously kayaked. Audrey has kayaked 8200 miles just in Alaska in all kinds of weather, camping on shore. This mileage does not include trips to Norway, New Zealand, France. "She's not into shameless self-promotion," Don says. "Otherwise she'd be passing out cards telling how many miles she's kayaked; but she just does her own thing."

Audrey is eighty-one and still going strong. Her white hair with its short pixie cut is attractive. She wears eye shadow and mascara when she's in town. We spoke a little French together. She did three weeks of intense French study in Bordeaux.

Howard Ulrich, a survivor of the July 9, 1958, tsunami in Lituya Bay: "It will happen again. I like to talk about it because it will happen again. It's happened five times in recorded history."

August 19: Dinner on *Gone with the Wind*, a beautiful thirty-six foot sailboat owned by Larry Gill, of Seattle. Larry is a retired court administrator and National Park Service "historian" with a law degree but a lively interest in history. His friend Heather Schreiber is a teacher of troubled students.

August 20, Wednesday night: Kathy Kyle and Ward Eldridge came by *Baidarka* to bring us a couple of sidebars (for our proposed Gulf of Alaska book) about their trip to Kodiak Island. They spent Fourth of July in Old Harbor, on the southeast side of Kodiak—the village which has the original Russian church. Kathy and Ward are gentle people; kind and without judgmental opinions. Ward seems so knowledgeable about history.

189

August 21, Thursday: *Royal Caribbean* pulls out of Sitka, which lacks a cruise ship dock. Cruising is a "maturing" industry here, though 800,000 passengers per season come to Alaska.

1800 hours. We are hobby-horsing east in Peril Strait at five and a half knots. The barometer reads about 1004 millibars. White caps cover the chop.

1840 hours. Heading into Appletone Cove, Baranof Island, on the south side of Peril Strait just past the entrance to Rodman Bay.

August 22: Up anchor at 1015 hours. Don and I argue over the route I took for exit from the anchorage. He criticizes today's blog entry, says it is badly written—I give too many details about the things I have to keep as "trade secrets"; or else, I don't give enough details. He says I have to study journalism to write or take notes quickly. The last I know. I also know that I do not promote myself. But I want to be correct and kind, not arrogant and egoistic and vain.

Later: "I think Baranof is the most beautiful of the islands in Alaska," Don says. Certainly it has the most dramatic peak with its year-round snow and steep high sides.

1845 hours. Frederick Sound. Sighted a half dozen whales at the west entrance. This is always a good place to see them. Chatham Strait was the calmest we've seen it. We had gentle swells from astern as we headed south on the ebb.

I'm struck by the numbers of islands that have a "thumb" or "tower" protruding from them. Magnificent sunsets tonight. I say sunsets plural because every fifteen minutes has brought a distinct new set of colors.

Anchor in Davidson Bay, 2115 hours.

August 23: Rocky Pass. With all the nav-aids (forty-three total) it's much easier than it used to be, but still it requires "heads up" and total vigilance.

Stopped at the Wooden Wheel Resort, in Port Protection, to see Starla (a woman we met on a previous trip). She says that last year they went through four cooks at the Wooden Wheel: the first one quit after two weeks, said it was too cold and rainy; the second got mad and started breaking up furniture; the third got drunk; number four got picked up by the State Patrol on an arrest warrant.

We visit for an hour and a half, then head east, down Sumner Strait and through Kashevarof Passage to Exchange Inlet, which we enter after dark under radar. Mercury shows itself just above the horizon as we set anchor. I confuse it for a small plane for a few moments. Before bed I go outside to look at the sky. It's a mass of stars—the sky as brilliant as that of the eastern Sierra.

August 24: Left Exchange Inlet at 1030 hours. Every day is a challenge. Today it's the gillnetters in Clarence Strait. We have to scan constantly with the binoculars to see their floats. At Ratz Harbor we were going to quit at 1315, but decided to continue on to Lyman Anchorage. A road comes in here; there are campers on shore.

I'm depressed today because of Don's impatience and my poor humor.

August 25: Leaving Meyers Chuck this morning I thought: if X leaves Port A at 0640 hours traveling at six knots, and Y leaves Port A at 0650 hours traveling at ten knots, how long will it takes Y to pass X, and at what point? This is the sort of algebraic formula I learned to do in high school but couldn't do to save me now.

Seiners are out along Cleveland Basin.

As we enter Tongass Narrows, the *Carnival Spirit* passes us—ten stories of apartments above the waterline deck. The aft section of the top deck has a blue water-slide that winds around, obviously into a pool. From a mile aft, the ship appears to be a skyscraper with a set of "wings" on its top. These are its smokestacks, out of which pours dark smoke.

We also hear the discourteous radio users: Courteously spoken: "Cruise ship shore boats, please slow down; you're causing too much wake along shore." No response. Request repeated. Finally a response: "Whine, whine, whine…"

I brought *Baidarka* into Foggy Bay under radar, Nobeltec and visual, going 1000 r.p.m., 0 r.p.m., 1000 r.p.m., 0 r.p.m., ad infinitum.

Tonight it's dark at 2040 hours. Tomorrow we advance our watches again to Pacific Daylight Time and it will be dark, instead, at 2140. We're getting farther east! 130°W now. From Kodiak to upper B.C., it's 152°W to 130°W.

Carnival Spirit.

August 26: Foggy Bay to Prince Rupert. Left 0830 hours, Alaska Daylight Time. A fishing seiner between Foggy Point and Tree Point caused us some consternation; we have to watch constantly for the red floats indicating end of their nets. I took us out of Foggy Bay, as I had entered, following the same track. This morning the tide was zero, so we had less depth even than yesterday. For the narrowest part I got too far to the west and had to back up and go forward till I had the boat on course again.

Arrived in Prince Rupert at 1730 hours. Don called in to Customs. No problem clearing by phone. They didn't care how much Canadian alcohol we had, asked only about the American stuff, and did not ask about produce.

August 31: Leave Prince Rupert at 0700 hours. I lie down at 0815 at the end of the Prince Rupert harbor limits, wake up at 0915. Don says, "Why are you getting up?"

"To check on you and see if you need anything."

"I'm fine. Why don't you sleep some more?"

I lie down again and he covers me with an army blanket. I sleep until 1050. I must have been exhausted.

A tug passes going north at 1430 off south end of Nabannah Bay, Grenville Channel. How do they determine length of cable to tow, I wonder. There must be a mathematical formula for determining length due to tonnage, height, etc.

Along Grenville Channel at 53°37.44, 129°43.45 there are about three spots of sea fog along the top of the water.

2000 hours. Anchored in Coghlan Anchorage, after 81.9 nautical miles.

September 1: Monday. Leave Coghlan at 0730 hours. Anchor in Rescue Bay, on the southeast side of Jackson Narrows Provincial Park. 77.7 nautical miles.

September 2: Leave Rescue Bay at 0915 hours. I take us through Gunboat Passage while Don snoozes. Nobeltec craps out—as it will again.

Ocean Falls is becoming an artists' community. This is "Paint Ocean Falls Weekend." Planks have been replaced; there's yellow paint on caution areas.

Supper: Rick, Nate and George on board for fish soup. They each have a Ranger 21 and are traveling as a convoy of three boats: *Kentucky Colonel, Wren,* and *Molly B.*

September 6: Wallace Bay. A recent rock and tree avalanche has wiped out the third house from north. The slide to bare rock started just below a 2000-foot ridge.

The three Ranger-21s are there: we have them aboard for more fish soup.

At 51°09.22'N, 127°46.65'W we sight Gary Lundgren, from Colorado, rowing a 20-foot lapstraked sailboat/rowboat with a blond dog. We ask if he needs anything. He hesitates, then says no. He's trying to get to Miles Inlet. He does say his hands hurt. Afterward, I wonder if we should have offered him a tow.

September 7: In Namu, Don jumped off *Baidarka* while the stern was still about five feet from the dock. The dock surged up and Don's left knee went crack and buckled beneath him. The three Ranger guys, who were at the dock too, secured the stern for me. I jumped off, worried that Don had broken his leg. He said, "No, it's my knee and I can't get up."

Rick and Nate helped me apply a knee brace from the medical kit, but Don still couldn't move. A nurse from an adjacent boat examined Don's leg. She didn't think anything was broken but said he should stay off it for a few days. That means I will have to be skipper and get us home, as well as being nurse, cook, etc.!

September 7: Queen Charlotte Sound was a pond, fortunately. I was able to engage the autopilot and run downstairs to Don on the saloon settee. He was full of questions about my course settings, asked for juice, then for the pee bottle.

"Take it slow, very slow, into Miles Inlet." Would there be room for us? Don gave me anchoring instructions. I dropped the hook, let out a hundred feet of chain, put the engine in reverse to test it. It held. Before this, I had been at the helm for ten hours straight. Don asked from the settee if I would fix him something to eat. "I'm kind of hungry." I fixed us both pea soup and crackers, changed the cold compress on his knee for the fourth time, set the depth alarm at two fathoms and the radio on Channel 16, and flopped on the pilothouse berth, exhausted.

In the dark, the VHF crackled. *Explorer*, sixty feet, ninety tons, asked if they could raft alongside us. Three other boats were in Miles Inlet with us. There was no room for *Explorer* anywhere else. Don was snoring, so I had to make the decision. I said yes. I hope the forecast for calm weather through the night is correct.

September 9: At 0500 hours, neither *Baidarka* nor *Explorer* had budged, but the inlet was shrouded in heavy fog. I would have to navigate by radar. This is okay with two people, but I would be at the helm on my own.

Richard aboard *Explorer* came to my rescue, instructing me over the VHF to follow him. Visibility in Queen Charlotte Strait was about 100 feet. I followed *Explorer* as close astern as I dared.

Three hours south of Miles Inlet, Nobeltec crashed. I radioed *Explorer* to slow down while I dug out the paper charts from under the pilothouse berth. The ones for Johnstone Strait and southward weren't there. Don has always said, "If your electronics haven't failed you yet, they will." Today he says, "We know this area like the backs of our hands so I didn't bring them. We had so many with the Gulf and Southeast Alaska there wasn't room for them anyway."

If Don wasn't already injured, I'd have done the job myself!

I demanded he get himself up to the pilothouse and help. Straight away he bombarded me with questions and instructions. Finally I told him to be quiet. I was the skipper, I would determine what was safe, what was not. His job was to keep his eyes on the radar and let me know if he saw anything that looked like a hazard. That shut him up. For the rest of the afternoon he did what I asked.

September 10: Cordero Lodge through Blind Channel to Discovery Passage. Seymour Narrows before slack. I'm at the helm, "riding" the whirlpools and ripples, when I look up at the SOG [speed over ground]. "Two knots. Shit! We're doing just two knots." Don and I both laugh. There's a three knot current against us.

We get through Ripple Rock area and pull around the corner to the west of Nymph Cove just to rest and have lunch. The current pushes us toward shore for the first twenty minutes. Then it finally reverses and we're more stable.

On to Campbell River, where we pull into a slip around 1330 hours, in pouring rain.

I tell Don, "I'm going uptown to buy a few things." At the marine store, I spend $300 on paper charts. Don is upset with me, says we have them all at home. "Yes, but I'm the skipper and I need them to get us there!"

The wind picks up and blows till around 2200 hours.

Bill and Madelyn Castle, M/V *Meridian*, homeport Sitka, AK. Madelyn: "Whenever we come to port there are always eight to ten people around you, so we've never had a chance to meet you." Bill: "We bought your books for a reason—to keep us off the rocks—and they do!" They've made thirteen trips to Alaska and back.

September 11: Leaving Campbell River, we spend the first couple of hours in fog. Campbell River to Nanaimo—eighty nautical miles. My navigation from lunch onward was not fun. I hit a log trying to set a waypoint on the electronic charting. Bad afternoon—and it's tough trying to be Don's feet as well as do all the normal first mate stuff!!

September 12: Barry and Irene McPhee, S/V *Morning Light*, from Lahaina, HI. They're on their way to the Broughton Islands. They have used our *South Coast of British Columbia* book, like it very much.

I see our friend Trish at the dock at Nanaimo. She compliments me —"Can't believe you two do what you do."

"I don't like to admit I'm seventy because I don't feel like seventy," I say. We talk about our grandmothers at age seventy—they seemed so OLD! Trish's mom and grandmother both died at seventy-one.

I maneuver the boat around and move to the north side of "J" dock, so we're facing out, not in as on "I" dock. We were the innermost vessel on south side of "I", so I would have had a terrible time trying to back out.

September 13: Winston Bushnell (Nanaimo-based world sailor), regarding *Exploring the North Coast of British Columbia*, and the places behind Ocean Falls: "If you die before I do (which I don't think is going to happen) I'm gonna put a monument to you up there... All those damn little coves. You were right on!" He adds, "Don, for all the anchoring you do and haven't got into trouble, you must be doing it right."

Don "waxes eloquent" (his words) as we sight Mt Baker. He says, "Write down xxxx."

"You write it down," I say (for the first time in five months). "I'm not your secretary."

"Are we partners or not?"

"Your idea of a partner is not the same as my idea of a partnership."

Don laughs.

EPILOGUE

At the end of each *Baidarka* voyage, our last stop before Anacortes was always Nanaimo. The boat was always filthy by then, as we had no means of cleaning it while we were cruising. In spite of this, at the end of our 2007 voyage a Canadian couple came up to us on the dock in Nanaimo, said they recognized our boat from our guidebooks and magazine articles, and offered to buy it! We told them it wasn't really for sale as we still had a book to finish, but we might consider selling it in a year or two. This was okay with the Canadians, who said they would have to sell both their own boat and their house before they could do the deal. Then they contacted us again in December of that year…

December 20, 2007: Don receives an email from Ian H. They've sold their house and boat and want to proceed with the purchase`of *Baidarka*. I burst into tears. "I'm not ready…" I sob for several minutes. It's not just giving up the boat, it's the entire process—of accepting Old Age, of ceding responsibility for ourselves, of losing our independence. I feel so young on the boat; alive; in charge. NOW WHAT?

APPENDICES

BOATS AND PEOPLE

1992

May 3	Nanaimo	*Sea Crews*, Icelandic Air employees
May 6	Squirrel Cove	*Divona Sea*, Sechelt, BC
May 7	Blind Channel	Edgar & Annemarie Richter, resort owners
May 8	Port Neville	Lorna Hansen Chesluk & family
May 17	Bishops Bay	*Julie Ann*, Margie & Frank Fletcher, Anacortes, WA
May 19	Lowe Inlet	Bob Sampson, solo kayaker, Gig Harbor, WA
May 21	Foggy Bay	*Kings Ransom*, Tom & Trudie King
May 31		*Frontier Queen*
May 31		*Rainbow*
Sept 23	Prince Rupert	Genevieve & Jean-Louis Doudeau, French travelers
Sept 28	Bishop Bay	*Coast Ranger* , Tom Frazer, B.C. Fisheries officer, and his friend Barry
Oct 1	Fury Cove	*Brigadoon*, Kathy Gallizio & Bill Lowe
Oct 4	Minstrel Island	Sylvia & Grant Douglas, resort owners
Oct 5	Port Neville	Lorna Hansen Chesluk
Oct 6	Lasqueti Island	Rena, German-born local resident

1994

April 22	Friday Harbor	Peter & Anita McMullen
April 28	Port Neville	Lorna Chesluk & family
May 4	Egg Island	Judy & Stan Westhaver, Lighthouse keepers
May 6	Addenbroke Island	Dawn & Mike Kovacs
May 10	Mathieson Channel	*Sidekick*

May 13	Kumealon Island	*Time Thief*
May 17	Ketchikan	*Sumdum*, Geoff Simmonds & Marzette Ellis, Ketchikan, AK
May 19	Point Baker	Joe Sebastian, fisherman
May 21	Warm Springs Bay	*Matatua*, Sydney, Australia
May 21	Warm Springs Bay	Emeric Fissett , French kayaker & adventurer
August 22	Hydaburg	Judy, owner, TJ's Café
August 24	Prince Rupert	*John Brix*, Ocean-going tug
August 27	Higgins Passage	*Nawitka*, Mel Bacon, and his dog, Stormy, Sidney, BC
August 28	Kynumpt Harbor	*Chrystal Vision*, Scott Davis, rower, Nordland, WA
August 28	Bella Bella	Alex Frid & Gail Rothenburg, kayakers, Haines Junction, YT
Aug 30-Sept 5	Bull Harbor	*Forevergreen*, Rod Nash, Ron Hayes, Crested Butte, CO
Sept 1	Julian Cove	Chris Bradley, Quatsino Boatyard
Sept 5	Nuchatlity	Dan & Fyffe DeVault and kids Janine & Evan
Sept 5	Nootka Mission	Kevin Hills; Anna & Gordon Lang, Earl & Louise Johnson
Sept 7	Kyuquot	Ray Williams
Oct 23	Friday Harbor	Barbara Marrett

1995

August 12	Prince Rupert	*Neuron II*, Harry & Barb Patton, Seattle, WA
August 18	Thurston Harbor	*Haida Crest* (Fishing vessel)
August 18	Thurston Harbor	*Ocean Light*
August 22	Juan Perez Sound	*Endeavour, Clavella*
August 26	Shearwater	Silveci & Del D'Ancangelo, Black Creek, BC
August 26	Shearwater	*Sara*, Lizzie & John Herchenrider, Granville, OH
August 26	Shearwater	*South Shore* , Newport, OR
August 28	Goldstream Harbor	*Sundowner*, Blaine, WA

| August 28 | Fury Cove | *Sabi, Sunshine Patriot, Alicia Marie* |
| Sept 1 | Port McNeill | Hiltje Binner, Harbourmaster |

1996

June 25	Port Neville	Lorna Hansen Chesluk & family
June 26	Port McNeill	*Metolius*, Cara & Bob Barringer, Hailey, ID
June 26	Port McNeill	*Summer Wind*, Bob & Dolores Rolfe, Mary Louise & Herb Stewart
June 27	Alert Bay	*Vixen*, Tom Stringfield & Vickie Nissen, Portland, OR
June 29-30	Echo Bay	*SacaLaurie*, Warren & Laurie Miller, Orcas Island, WA
June 30	Sullivan Bay	*Carousel*, Gloria & Tom Burke
June 30	Sullivan Bay	*High Flight*, Bill Swain
June 30	Sullivan Bay	Pat Finnerty & Lynn Whitehead, local residents
July 1	Duncanby Landing	Ken & Judy Gillis, resort owners
July 1	Duncanby Landing	John & Randi Sanger
July 1	Duncanby Landing	*Sundowner*, Del & Inez
July 2	Big Frypan Bay	*Sagebrush Sailor*, Betty & Bob Lynch
July 3	Fitz Hugh Sound	*Illahee*
July 4	Bella Coola	Kevin O'Neill, Assistant Harbourmaster
July 7	Ellerslie Lagoon	*Evergreen, Starlite, Charisma*
July 7	Ellerslie Lagoon	*Lucky Girl*, George & Evelyn Rasmussen, Bremerton, WA
July 19	Lawson Harbor	*Sage Hen*, Sandy & Alan Rawson, Fargo, ND
July 20	Prince Rupert	*Diamond Sea*, Frank Kelly & Liz Cochien, Vancouver, BC

2000

| July 20 | Tenakee Hot Springs | *Northern Trawler*, Carlene & Keith, Port Townsened, WA |
| August 5 | El Capitan Cave | Kevin Casey, Ranger |

August 29	Shearwater	Don & JoAnne Kumpula, Ocean Falls, BC
August 29	Shearwater	*Raison d'Etre*, Kathy & Serge, Hileah, HI
August 29	Shearwater	Rick Andrews (BC Electric); Jim Nyland (Ocean Falls); Beth (nurse)
Sept 5	Kelsey Bay	*Panasea*, Marina del Rey, CA
Sept 7	Lasqueti Island	*Beverly K*
Dec 23	Victoria	*Sheer Folly*

2001

May 19	Port Neville	Hansen family
May 20-21	Blunden Harbour	*Pacific High*, Lou & Geoff Thompson, Sunnyvale, CA
May 22	Nakwakto Rapids	*Pacific Sunrise*, Tilly & Anton, Ladner, BC
May 23	Strachan Channel	Charlie Chilson, local resident
May 23	Nakwakto Rapids	*Inlet Charger*
May 23	Finn Bay Retreat	Peter & Renée, owners
May 24	Ocean Falls	*Cyndyn*, Judy
May 24	Ocean Falls	Herb Carpenter, Harbourmaster
June 2	Ketchikan	Holly Churchill, Haida basketmaker
June 2	Meyers Chuck	Cassie & Steve Peavey, local residents
June 3	Deception Pt Cove	*Galaxy*, Vic
June 4	Petersburg	*Caron*, Ron
June 5	Cape Fanshaw	*Shemyu*, Brooks Hollern & Aaron Cummins
June 6, 8	Sandborn Channel	*Raven*, Sunny & Bob Johnson
June 8	Tracy Arm	*Ghost Rider*, Lowell & Sue Marsh, Cathalmet, WA
June 8	Taku	*Sanctuary*, Sue & Dave Kjome, Rancho Murieta, CA
June 9	Juneau	*Cat's Paw*, Kennewick, WA
June 11	Swanson Harbor	*Amorosa*, Judy & Allan Reese, Seattle, WA

June 11	Swanson Harbor	Greg Cook, kayaker & Pomona College graduate
June 13	Glacier Bay	Karen Platt, ANHA manager, and Chuck Young, Chief Ranger
June 14	Glacier Bay	*Northern Exposure*, Larry Edgerton & Charleen Folly
June 15	Glacier Bay	Tom & Gloria Burke
June 15	Glacier Bay	*Cat's Paw, Winddancer*
June 16	North Sandy Inlet	*Norma Jean* , Reno, NV
June 17	Elfin Cove	Dave Walton, Harbormaster
June 17	Lisianski Strait	*Home Shore*, Jim Kyle
June 19	Kalinin Bay	*Miniship, White Star, Locassos*
July 18	Sitka	*Raven*, Bob & Sunny Johnson
July 19	Sitka	*Hawkeye II* , Thad Wardell; Clark & Maggie Oster
July 19	Sitka	*Moonlight*, Leo Nigg, Switzerland
July 22	Craig	Julius ("Doug") & Georgie Douglas, Ketchikan, AK
July 23	Craig	*Raven*, Don & Red McVittie, Seattle, WA
July 23	Craig	*Jazz, Gairloch*,
July 23	Craig	*Sea Web II*, Derek Ingram, North Vancouver, BC
August 4	Armentieres Ch.	CCGS *Arrow Post*, Gordie Usher, Ron Paziac & Darrell Robertson
August 4	Armentieres Ch.	*Mithrandir*, Rick & Elke Cunningham, British Virgin Islands
August 18	Tcuga Cove	*Gwaii Haanas II,* Ken Brillon, Wally Pelton, Heather Toews, Parks Canada; Richard Scott, Richelle Leonard, Ernie Gladstone
August 23	Dolomite Narrows	*Tasman*, Alan Brown
August 24	Hoya Passage	*Island Roamer*, Natalie, Director of Skidegate Museum
Sept 1	Ocean Falls	*Coastal Messenger*, Brian, Tom and Debbie
Sept 2	Frypan Bay	*Sundown*, John & Midge Stapleton
Sept 2	Frypan Bay	*Cadenza, Rhapsody*
Sept 5	Nanaimo	*Tapawingo*, Bruce & Margaret Evertz

2003

May 2	Port Neville	Lorna Hansen Chesluk & Erica
May 3	Fury Cove	*Pelorus,* Joe & Margy Orem, Bellingham, WA
May 7	Ethelda Bay	Danielle, Dan, Mikal, Ilene & Nicole Pollack
May 12	Prince Rupert	*Nellie Juan,* Ken & Judy Carpenter, Seward, AK
May 12	Prince Rupert	*Uno Mas,* John & Sue Spencer, San Antonio, TX
May 12	Prince Rupert	*Ciao,* Peter & Marilyn Copeland
May 17	Sitka	*Blue Merlin,* Ward Eldridge
May 21	Yakutat	Brandt Petersen, Harbormaster, & Tina, his wife
May 21	Yakutat	*Taz, Pazzo*
May 21	Yakutat	*Sea Raven,* Geoff Widdows
May 22	Yakutat	Jacqueline Lott, NPS Ranger
May 22	Yakutat	Steve Estes & Josh Stachnik, Univ. of AK Fairbanks, seismologists
May 25	Icy Bay	*Peril Strait* (tug)
May 31	Sawmill Bay	*Rose,* Unalaska, AK
May 31	Sawmill Bay	*Billie Sue*
June 1-24	Sawmill Bay	*Enetai,* Dave and Evie Frisby, Duncan, BC
June 7	Agaguat Bay	Susie & Dave Scawinski, oyster farmers
June 8	Cascade Bay	*For Play,* Cliff & Linda Ricketts, Eagle River, AK
June 8	Cascade Bay	*Sea Alaska,* Barbara & Dick Crittenden, Eagle River, AK
June 8	Esther Passage	Kip Melling, kayaker, Eagle River, AK
June 10	Whittier	*Caspar,* Debbie
June 10	Whittier	Leonard Jones, Harbormaster
June 25	Tonsina Bay	*Perspective,* Dave & Karen Summerfeld & kids Jaden & Danielle, Anchorage/Seward AK
June 26	Port Chatham	*Meander*
June 28	Shuyak Harbor	Sven Kelly, Alaska State Trooper, Kodiak, AK

June 28	Shuyak Harbor	Kevin Murphy, Ranger, Big Bay
June 28	Shuyak Harbor	*Sea Eagle* (kayak), Sam Barber & Fran Wilson, Anchorage, AK
July 1	Kodiak	Sylvie & Jean-François André, France
July 3-4	Kodiak	*Viking Star* , Thor & Connie Olsen & family
July 3	Kodiak	Marty Owens, Harbormaster
August 18	Sitka	*Home Shore*, Jim Kyle; Audrey Sutherland, kayaker
August 18	Sitka	Howard Ulrich, 1958 Lituya Bay tsunami survivor
August 19	Sitka	*Gone with the Wind*, Larry Gill & Heather Schreiber
August 20	Sitka	Kathy Kyle & Ward Eldridge, local residents
August 23	Port Protection	Starla, Wooden Wheel Resort
Sept 6	Wallace Bay	Rick, Nate & George, *Wren, Molly B, Kentucky Colonel* (all Ranger 21s)
Sept 10	Cordero Lodge	*Meridian*, Bill & Madelyn Castle, Sitka
Sept 12	Nanaimo	*Morning Light*, Barry & Irene McPhee, Lahaina, HI
Sept 13	Nanaimo	Winston Bushnell, world sailor

BAIDARKA CREW

1992

May 3	Geza & Rusty Dienes
May 23	Sally Ridley
June 8	Dawn & Jeff Mach
Sept 21	Bob & AnnaMae Botley

1994

May 5	Geza & Rusty Dienes
May 20	Jeff Mach
August 23	Herb Nickles
August 29	Al Ryan

1995

Sept 2	Kathy Wells

2000

August 5	Joel & Jean Gillingwaters

2001

May 19	John Leone
June 12	Jean & Genevieve Doudeau
July 30	Frank Caldwell
August 11	Kevin Monahan

2003

Gulf of Alaska John Leone; (also Richard Spore, Don Odegard and Mark Bunzel)

NAUTICAL CRUISING GUIDEBOOKS
By Don Douglass and Réanne Hemingway-Douglass
Published by Fine Edge, Anacortes, WA
www.fineedge.com

Exploring Vancouver Island's West Coast. Douglass & Hemingway-Douglass (1995, 1st ed.; 1999, 2nd ed.)

Exploring the Inside Passage to Alaska. Douglass & Hemingway-Douglass (1995, 1st ed.)

Exploring the South Coast of British Columbia: Gulf Islands & Desolation Sound to Port Hardy [Broughton Archipelago for 2nd ed] & Blunden Harbour. Douglass & Hemingway-Douglass (1996, 1st ed.; 1999, 2nd ed; 2009, 3rd ed.)

Exploring the North Coast of British Columbia: Blunden Harbour to Dixon Entrance including the Queen Charlotte Islands. Douglass & Hemingway-Douglass (1997, 1st ed.; 2002, 2nd ed.; 2017, 3rd ed.)

Proven Cruising Routes: Seattle to Ketchikan. Kevin Monahan & Don Douglass (2000)

Exploring the San Juan & Gulf Islands. Douglass & Hemingway-Douglass (1998, 1st ed.; 2003, 2nd ed.; 2011, 3rd ed.)

Exploring Southeast Alaska: Dixon Entrance to Skagway. Douglass & Hemingway-Douglass (1999, 1st ed.; 2007, 2nd ed; 2018, 3rd ed.)

Exploring the Pacific Coast: San Diego to Seattle. Douglass & Hemingway-Douglass (2002, 1st ed.; 2009, 2nd ed.)

ABOUT THE AUTHOR

Réanne Hemingway-Douglass grew up in the Great Lakes region and Washington D.C. She attended Pomona College, Claremont Graduate University in Southern California, and the Université de Grenoble, France. After teaching French for twenty years, she joined her husband, Don Douglass, in their manufacturing and backpacking business. In the 1970s she and Don were the first American couple to attempt a circumnavigation of the Southern Hemisphere by sailboat. Réanne's best-selling book, *Cape Horn: One Man's Dream, One Woman's Nightmare*, tells the story of their pitch-poling near Cape Horn and has become a classic in nautical survival literature.

As sailors and cruisers, the Douglasses have logged over 175,000 nautical miles in the Southern Ocean, South Atlantic, New Zealand, and France. In 1986 they began in-depth exploring of the West Coast of America from Mexico to the Alaska Peninsula. Their explorations led them to write the *Exploring* series of nautical guidebooks and planning maps that cover areas from Baja California to the Gulf of Alaska. In the 1980s and '90s they published numerous other outdoor guidebooks through their company, Fine Edge Productions.

Réanne is also the author of *The Shelburne Escape Line - Secret Rescues of Allied Aviators by the French Underground, the British Royal Navy and London's MI-9*, and *Two Women Against the Wind – A Tierra del Fuego Bicycling Adventure*. She has written numerous articles on cruising, bicycling and women's issues for outdoor magazines, and has been a featured speaker at Boat Shows, Trawler Fests, yacht clubs and civic organizations.

Réanne and Don live in Anacortes, Washington State, and are the owners of Cave Art Press.

www.ingramcontent.com/pod-product-compliance
Lightning Source LLC
Chambersburg PA
CBHW051958090426
42741CB00008B/1454